© 2004 Russ Kick
Each "guest list" © 2004 by its author

Published by The Disinformation Company Ltd.
163 Third Avenue, Suite 108
New York, NY 10003
Tel.: +1.212.691.1605
Fax: +1.212.473.8096
www.disinfo.com

Design & Layout: Paul Pollard Tomo Makiura and Mary McDonnell for P⸱M, NYC

Library of Congress Control Number: 2003113894

ISBN 0-9729529-4-2

Printed in USA

Distributed in the USA and Canada by:
Consortium Book Sales and Distribution
1045 Westgate Drive, Suite 90
St Paul, MN 55114
Toll Free: +1.800.283.3572
Local: +1.651.221.9035
Fax: +1.651.221.0124
www.cbsd.com

Distributed in the United Kingdom and Eire by:
Turnaround Publisher Services Ltd.
Unit 3, Olympia Trading Estate
Coburg Road
London, N22 6TZ
Tel.: +44.(0)20.8829.3000
Fax: +44.(0)20.8881.5088
www.turnaround-uk.com

Attention colleges and universities, corporations and other organizations: Quantity discounts are available
on bulk purchases of this book for educational training purposes, fund-raising, or gift-giving. Special
books, booklets, or book excerpts can also be created to fit your specific needs. For information contact
Marketing Department of The Disinformation Company Ltd.

Disinformation is a registered trademark of The Disinformation Company Ltd.

disinformation®

BOOK OF LISTS

SUBVERSIVE FACTS AND HIDDEN INFORMATION IN RAPID-FIRE FORMAT

RUSS KICK

INTRODUCTION

A book of lists? Maybe some of you whippersnappers out there are scratching your heads in puzzlement. Those of us who are a tad older fondly recall the original *Book of Lists* series from the mid-1970s to early 1980s (with a fourth volume in 1994). I was only a lad then, but I devoured them.

David Wallechinsky, Amy Wallace, and Irving Wallace were ahead of their time when they first put together these compendiums of rapid-fire facts. We had yet to enter the era of the short attention span—MTV-style hyperediting, *USA Today*, Headline News Network, soundbites, blogs, Nintendo and Xbox, fast food domination, and microwave everything (not to mention the resulting Attention Deficit Disorder)—but they and their many, many contributors, researchers, and editors gave us a mountain of knowledge in an easily digestible format. We could read about "12 Famous People Who Changed Their Birthdays," "8 Generals Who Never Won a Battle," "18 Words Worth Reviving," "6 UFO Encounters of a Sexual Kind," "18 Health Experts and How They Died," and "9 Famous Hemorrhoid Sufferers."

The format caught on like wildfire. Amazon currently returns 267 hits for the title search "book of lists." This mini-library includes *The Art Teacher's Book of Lists*, *The Southern Gardener's Book of Lists*, *The Marine Corps Book of Lists*, *The Gay Book of Lists*, *The Bride's Book of Lists*, *Civil War Book of Lists*, and *The Celebrity Sex Book of Lists*. Could there be a more versatile format for presenting facts? I doubt it, which is why I'm surprised that it took me this long to think of doing a book of lists for subversive and unusual information—pot-smoking politicians, criminal cops, corporate crooks, CIA cryptonyms, gay animals, biblical contradictions, banned movies, and health problems that cause or mimic so-called mental illnesses. In the tradition of the original *Books of Lists*, I asked some contributors to join in, and they gave me rosters of botched executions, Disneyland deaths, sex spam, modern magicians, and more.

So jump right in anywhere—no need to worry about whether you can devote a long stretch to your reading. The disparate info has been condensed into a super-concentrated form. Simply apply to your brain.

—Russ Kick
Tucson, Arizona

ABOUT THE AUTHOR

Besides the books below, Russ has written articles and a column for the *Village Voice*. The Memory Hole [www.thememoryhole.org], a website devoted to rescuing knowledge and freeing information, is his labor of love. Russ made the front page of the *New York Times* when he digitally uncensored a heavily redacted Justice Department report.

9 BOOKS BY RUSS

1. *Outposts: A Catalogue of Rare and Disturbing Alternative Information* (author)

2. *Psychotropedia: Publications from the Periphery* (author)

3. *Hot Off the Net: Erotica and Other Sex Writings From the Internet* (editor)

4. *You Are Being Lied To: The Disinformation Guide to Media Distortion, Historical Whitewashes and Cultural Myths* (editor)

5. *Everything You Know Is Wrong: The Disinformation Guide to Secrets and Lies* (editor)

6. *Abuse Your Illusions: The Disinformation Guide to Media Mirages and Establishment Lies* (editor)

7. *50 Things You're Not Supposed to Know* (author)

8. *The Disinformation Book of Lists* (author)

9. *50 Things You're Not Supposed to Know, Volume 2* (author) [forthcoming]

ロ

CONTENTS

War ~~and Peace~~ +

Corporate Responsibility +

Sex +

Religion +

Movies, Music, and Pulp Fiction +

Odds & Ends +

ACKNOWLEDGMENTS

Personal thanks to ▶

1	Anne
2–3	Mom and Dad
4	Ruthanne
5	Jennifer
6	Billy Dale
7–8	Brett and Cristy
9	Darrell
10–11	Terry and Rebekah

Research thanks to ▶

1	Michael Ravnitzky
2	Richard Metzger
3	Matt Silvey
4	Beau Gunderson
5	Kevin Saylor
6	Hilary Claire Carmody
7	"rvdh0"
8	"walrus and carpenter"

Publishing thanks to ▶

1	Gary Baddeley
2	Richard Metzger
3	Ralph Bernardo
4	Alex Burns
5	The rest of the Disinfo gang
6–8	Paul, Tomo, and Mary

Trade thanks to ▶

1	Consortium Distribution
2+	All booksellers

Ultimate thanks to ▶

1+	My readers

+Drugs

Maybe the title of this list should be "39 Famous but Unexpected People Who Took Drugs," because the idea is not to document every well-known person who smoked pot or popped a pill. Instead, the list concerns famous figures whose usage might be somewhat surprising to the average person (of course, no readers of this book are merely average, but you know what I mean!). We won't look at people who were *expected* to do drugs, which means you won't read about anybody from the Beat movement or the Counterculture, nor any rock or jazz musicians. Instead, we'll focus on scientists, old-school literary giants, Nobel laureates, legendary actors, physicians (and a nurse), etc. These are the people you probably read about in school or college, but you didn't hear about their fondness for opium, LSD, hash, laughing gas, and other such substances.

1

Mathematician **Ralph Abraham**—the primary developer of chaos theory—said in a 1991 interview:

In the 1960s a lot of people on the frontiers of math experimented with psychedelic substances. There was a brief and extremely creative kiss between the community of hippies and top mathematicians. I know this because I was a purveyor of psychedelics to the mathematical community.

To be creative in mathematics you have to start from a point of total oblivion. Basically, math is revealed in a totally unconscious process in which one is completely ignorant of the social climate. And mathematical advance has always been the motor behind the advancement of consciousness.

2

Social reformer, founder of Hull House, and Nobel laureate **Jane Addams** wrote that she and some friends took opium once while in seminary-college. "We solemnly consumed small white powders at intervals during the entire long holiday, but no mental reorientation took place, and the suspense and excitement did not even permit us to grow sleepy."

3

Little woman **Louisa May Alcott** was addicted to morphine.

LIST 1   39 Famous People Who Used Drugs

4

Marcus Aurelius, Roman Emperor and philosopher, took opium.

5

Honoré de Balzac, one of France's literary giants, smoked hash at least once.

6

Victorian poet **Elizabeth Barrett Browning** suffered from numerous physical maladies and was no stranger to the use of opiates. When she and Robert Browning became involved, she was heavily addicted to laudanum (a tincture of opium in alcohol), morphine, and her own special brew, a mixture of morphine and ether. With his help, she was able to gradually reduce her intake, but because of an abscess on her lung, her doctor increased her dosage of morphine, which is probably what killed her. Thus, much of Elizabeth's verse—including all of her immortal love poems to Robert—were written while opium coursed through her veins.

7

Samuel Taylor Coleridge, the Romantic poet, gave us what is probably the most well-known piece of literature written while tripping. After taking two grains of opium and falling into a hazy state of mind in 1797, Coleridge saw vivid images with a corresponding poem of 200 to 300 lines. Coming out of his reverie, he wrote—or perhaps transcribed—54 lines that became the classic poem "Kubla Khan." At that moment, though, "a visitor on business" from a nearby town knocked on the poet's door. Unfortunately for literature,

Coleridge answered his visitor. By the time the salesman left over an hour later, the images and poem had fled Coleridge, except for a few scattered lines. He tried many times to retrieve the lost portion of the poem but never could. (It should be noted that some experts think this account is bogus, saying that "Kubla Khan" was written like any other poem, though perhaps based on images Coleridge saw while tripping.)

Around this time (the final years of the 1700s), the poet described laudanum as taking him to "a spot of enchantment, a green spot of fountains, & flowers & trees, in the very heart of a waste of Sands!" The liquid opium would let him "float about along an infinite ocean cradled in the flower of the Lotos."

But Coleridge soon changed his tune when he became addicted to the milk of paradise, taking huge doses of laudanum every day by 1801. In letters written in May 1814, he speaks of "this wicked direful practice of taking Opium or Laudanum" and refers to the tincture as a "*free-agency-annihilating Poison.*" At this time, he tried going cold turkey, but he went through sheer hell and was put on a suicide watch (all sharp objects were removed and someone stayed with him 24 hours a day). He never completely kicked the habit and used small doses for the rest of his life.

Opium may have been Coleridge's master, but his play pals included ether, hash, henbane, and belladonna.

8

Philip K. Dick was a pulp sci-fi writer whose dystopian stories of government-corporate-media control, strange drugs, and the subjective natures of reality and identity have achieved cult, even classic, status. Nine of his works have been made into movies, most notably, "Minority Report," *Do Androids Dream of Electric Sheep?* (filmed as *Blade Runner*), and "We Can Remember It for You Wholesale" (turned into the film *Total Recall*).

Throughout most of his writing years, Dick was fuelled by amphetamines, which allowed him to crank out 60 pages a day. His need for speed undoubtedly contributed to his paranoia, visions, and breaks with reality.

Dick also dropped acid, although he said it didn't contribute to the hallucinatory quality of his work, especially since much of it was written before he took LSD. When asked if one of his stories was written while he was high, he replied: "That really is not true. First of all, you can't write anything when you're on acid. I did one page once while on an acid trip, but it was in Latin. Whole damn thing was in Latin and a little tiny bit in Sanskrit, and there's not much market for that." Summing up his experiences in 1974, he said: "All I ever found out about acid was that I was where I wanted to get out of fast. It didn't seem more real than anything else; it just seemed more awful."

9

Charles Dickens—Victorian England's greatest novelist—drank quite a bit of laudanum to help him sleep and to ease a painful foot condition.

10

In 1970, Pittsburgh Pirates pitcher **Dock Ellis** hurled a no-hitter while under the influence of LSD. He and his girlfriend had dropped acid the night before. Ellis got up around nine or ten and downed another half a tab. Looking at a newspaper, his girlfriend informed him that he was supposed to pitch in a little while, which was news to him. At the clubhouse, Ellis took Dexamyl and Benzedrine to counter the acid. The coauthor of his autobiography, Donald Hall, later admitted that he and Ellis bowdlerized this story. Instead of "taking tabs," the pitcher was said to have drunk screwdrivers the night before.

11

Physician **Havelock Ellis**, a pioneer of sexual studies in the late 1800s up to the 1930s, was a devotee of mescal. Of his first trip, he wrote:

> I was further impressed, not only by the brilliance, delicacy, and variety of the colours, but even more by their lovely and various textures; fibrous, woven, polished, glowing, dull-veined, semitransparent. The glowing effects, as of jewels and the fibrous, as of insect's wings, being perhaps the most prevalent.

12

In *Opium: A History*, Martin Booth writes that **Benjamin Franklin** "was almost certainly addicted to opium in his declining years."

13

In his first paper of several on the subject, "On Coca"—which in 1884 simultaneously helped make **Sigmund Freud**'s name and introduce the general populace to coke—the father of psychoanalysis writes: "I have tested this effect of coca, which wards off hunger, sleep, and fatigue, and steels one to intellectual effort, some dozen times upon myself..." He elaborates:

> A few minutes after taking cocaine, one experiences a certain exhilaration and feeling of lightness. One feels a certain furriness on the lips and palate, followed by a feeling of warmth in the same areas; if one now drinks cold water, it feels warm on the lips and cold in the throat. One other occasions the predominant feeling is a rather pleasant coolness in the mouth and throat.
>
> During this first trial I experienced a short period of toxic effects, which did not recur in subsequent experiments. Breathing became slower and deeper and I felt tired and sleepy; I yawned frequently and felt somewhat dull. After a few minutes the actual cocaine euphoria began, introduced by repeated cooling eructation. Immediately after taking the cocaine I noticed a slight slackening of the pulse and later a moderate increase.

From our current perspective, it's wince-inducing to read this soon-to-be-eminent physician making guesses that are 100 percent wrong: "It seems probable, in the light of reports which I shall refer to later, that coca, if used protractedly but in moderation, is not detrimental to the body." And this clunker: "I have the impression that protracted use of coca can lead to a lasting improvement [in the user's mental powers]..."

Cocaine's addictive properties soon became apparent to the world at large, but Freud was gung-ho for blow for several years. Finally he quit lauding it and using it.

14

King George IV believed that laudanum was a cure for his hangovers.

15

Like Carl Sagan and Stephen Hawking, **Stephen Jay Gould** became famous as a superb popularizer of science, in this case evolutionary biology, with his books *The Mismeasure of Man* and *The Panda's Thumb*, among others. Gould developed a cancer known as abdominal mesothelioma, and his chemotherapy gave him horrendous nausea that couldn't be tamed by any medications. As a last resort, he tried pot:

> Marihuana worked like a charm. I disliked the "side effect" of mental blurring (the "main effect" for recreational users), but the sheer bliss of not experiencing nausea—and then not having to fear it for all the days intervening between treatments—was the greatest boost I received in all my years of treatment, and surely had a most important effect upon my eventual cure. It is beyond my comprehension—and I fancy I am able to comprehend a lot, including much nonsense—that any humane person would withhold such a beneficial substance from people in such great need simply because others use it for different purposes.

16

One of the greatest idols of the silver screen, **Cary Grant** starred in many classic films, including *North by Northwest*, *An Affair to Remember*, *Notorious*, *Arsenic and Old Lace*, *Gunga Din*, and *Monkey Business*. Starting in the late 1950s, Grant dropped LSD during 100 therapy sessions with pioneering shrinks Dr. Mortimer Hartmann and Dr. Oscar Janiger. In *CG: A Touch of Elegance*, the matinee idol is quoted from that time period:

> I have been born again. I have just been through a psychiatric experience that has

completely changed me. It was horrendous. I had to face things about myself which I never admitted, which I didn't know were there. Now I know that I hurt every woman I loved. I was an utter fake, a self-opinionated boor, a know-all who knew very little.

Once you realize that you have all things inside you, love and hate alike, and you learn to accept them, then you can use your love to exhaust your hate. That power is inside you, but it can be assimilated into your power to love. You can relax. Then you can do more than you ever dreamed you could do. I found I was hiding behind all kinds of defenses, hypocrisies and vanities. I had to get rid of them layer by layer. That moment when your conscious meets your subconscious is a helluva wrench. You feel the whole top of your head is lifting off.

Also in *CG*, Grant says:

The experience was just like being born the first time; I imagined all the blood and urine, and I emerged with the flush of birth. It was absolute release. You are still able to feed yourself, of course, drive your car, that kind of thing, but you've lost a lot of the tension.

It releases inhibition. You know, we are all unconsciously holding our anus. In one LSD dream I shit all over the rug and shit all over the floor. Another time I imagined myself as a giant penis launching off from Earth like a spaceship.

In his short autobiography, Grant wrote: "The shock of each revelation brings with it an anguish of sadness for what was not known before in the wasted years of ignorance and, at the same time, an ecstasy of joy at being freed from the shackles of such ignorance." When he was 70 years old, he told his former flame Maureen Donaldson: "But you don't understand. LSD is a chemical, not a drug. People who take drugs are trying to escape from their lives. LSD is a hallucinogen, and people who take it are trying to look within their lives. That's what I did."

17

Novelist **Graham Greene** (*The Quiet American*) smoked opium in dens throughout Southeast Asia

18

Hippocrates, the Greek doctor considered the founder of Western medicine, recommended opium for numerous complaints.

19

Ask any first-year psychology student about **William James**, and you'll find out that he's a giant in the field, the psychologist who formed the school of thought called functionalism. Ask any first-year philosophy student about William James, and you'll find out that he's a giant in the field, the philosopher who formed the school of thought called Pragmatism. What you're less likely to hear is that he was a user of mind-altering drugs who penned the seminal work on altered states of consciousness—*Varieties of Religious Experience*. Nitrous oxide was his substance of choice. From the first time James inhaled it, his thinking was changed and he was set on his path. As he wrote in *Varieties*:

One conclusion was forced upon my mind at that time, and my impression of its truth has ever since remained unshaken. It is that our normal waking consciousness, rational consciousness as we call it, is but one special type of consciousness, whilst all about it, parted from it by the filmiest of screens, there lie potential forms of consciousness entirely different.

About his encounters with laughing gas, he also wrote:

> Looking back on my own experiences, they all converge towards a kind of insight to which I cannot help ascribing some metaphysical significance. The keynote of it is invariably a reconciliation. It is as if the opposites of the world, whose contradictoriness and conflict make all our difficulties and troubles, were melted into unity.

James also took peyote, which didn't do much for him, and chloral hydrate, the hypnotic that puts the knock-out in a Mickey Finn.

20

Mitch Kapor—pioneering software developer (Lotus 1-2-3), founder of Lotus Development, cofounder of the Electronic Frontier Foundation—told the Buddhist magazine *Tricycle*:

> I had gotten to college in the 60's and started experimenting with marijuana and psychedelics, fairly heavily. I had some distressing experiences with LSD. Bad trips. So I stopped doing drugs and then started getting acid flashbacks. I decided to give meditation a serious try to see if that could have some calming effect. I got hooked in to TM and eventually made the decision to go through advanced training to become an initiator, an instructor.

21

Famed comedian **Groucho Marx** first took LSD in 1967 or 1968 with counterculture icon Paul Krassner. Soon after, Marx smoked pot with extras on the set of the all-star comedy *Skidoo*, and he even tokes a little on-screen. Krassner relates the following exchange:

I said to him, "My mother once told me she was concerned that LSD would lead to marijuana."

Groucho replied, "Your mother was right."

22

Opiate historian Barbara Hodgson says of **Guy de Maupassant**, France's greatest writer of short stories: "Much of the ill health that plagued him through his adult years could be blamed on syphilis, against which he tried ether, hashish, cocaine and morphine."

23

Weir Mitchell—the most illustrious neurologist of his day (a nineteenth-century Oliver Sacks), who also wrote popular novels and short stories and was friends with Walt Whitman, Oliver Wendell Holmes, William James, and other notables—seems to be the first Westerner to try peyote and write about his experiences:

> Stars, delicate floating films of colour, then an abrupt rush of countless points of white light swept across the field of view, as if the unseen millions of the Milky Way were to flow in a sparkling river before my eyes; Zigzag lines of very bright colours...

24

Kary Mullis won the 1993 Nobel Prize for Chemistry for developing the polymerase chain reaction (PCR) method for studying DNA molecules. In his autobiography, *Dancing Naked in the Mind Field*, Mullis describes the first time he smoked a joint, in 1966 when he was attending grad school: "I looked at Richards, my wife, with new eyes.

She was the same Richards, but not to me. I grabbed her in a primitive way, rolled her onto our enhanced bed, and felt the surging power of bliss."

The next week, Mullis dropped acid with a friend to guide him. At that point, the "double-domed 1000-microgram Owsley" he took was legal.

> I started laughing. I got up from the table and realized, on the way to the couch, that everything I knew was based on a false premise. I fell down through the couch into another world....
>
> I wasn't afraid. I wasn't anything. I noticed that time did not extend smoothly—that it was punctuated by moments—and I fell down into a crack between two moments and was gone....
>
> I felt like I was everywhere. I was thrilled. I'd been trapped in my own experiences—now I was free.

Mullis describes the immediate after-effects of his inaugural trip: "I appreciated my life in a way I never had before. On the following Monday I went to school. I remember sitting on a bench, waiting for a class to begin, thinking, 'That was the most incredible thing I've ever done.'"

It wasn't always rosy, though. The outspoken chemist reports feeling overwhelming feelings of guilt and ugliness when he dropped acid after leaving his wife and daughter. During a previous experiment, he synthesized an LSD analogue and accidentally took ten times the proper dose, which "annihilated" his personality. The next morning he couldn't recognize his wife or child. "I couldn't remember who I was, what I did, what I liked.... I had no preferences. I didn't recognize my body." Twenty-four hours later, his memories and personality started to return, and in another day he was fully integrated again.

25

That nurse among nurses, **Florence Nightingale**, used morphine, though we don't know how often.

26

Anaïs Nin—experimental/erotic novelist, diarist, consort of Henry and June Miller—engaged one time in LSD therapy under its pioneer, psychiatrist Oscar Janiger. Although she enjoyed the experience, she realized afterward that what she had experienced was already within her. "Therefore, I felt, the chemical did not reveal an unknown world. What it did was shut out the quotidian world as an interference and leave you alone with your dreams and fantasies and memories."

27

Paracelcus, the physician and alchemist whose contributions to Western medicine are paramount, was a proponent of opium. PBS notes that in 1527: "During the height of the Reformation, opium is reintroduced into European medical literature by Paracelsus as laudanum. These black pills or 'Stones of Immortality' were made of opium thebaicum, citrus juice and quintessence of gold and prescribed as painkillers."

28

Of mescaline, the celebrated Mexican poet **Octavio Paz**—winner of the 1990 Nobel Prize for Literature—wrote:

An encounter with mescaline: an encounter with our own selves, with the known-unknown. The double that wears our own face as its mask. The face that is gradually obliterated and transformed into an immense mocking grimace. The devil. The clown. This thing that I am not. This thing that I am. A martyrissible apparition. And when my own face reappears, there is nobody there. I too have left myself. Space, space, pure vibration. A great gift of the gods, mescaline is a window through which we look out upon endless distances where nothing ever meets our eye but our own gaze. There is no I: there is space, vibration, perpetual animation.

29

Plotinus, the ancient Roman philosopher who founded Neoplatonism, is said to have used opium.

30

We know that **Edgar Allen Poe** liked to quaff absinthe, sometimes mixed with brandy, but whether or not he used opium has been the subject of intense debate. Martin Booth, author of *Opium: A History*, believes that Poe was a user, possibly an addict.

31

Marcel Proust may have had a hard time remembering things past, considering his fondness for opium, morphine, hypnotics, camphor cigarettes, and possibly heroin, not to mention booze.

32

Living during the second half of the 1700s, **Mary Robinson** started out as a popular Shakespearean actress, but her career was aborted by scandal when she temporarily became the mistress of the Prince of Wales. However, she found a second life as a poet and novelist. For her rheumatism, she took heroic doses of laudanum. One night when she was 34, she had an opium dream about a menacing lunatic. Calling her daughter to her bedside, she dictated a poem ("The Maniac"); the next day, she didn't remember doing this. Thus, we have the first poem known to have crossed over from an opium dream. Samuel Taylor Coleridge was friends with Robinson, and skeptics think he might've made up the creation story of "Kubla Khan" in imitation of her.

33

Carl Sagan: Pulitzer Prize-winning astronomer and biologist; famous popularizer of science; creator and host of the *Cosmos* TV series; author of *Cosmos*, *Dragons of Eden*, *Broca's Brain*, and other books; avid potsmoker. As discussed in *Carl Sagan: A Life* (and subsequently in my *50 Things You're Not Supposed to Know*), Sagan loved to toke reefer. He said that it enhanced his productivity, creativity, and insights, among other things. In his anonymous ode to Mary Jane in the classic *Marihuana Reconsidered*, he wrote: "My high is always reflective, peaceable, intellectually exciting, and sociable, unlike most alcohol highs, and there is never a hangover.... [T]he illegality of cannabis is outrageous, an impediment to full utilization of a drug which helps produce the serenity and insight, sensitivity and fellowship so desperately needed in this increasingly mad and dangerous world."

34

Sir Walter Scott, the Scottish novelist and poet, drank massive amounts of laudanum to combat stomach cramps. He wrote many works under the drug's influence, including *Rob Roy* and *The Bride of Lammermoor*.

35

When being interviewed by *High Times*, the intellectual-philosopher-theorist **Susan Sontag** was asked if she wrote while stoned on pot. She replied: "I've tried, but I find it too relaxing. I use speed to write, which is the opposite of grass."

36

Robert Louis Stevenson wrote *Strange Case of Dr. Jekyll and Mr. Hyde* on a six-day cocaine binge in 1886. Many commentators have noticed the uncanny similarity between Stevenson's drug of choice and the potion that turns nice guy Dr. Jekyll into the uncontrollable bastard Mr. Hyde.

37

Pancho Villa, the bandit who became a general and leader of the Mexican Revolution, was a party animal. Villa and his men were well-known for their copious use of marijuana, mescal, and sotol (psychedelic cactus whiskey).

38

Andrew Weil, M.D., is one of the biggest names in alternative medicine. Along with Deepak Chopra, his is the bearded face of holistic health in America. Combining his mainstream medical training (from Harvard) and scientific outlook with botany, natural healing, Eastern approaches, and consciousness studies has resulted in numerous best-selling books (including *Spontaneous Healing* and *Natural Health, Natural Medicine*), repeat appearances on Oprah and Larry King, and a professorship at the University of Arizona, where he founded and heads the Program in Integrative Medicine.

Weil has always been up-front and unapologetic about his professional and personal interest in psychoactive substances (among other methods of altering consciousness). Several of his early books addressed the topic, including the classics *From Chocolate to Morphine: Everything You Need to Know About Mind-Altering Drugs* and *The Natural Mind: A New Way of Looking at Drugs and the Higher Consciousness*. In the course of his writings, he has discussed his usage of marijuana, yage, MDA (a close cousin of ecstasy), Jimsonweed, coca leaf, cocaine, LSD, magic mushrooms, toad venom, and others that I've probably overlooked.

In March 2001, he briefly made headlines when he told *60 Minutes* that LSD had cured his lifelong allergy to cats. If only acid were legal, he said, "I think I would recommend that some patients do it." Not that he recommends all the drugs he's tried. His experience with Jimsonweed, for one, was horrible, and he advises against taking any plants of the *Datura* variety. "Its physical toxicity is, at best, uncomfortable and, at worst, very dangerous. Its mental effects are unpredictable, often unpleasant, and always uncontrollable."

39

Besides imbibing absinthe, **Oscar Wilde** smoked tobacco steeped in laudanum.

Honorable Mention

When we think of **Sherlock Holmes**, we imagine the pipe in his mouth, not the needle in his arm. Yet Arthur Conan Doyle's archetypal detective was a devotee of blow. Only one work contains a scene of Holmes' cocaine use, while eight others refer in passing to his habit. (Meanwhile, his fondness for morphine is only alluded to.) The second novel featuring the super-sleuth literally opens and closes with coke. These are the very first paragraphs of *Sign of the Four*:

> Sherlock Holmes took his bottle from the corner of the mantelpiece, and his hypodermic syringe from its neat morocco case. With his long, white, nervous fingers he adjusted the delicate needle and rolled back his left shirtcuff. For some little time his eyes rested thoughtfully upon the sinewy forearm and wrist, all dotted and scarred with innumerable puncture-marks. Finally, he thrust the sharp point home, pressed down the tiny piston, and sank back into the velvet-lined armchair with a long sigh of satisfaction.

Dr. John Watson, who is narrating the story, tells us that Holmes has been shooting up three times a day "for many months." He asks Holmes: "Which is it to-day, morphine or cocaine?" The detective replies that it's the latter. At the time the book was written, the addictive, destructive aspects of the drug weren't widely known, so Doyle was going very much against the current when he had Watson give his friend a tongue-lashing over his jones. Holmes replies that he only mainlines coke when there is nothing else, such as a case, to keep him busy. "I suppose that its influence is physically a bad one. I find it, however, so transcendently stimulating and clarifying to the mind that its secondary action is a matter of small moment."

The novel closes with these paragraphs:

> "The division seems rather unfair," I remarked. "You have done all the work in this business. I get a wife out of it, Jones gets the credit, pray what remains for you?"
>
> "For me," said Sherlock Holmes, "there still remains the cocaine-bottle." And he stretched his long white hand up for it.

After Doyle killed off Holmes in 1893 and brought him back eight years later for an additional two novels and 30-plus short stories, the detective is never again mentioned as using drugs. ⌺

> **Drug Quote #1**
> "Among the hundreds of cocaine users I have known, I have only seen the drug induce good moods."
> —Andrew Weil, M.D.

Vin Mariani was made by steeping coca leaves in Bordeaux wine, resulting in 150 to 300 mg of cocaine per liter. Due to creator Angelo Mariani's groundbreaking publicity efforts—which included testimonials from popes, royalty, presidents, doctors, artists, athletes, and hundreds of other notables—he sold huge amounts of the stuff in France and America from the late 1860s to at least 1913. Among those who publicly toasted the cocaine-wine:

2 | 42 Famous Drinkers of Vin Mariani

1. **Albert I, Prince of Monaco**

2. **King Alphonse XIII of Spain**

3. **Frédéric-Auguste Bartholdi**

    The creator of the Statue of Liberty enthused: "Vin Mariani seems to brighten and increase all our faculties; it is very probable that had I taken it twenty years ago, the Statue of Liberty would have attained the height of several hundred meters."

4. **Sarah Bernhardt**

5. **Louis Bleriot**

    Bleriot was the first person to fly over an ocean in a plane, and he did it with a flask of Vin Mariani.

6. **"Buffalo Bill" Cody**

7. **Thomas Edison**

8. **Anatole France**

9. **King George I of Greece**

10. **Ulysses S. Grant**

11. **Zadoc Kahn**

    The Grand Rabbi of France wrote: "My conversion is complete. Praise be to Mariani's wine!"

12. **Cardinal Lavigerie**

    "Your coca from America gave my European priests the strength to civilise Asia and Africa."

13. **Pope Leo III**

14-15. **Auguste and Louis Lumière**

16. **Pope Pius X**

17. **Auguste Rodin**

18. **Jules Verne**

19. **Queen Victoria**

20. **The Shah of Persia**

21. **H.G. Wells**

22. **Emile Zola**

23-36. **Fourteen kings and queens**

37-42. **Six Presidents of France**

Honorable Mention

Mariani sent a case of his coca wine to **President William McKinley**, whose secretary wrote a thank-you note saying that the wine would be used. It's not known whether McKinley and guests ever drank it. ⌁

> *Drug Quote # 2*
> *"Creative people probably do run a greater risk of alcoholism and addiction than those in some other jobs, but so what? We all look pretty much the same when we're puking in the gutter."*
> *—Stephen King*

Absinthe is a greenish alcoholic brew containing the herbs anise, which gives it a licorice-like flavor, and wormwood, which gives the drinker a buzz unlike any other liquor or drug. The decadent drink became extremely prevalent in France in the 1840s. Its popularity only climbed as decades went by and the Green Fairy—as absinthe was known—spread abroad. Around 1915, it was banned in most countries, the temperance movement having convinced people that it was even more dangerous than regular booze.

In recent times, absinthe has taken on a romantic, outlaw image for several reasons. First, it's rumored to drive drinkers insane. This is mostly myth, although if you drank it by the truckload, as with most alcohol, you'd probably end up a wreck. And eating handfuls of wormwood isn't advisable, so ingesting gigantic doses via absinthe isn't too smart, either. The second alluring factor is that the Green Fairy was the drink of choice for the Impressionists, Decadents, Symbolists, and other renegade artists, writers, and poets, particularly those of *fin-de-siècle* France. Finally, the fact that it really is illegal in the US and almost all of Europe makes it all the more appealing.

Absinthe Robette (1896) by Privat Livemont

LIST 3 | 20 Famous Drinkers of Absinthe

1. **Charles Baudelaire**

2. **Aleister Crowley**

3. **Edgar Degas**

4. **Havelock Ellis**

5. **Paul Gauguin**

6. **Ernest Hemingway**

   Hemingway mixed absinthe with champagne for a concoction he called "death in the afternoon."

7. **Alfred Jarry**

   (the playwright who created the Absurdist movement)

8. **Jack London**

9. **Edouard Manet**

10. **Eugene O'Neill**

11. **Pablo Picasso**

12. **Edgar Allen Poe**

    Poe sometimes drank his absinthe mixed with brandy, which must've strained the liver of even a dedicated alcoholic.

13. **Pierre Auguste-Renoir**

14. **Arthur Rimbaud**

15. **Henri de Toulouse-Lautrec**

16. **Mark Twain**

17. **Vincent Van Gogh**

18. **Paul Verlaine**

19. **Walt Whitman**

20. **Oscar Wilde**

    Wilde penned the following lines on the successive stages of absinthe inebriation, which are quoted by everyone who writes about the Green Fairy: "The first stage is like ordinary drinking, the second when you begin to see monstrous and cruel things, but if you can persevere, you will enter in upon the third stage where you see things that you want to see, wonderful, curious things."

Honorable Mentions

Absinthe is making a comeback of sorts. At least a dozen legal brands are available in Britain and Spain. **Johnny Depp** and **Marilyn Manson** are admitted contemporary devotees. **Hunter S. Thompson** and **Eminem** are reputed to have drunk it at least once. Although not known for sure, it's likely that **Trent Reznor** imbibes, as well. He's close to Manson, and the video for Nine Inch Nails' "The Perfect Drug" prominently features the green liquor. And what to make of the photograph showing then-First Lady **Hillary Clinton** in Prague, with a glass of absinthe in front of her? Was she drinking it, or did it just happen to be there? □

> *Drug Quote # 3*
> *"God is unjust because he made man incapable of sustaining the effect of coca all life long."*
> *—Paolo Mantegazza, nineteenth-century Italian neurologist*

1. **Michael Bloomberg**, Mayor of New York City

2. **Bill Clinton**, former President of the US

3. **Howard Dean**, former Governor of Vermont

4. **John Edwards**, Senator from North Carolina

5. **Newt Gingrich**, former Speaker of the House of Representatives

6. **Al Gore**, former Vice President of the US

7. **Gary Johnson**, former Governor of New Mexico

8. **John Kerry**, Senator from Massachusetts

9. **George Pataki**, Governor of New York

10. **Arnold Schwarzenegger**, Governor of California

11. **Clarence Thomas**, Supreme Court Justice

12. **Jesse Ventura**, former Governor of Minnesota

Drug Quote #4

"Pot is marvelous for getting new connections in the brain. It's divine for that. You can think associatively on pot, so you can really have extraordinary thoughts."
—Norman Mailer

LIST 4 : A Dozen US Politicians Who Have Smoked Pot

1. Coca-Cola

From 1886 to 1902, Coke contained coke. John Pemberton, the Atlanta pharmacist who created it, first made a different drink. French Coca Wine was a knock-off of France's insanely successful Vin Mariani that added another pick-me-up—the kola nut. Pemberton's alcoholic cocaine-caffeine brew was selling well (no surprise there), but the temperance movement pressured Atlanta into banning booze starting July 1886. Scrambling madly, Pemberton came up with a drink that kept the coca and the kola, lost the wine, and added sugar, citric acid, and carbonation. Coca-Cola was born. The company's official history denies that Coke ever contained cocaine, but the drink's drug-induced beginnings are just too well documented. For instance, an 1896 ad for Coke begins:

> It seems to be a law of nature that the more valuable and efficacious a drug is, the nastier and more unpleasant its taste. It is therefore

31 Products Containing Hard Drugs

quite a triumph over nature that the Coca-Cola Co. of Atlanta, Ga., have achieved in their success in robbing both coca leaves and the kola nut of the exceedingly nauseous and disagreeable taste while retaining their wonderful medicinal properties, and the power of restoring vitality and raising the spirits of the weary and debilitated.

By the early 1900s, though, a backlash against cocaine was storming society, so the company started phasing it out in 1901, and by 1903 the drink was blow-free.

2. **Atkinson's Infants' Preservatives**

3. **Battley's Drops** (a brand of laudanum)

4. **Battley's Sedative Solution** (morphine)

5. **Bullard & Shedd's Wine of Coca**

6. **Café-Coca Compound**

7. **Cassebeer's Coca Calisaya** (cocaine, 42 percent alcohol)

8. **Coca-Bola**
During the heyday of products containing cocaine, a doctor in Philadelphia marketed a gum called Coca-Bola. Each ounce contained a whopping 710 milligrams of nose candy, meaning that each stick was infused with the equivalent of several lines of snorted coke.

9. **Cocaine Tooth Drops**

10. **Dope Cola**

11. **Dover's Powder** (morphine)

12. **Dr. Don's Kola**

13. **Dr. Fahrney's Teething Syrup** (morphine)

14. **Dr. James' Soothing Syrup** (heroin)

15. **Dr. Moffett's Teething Powder** (opium)

16. **Dr. Tucker's Asthma Specific** (420 mg/cocaine per ounce)

17. **Fraser's Antiasthmatic Tablets** (heroin)

18. **Glyco-Heroin**

19. **Godfrey's Cordial** (sweetened laudanum for babies)

20. **Koca Nola**

21. **Kola-Ade**

22. **Kos Kola**

23. **Maltine with Coca Wine**

24. **Metcalf's Coca Wine**

25. **Mrs. Winslow's Soothing Syrup** (morphine)

26. **Rococola**

27. **Street's Infants' Quietness**

28. **Vapor-OL Treatment No. 6** (opium)

29. **Vélo-Coca**

30. **Vin Mariani** (see the second list in this chapter)

31. **Wiseola**

A small number of companies in the US are permitted by the Drug Enforcement Administration to manufacturer or grow illegal substances. Why? Some drugs, such as pot and coke, are prescribed to an extremely limited number of people. In other cases, the drugs are used as chemical references, so labs that test seized illegal drugs have a standard for comparison. Some of the legally-created drugs are used in the manufacture of home narc kits, which parents use to find out if their kids are druggies. Still others are an intermediate step in the creation of industrial chemicals. I would imagine that employee pilfering is more of a problem at these companies than most.

One of the two most well-versed chemical companies, **Accustandard, Inc.** (Connecticut) is allowed to create practically every drug on Schedule I and nine on Schedule II. It is the only American company allowed to produce opium.

2

Aldrich Chemical Company, Inc. (Ohio) is permitted to brew LSD, ecstasy, GHB, mescaline, psilocybin, oxycodone, and meth. Call them for your next rave!

3

Cerilliant Corporation (Texas) has permission to cook up almost any Schedule I or II drug. It and Accustandard are the only two companies that can legally make bufotenine (a psychoactive substance occurring naturally in some Amazonian plants and the venom of Bufo toads).

LIST 6

9 US Companies Allowed to Manufacture Illegal Drugs

4

The New Age-sounding **Lifepoint, Inc.** (California) produces speed.

5

Organix, Inc. (Massachusetts) is one of fourteen corporations (five in Massachusetts alone) allowed to make cocaine. Perhaps that state's slogan could be changed to, "The coke capitol of the US."

6

The Polaroid Corporation (Massachusetts), of camera fame, is allowed to produce 2,5-dimethoxyamphetamine, a psychedelic amphetamine in the same class as ecstasy and DOM. According to the DEA, this phenythylamine is then converted into a "non-controlled substance."

7

The US division of **Roche Diagnostics Corporation**, itself a division of the Swiss pharmaceutical giant, can create morphine, LSD, and several other drugs for use in its home drug-test kits. (Are there really teenagers out there using morphine?)

8

Sigma Aldrich Research (Massachusetts) produces heroin, much like Bayer did when it introduced smack to the world in 1898. It also offers LSD, coke, meth, and ice (a/k/a U4Euh).

9

The University of Mississippi, through its National Center for Development of Natural Products, is one of only three US entities allowed to grow pot. ⌂

Drug Quote #5
"Coffee is a strong psychoactive drug; its direct pharmacological effects are more powerful than those of cannabis."
—Andrew Weil, M.D.

The basic reason that certain drugs make us feel so good is that they fit into receptors in our nervous systems. These receptors aren't there by accident—our bodies already create chemicals meant to bind at these points. Dr. Candace Pert—the Johns Hopkins researcher who discovered the brain's opiate receptors in the 1970s—has pointed out that feel-good drugs simply mimic the chemicals we already have.

Since current drug laws target analogues of illegal substances, this means that any chemical in our bodies that is molecularly similar to a scheduled drug is outlawed. In other words, each one of us—infants, gray-haired grannies, the President—has illegal substances coursing through our veins every minute of the day.

1

The neurotransmitter **anandamide** binds to the same receptors as tetrahydrocannabinol (THC), the chemical that gives weed its kick. The National Institutes of Health has referred to it as the "brain's marijuana-like compound." Some scientists theorize that anandamide can give people the munchies, with high levels contributing to obesity.

2

DMT is a potent, fast-acting psychedelic that forms the basis of many South American snuffs and brews, and is popular among connoisseurs of mind-expanding drugs. Professor of psychiatry Samuel L. Christian writes that "studies in both human spinal fluid and animal brain conclusively demonstrated the production of dimethyltryptamine (DMT) from the precursor amino acid [tryptophane]." This means that we don't have a mere analogue of DMT in our bodies, we have the actual substance itself inside us. That includes you, Mr. Drug Czar.

LIST 7

6 Illegal Substances That Occur Naturally in Our Bodies

3

The neurotransmitters known as **endorphins** have effects similar to morphine. The *Columbia Encyclopedia* explains: "Endorphins interact with opiate receptor neurons to reduce the intensity of pain: among individuals afflicted with chronic pain disorders, endorphins are often found in high numbers. Many painkilling drugs, such as morphine and codeine, act like endorphins and actually activate opiate receptors." In fact, this is how endorphins were discovered; scientists examining addiction to opiates noticed that the human brain has receptors for opium and its derivatives, which led them to believe that our bodies must already make biochemicals that fit these receptors. Sure enough, in the early 1970s, the endorphins were isolated.

4

Also known as noradrenaline, the neurotransmitter **norepinephrine** kicks your central nervous system into overdrive, resulting in higher levels of energy, awareness, and arousal. In other words, it's speed. When amphetamines, including meth, are put into your body, the central nervous system thinks they're norepinephrine and acts accordingly.

5 6

Serotonin—the neurotransmitter crucial to so many bodily processes, and a key factor in mood—is chemically similar to LSD and phenethylamines, which include ecstasy and mescaline. Likewise, the hormone **melatonin**—crucial to our sleep patterns—is derived from serotonin, making it similar to LSD. Despite the fact that LSD acts on the same receptor sites as serotonin and melatonin, however, injections of these two substances haven't triggered psychedelic states in volunteers.

Honorable Mentions

Glutemorphin (a peptide formed when gluten breaks down) and **casomorphin** (a peptide formed when milk breaks down) are opioids. If you eat grains, particularly wheat, or milk products, you have these morphine-like substances in your body. ◻

> **Drug Quote #6**
> "One cannot help but ponder the strange dichotomy that the nation based on establishing individual freedom has now outlawed every substance which might aid in the exploration of that last and most important frontier, the human mind. Alexander Shulgin, world-renowned chemist in the field of psychoactive drugs, is quoted in a recent periodical: 'Our generation is the first ever to have made the search for self-awareness a crime.'"
> —Myron Stolaroff

1

"Cocaine"

Arguably the most well-known pro-drug song, Eric Clapton's ode to nose candy sounds surprisingly downbeat and melancholy, given its glowing lyrics about the ultimate upper. "She don't lie, she don't lie, she don't lie…"

2

"Cocaine Blues"

Blues and jazz musicians performed lots of songs about drugs. (Even Ella Fitzgerald sang about "Wacky Dust": "Puttin' a buzz in your heart.") East Coast Blues pioneer Luke Jordan recorded at least two versions of "Cocaine Blues" in 1927 and/or 1929 (accounts vary). In one version the Virginia bluesman sings:

> I called my Cora, hey hey
> She come on sniffin' with her nose all sore,
> Doctor swore [she's] gonna smell no more
> Sayin' coke's for horses, not women nor men
> The doctor said it will kill you, but he didn't say when
> I'm simply wild about my good cocaine

The other version has ten verses with the same basic structure (a rhyming couplet and the same third line):

> You take Mary, I'll take Sue,
> Ain't no difference 'twixt the two.
> Cocaine run all 'round my brain.

3

"Cold Turkey"

When John Lennon and Yoko Ono wanted to kick heroin, they took an ocean cruise, didn't bring any junk with them, and locked themselves in their cabin for the duration. At the end of the voyage, they were clean. Lennon wrote "Cold Turkey" about the hellish experience in 1969, but the other Beatles didn't want to record it, so he, Ono, Eric Clapton, and a couple of other musicians laid it down. The lyrics are heavy-handed and straight-forward (the only clever turn of phrase being "goose-pimple bone"), but what makes the song are Lennon's convincing screams, groans, and panting—sounds that must've been coming from the cabin during the cruise.

 **LIST 8** | **12 Songs About Drugs**

4

"Coma White"

Marilyn Manson's songs are rife with imaginative drug references like "my phenobarbi-doll," "cocaingels," and, "You're kissing me like benzocaine with your sleeping pill eyes." But surprisingly, Manson has hardly done any songs entirely about drugs. Even "I Don't Like the Drugs (But the Drugs Like Me)" is really about—like most of his output—the shallowness of society, the hypocrisy of the bourgeoisie, and the overall suckiness of the world. The only one that qualifies as a full-fledged drug song is "Coma White," which is summed up by the line: "all the drugs in this world won't save her from herself."

5

"Easy Skanking"

One of Bob Marley's many odes to pot, "Easy Skanking" basically recreates the feeling of slowly descending into a warm, mellow buzz. Just in case there's any confusion about what's going on, Marley says: "Excuse me while I light my spliff."

6

"Heroin"

In this song, penned by Lou Reed, The Velvet Underground captures some of the ambivalence of smack—the way it helps you escape, the way it kills you—but in the end, it leans more toward the positives. Compare the opening lines of the second verse ("When I'm rushing on my run / And I feel just like Jesus' son") with the opening lines of the next verse ("I have made a very big decision / I'm goin' to try to nullify my life").

7

"Hits From the Bong"

Cypress Hill's breakthrough record, *Black Sunday*, is practically a concept album about chronic. The big hit, "Insane in the Brain," contains the lines: "I got to get my props / Cops come and try to snatch my crops." The most memorable line in "I Wanna Get High" is: "Tell Bill Clinton to go and inhale."

"Hits From the Bong" gets into the minutiae of the act of smoking: "I like a blunt or a big fat cone / But my double-barrel bong is gettin' me stoned." Plus: "And then take that finger off of that hole / Plug it, unplug it." B-Real even offers care and maintenance tips like: "when I pack a fresh bowl I clean the screen."

8

"Hurt"

Trent Reznor's unsparing song about heroin addiction gained a second life when it was improbably covered by Johnny Cash. The Man in Black stripped down the Nine Inch Nails tune to its bare bones, singing it toward the end of his hard-bitten life. Though Cash apparently was never a smack addict, he did battle the bottle and speed. He proclaimed "Hurt" to be the best anti-drug song ever written. The lyrics are rife with images of waste and decay: "You could have it all / My empire of dirt," and, "I wear this crown of shit / Upon my liar's chair."

9

"Lit Up"

While Clapton's "Cocaine" sounds so mellow that it should be about 'Ludes, Buckcherry's "Lit Up" is fueled by coke. Loud, aggressive, and bouncing off the walls, it's the musical equivalent of snorting a line. When Josh Todd shouts, "You're at ten but, money, I'm on eleven," you know he means it. If the Medellin Cartel licensed an official song for their product, it would be "Lit Up."

10

"Mother's Little Helper"

Like Marilyn Manson, the Rolling Stones did very few songs completely about drugs, though their oeuvre is littered with drug references. Their masterpiece *Exile on Main Street* crackles with lines like, "I need a shot of salvation, baby, once in a while," and, "Doctor prescribes drug store supplies / Who's gonna help him to kick it?"

Their 1966 hit "Mother's Little Helper" is a catchy, condescending number that rakes women over the coals for their heavy use of tranquilizers in the 1950s and 1960s. These housewives and proto-soccer moms are so bored or stressed out by their domestic chores that they wolf down barbiturates to cope. We can imagine the Glimmer Twins writing these disapproving lyrics as Mick rolls another joint and Keith mainlines some H.

11

"Semi-Charmed Life"

A huge hit for Third Eye Blind in 1997, it might take repeated listenings to realize this song is about methamphetamine. Sure, the line "Doing crystal meth will lift you up until you break" is the giveaway, but between the oft-bleeped words and semi-intelligible delivery, you might not hear it. "Semi-Charmed" contains some of the cleverest lyrics in a drug song, including: "And I speak to you like the chorus to the verse / Chop another line like a coda with a curse," and, "The sky it was gold, it was rose / I was taking sips of it through my nose."

12

"Who Put the Benzedrine in Mrs. Murphy's Ovaltine?"

If you think rock songs about drugs began appearing in the 1960s, better think again. Back in those blissful, bygone days that Tipper Gore dreams about, Henry "The Hipster" Gibson—basically a proto-Jerry Lewis who never lived up to his potential—had a hit with a novelty song about an old lady who drinks a cup of Ovaltine every night before bed. Suddenly she's having trouble sleeping, and it turns out that some prankster has been slipping speed into her bedtime drink. The year of this degenerate song? 1944.

Honorable Mentions

"Lucy in the Sky With Diamonds"

Britain banned the third track on the Beatles' epochal *Sergeant Pepper's Lonely Hearts Club Band*, John Lennon's "Lucy in the Sky With Diamonds." The rationale was that the hallucinatory song vividly describes an acid trip, and the initials of the title are "L.S.D." Lennon always denied this interpretation of the song, saying that the lyrics, including the title, were based on a drawing that his then-young son Julian created. In support of this, notice that the imagery fits right in with Lewis Carroll's "Alice in Wonderland" books, which also influenced Lennon's Beatlesongs "I Am the Walrus" and "Cry Baby Cry." Then again, some have argued that the Alice books are themselves descriptions of drug trips, so maybe we're right back where we started.

"Puff the Magic Dragon"

In a similar manner, folk trio Peter, Paul and Mary have always denied that their signature 1963 song is about marijuana, when signs seem to point to this interpretation: the word "puff"; dragons are generally visualized as green (same as pot); the name of the boy in the song is Jackie *Paper*; he eventually grows up and has nothing more to do with Puff.

> **Drug Quote # 7**
> "I don't like drugs. I think cocaine is a very bad, habit-forming drug. It's about the most boring drug ever invented. [Laughs.] I mean, it's very bad and very debilitating. I can't understand the fashion for it. 'Cause it's so expensive."
> –Mick Jagger, 1980

1

Hemp oil—a nutritious substance derived from hemp seed—is sold in health food stores and even some mainstream grocery stores. *The Journal of Analytical Toxicology* spells out the problem: "A dose consistent with the manufacturer's recommendation of one to four tablespoons per day (15-60 mL) would be sufficient to cause a positive finding for cannabinoid metabolites in a workplace urine drug-testing procedure designed to detect marijuana use." An Air Force master sergeant was court martialed when drug tests labeled him a pot-smoker, but in late 1997 a jury acquitted him on all charges after his use of hemp oil was presented.

2

Newer **antibiotics** from the –cillin family (e.g., amoxicillin) can test as coke.

3

Diazepam, a tranquilizer, triggers PCP-positive results.

LIST 9

16 Legal Substances That Can Cause False Positives on Drug Tests

4 5 6

Cold remedies, decongestants, and diet pills can show up as speed due to the presence of **ephedrine, pseudoephedrine, phenypropanolamine**, and similar substances.

7

Some **cough suppressants** can look like opiates to drug tests.

8

Some **antidepressants** cause false positives for opiates within three days of use.

9

The common pain reliever **ibuprofen**, at least in the past, would show up as THC (the active ingredient in pot) on some drug tests, and, in high doses, it might still be causing some false positives.

10

DHEA, taken by people with AIDS, shows up as anabolic steroids.

11

Testosterone supplements also can make you look like a 'roid user.

12 13

Novocaine and **lidocaine**—two synthetic anesthetics based on cocaine and commonly used in medical and dental procedures—can, not surprisingly, give a false positive for coke.

14

Nyquil Nighttime Cold Medicine and other over-the-counter formulations containing **doxylamine** can show up as methadone for 48 hours.

15

Because pastries and breads with **poppy seeds** contain so few of them, you'd have to eat a lot before you show up positive for opiates, and, regardless, drug tests can now differentiate between baked goods and the stuff that gets you high.

16

Second-hand **pot smoke** can be enough to trigger a false positive. ◘

Drug Quote # 8
"I love what speed and coke do to my weight. It's unnatural, I know. I could just exercise..."
–Carrie Fisher

1

C-4 explosive

It's hard to know what to make of the claim that you can get high from this plastic explosive. It appears in only one place that I've seen, a fairly level-headed book titled *Uppers, Downers, All-Arounders*, written by two people from the Haight-Ashbury Free Clinic. They devote two sentences to the topic:

> Modern veterans have been known to ingest C4 or cyclonite plastic explosives for their psychedelic effects. Tremors and seizure activity can result but usually not an explosion as it takes a blasting cap to set off the chemical.

Seems pretty outlandish, but perhaps it's true. A Marine Corps training document on explosives contains the following warning: "Do not ingest any explosive material."

2

carbogen

When you inhale this mixture of oxygen (70 percent) and carbon dioxide (30 percent), your brain thinks that you're dying of suffocation,

LIST 10 · 12 Strange Drugs

although you're actually getting enough oxygen to function normally. In the Seventh Day Adventist magazine *Signs of the Times* (of all places), Dr. Jack Provonsha writes: "Subjects on carbon dioxide report separation of the self from the body. And as with the [psychedelic] drugs and NDEs [near death experiences], there were reports of caves, tunnels, intensely bright lights, visions of other persons, luminaries, reliving of the past, and 'spiritual' experiences." He then reprints the experience of a carbogen user as first relayed in Dr. L.J. Meduna's pioneering work on the subject, *Carbon Dioxide Therapy* (1950):

> I felt myself being separated; my soul, drawing apart from the physical being, was drawn...seemingly to leave the earth and to go upward where it reached a greater Spirit with whom there was a communion, producing a remarkable new relaxation and deep security.... I felt the Greater Spirit even smiling indulgently upon me in my vain little efforts to carry on by myself, and I pressed close [to] the warmth and tender strength and felt assurance of enough power to overcome whatever lay ahead for me.

Psychonaut Myron Stolaroff took carbogen once a week for two years under a doctor's supervision. "I always approached the experience with enormous anxiety," he wrote, "but got considerable relief when I explosively discharged repressed material. I would then feel great for a few days, but then relapse back to my previous condition."

During the same time that LSD was being introduced into psychotherapy, carbogen was also used. Stolaroff says that around 200 therapists employed the procedure, and they even formed a short-lived professional organization.

3
catnip

Catnip isn't just for felines anymore. Most humans who've smoked it say that it's like a mild, mellow pot buzz. Nothing to get too excited about, but since it's cheap and legal, most recommend it.

4
clomipramine (trade name: Anafranil)

The strange thing about this prescription antidepressant—most often prescribed for obsessive-compulsive disorder—is the side effect it causes in a few people: spontaneous orgasms while yawning. A 1983 article in the *Canadian Journal of Psychiatry* presents the cases of three people who experience this pleasurable but disconcerting phenomenon. A woman in her late twenties said that she came *every time* she yawned. "She found she was able to experience orgasm by deliberate yawning," the authors note. A man in his mid-twenties reported that sometimes when he yawned, he would ejaculate, even though he wasn't turned on at the time. "The awkwardness and embarrassment was overcome by continuously wearing a condom." The final patient, a woman in her forties, didn't necessarily cream each time she yawned, but she would get so intensely horny that she'd often have to masturbate. In all cases, the effects stopped soon after the patients quit popping clomipramine.

5

DDT

When it was still thought to be pretty safe for humans, the now-banned pesticide DDT was used for kicks. As inconceivable as it now seems, a popular cocktail of the 1950s, a Mickey Slim, was made by adding a very small amount of DDT to gin. Since it attacks the nervous system, a dollop produced sensations that were kinda pleasurable in a fucked-up way.

6

DIPT

A tryptamine that's known for mainly affecting auditory sensations. An experiment in the classic book *TIHKAL* by Alexander and Ann Shulgin relates: "Radio voices are all low, music out of key. Piano sounds like a bar-room disaster. The telephone ringing sounds partly underwater." Orally taking a larger amount results in: "Abrupt sounds have golden spikes attached to them as after-sounds, but I can't focus in on any other sensory changes." At a much higher dosage: "The voices of people were extremely distorted—males sounded like frogs—children sounded like they were talking through synthesizers to imitate outer space people in science fiction movies."

A user named Borkhane writes: "At this level of DIPT effects, all music sounded absolutely terrible, with no harmonic structure intact at all. Music that was normally quite familiar sounded totally foreign. It was really like listening to a totally different version of the song, with the only familiar elements being the lyrics."

7

poisons and venom

Several plants known for their hallucinogenic effects are quite toxic, such as the *Datura* family, which includes Jimsonweed. And, of course, you can make the argument that any substance is toxic if you ingest enough of it. Still, some natural substances known *primarily* as poisons—arsenic, strychnine, and venom—have been used in sublethal doses for their mind-altering effects. Information on this is hard to come by, and an in-depth study would prove fascinating. For now, we have these bits and pieces:

☙ In 1817, when the Queen of Portugal was dying a slow, painful death, one of her slaves gave her a mixture of pot and arsenic which completely relieved her suffering.

☙ In his classic 1885 book *Plant Intoxicants*, Baron Ernst von Bibra discusses the eating of arsenic by the mountain-dwellers of Austria. The two reasons given are that the poison "facilitates breathing while climbing...it makes them well ventilated" and "to obtain healthy and sturdy looks, to appear strong and robust."

☙ Also in 1885, *Chambers Journal of Popular Literature, Science and Art* carried an article discussing arsenic use:

> When a man has once begun to indulge in it he must continue to indulge; or, as it is popularly expressed, the last dose kills him. Indeed the arsenic eater must not only continue his indulgence, he must also increase the quantity of the drug, so that it is extraordinarily difficult to stop the habit; for, as the sudden cessation causes death, the gradual cessation produces such a terrible heart knowing that it may probably be said that no genuine arsenic eater ever ceased to eat arsenic while life lasted.

☠ The 1902 book *Morphinism and Narcomanias From Other Drugs* discusses arsenic addiction.

☠ Victorian-era cotton farmer James Maybrick achieved notoriety in 1992 when *The Diary of Jack the Ripper* was published. Now widely (though not universally) regarded as a forgery, this diary supposedly was written by Maybrick, who supposedly was Jack the Ripper. Whether or not Maybrick was the Ripper, he was an actual person who—as the diaries relate—was addicted to arsenic.

☠ In his article theorizing that Napoleon Bonaparte may have been an arsenic junkie, Napoleonic expert Bob Elmer writes: "Arsenic was also used by some as a mind-altering drug, much as marijuana or cocaine is used today. In small doses it gave the user a feeling of well-being, strength, and sexual staying power."

☠ In 1909, while discussing drug use in the United States, the *New York Times* bemoaned: "...a legion of others habitually use belladonna, arsenic, and strychnine without consulting a physician."

☠ *The Encyclopedia of Psychoactive Substances* reveals: "Holy men in India are reported to smoke cobra venom for its psychoactive effects.... [T]heir dried venom glands or crystallized venom is often mixed with cannabis when smoked."

☠ The *Encyclopedia* further notes that ten Native American tribes in California are known to swallow live ants as means of inducing visions. The ants bite the stomach lining, injecting their venom, and later may be vomited up, still alive.

8

rhododendron

A single species of rhododendron, the lavender *ponticum*, is known to create trips when its smoke is inhaled. The plant is quite poisonous, though, so this seems to be a case where ingesting sublethal doses of harmful plants—*a la* Jimsonweed and belladonna—gets you high by attacking the hell out of your nervous system.

9

saffron

The expensive flavoring saffron—the dried, crushed stamen of the *Crocus sativas*—is not often mentioned in the canon of mind-altering drugs, but it was the most oft-used ingredient in laudanum, after opium and alcohol, of course. *The Encyclopedia of Psychoactive Substances* notes that the famously orange-yellow flower "is known to have soporific and narcotic effects similar to those of opium."

10

salamander brandy

Not be found on the shelves of your local liquor store, salamander brandy is noncommercially produced in parts of Slovenia. At least four ways—all involving cruelty toward the amphibians—are used. In one, the salamanders are placed on a sieve and brandy is poured over them until they drown. In another approach, the poor beasts are suspended by their back legs as brandy drips down the string and over their bodies. In all cases, the salamanders are so frightened and distressed that they excrete large amounts of poisonous slime, which then infuses the brandy. A reporter who tried the concoction describes his trip:

> And then it...started unnaturally, colorfully glittering around the treetops and trees, which were weirdly, hysterically rushing into the depths of gorges... It was as if I were totally unburdened by the biology of extraterrestrial beings from some other planet and watched everything, the grass, the insects or a grazing cow in the vicinity...and absolutely everything seemed new and strange, and I wished to fuck something, anything. And in this almost full absence from this world...I chose the beech tree. Their trunks...seemed horribly erotic to me. ...After this I finally crashed into the wet leaves and maybe even slept for a while. But damn, a few salamanders walked near by. And they said with their mysterious voices: look, look, who's there, not a salamander for sure...

Slovenian academic Miha Kozorog contests the view that this beverage is a traditional hallucinogenic drug. Instead, he believes it's a deceitful way of making brandy—the punch of the salamander mucus supposedly makes up for low alcohol content.

11

urine

Not just any urine, of course, but the wizz of a person who has partaken of the *amanita muscaria* mushroom (a/k/a fly agaric). At one time, Eskimos and tribes in Siberia were known to use this trick for a couple of reasons. First, since there wasn't an endless supply of 'shrooms, this approach helped economize them. Not only would drinking the pee of someone who had eaten the mushroom get you high, drinking the urine of the first piss-sipper would also work. And so on, down through five people. An added benefit was that the more the mushrooms were processed through digestive systems, the less they caused cramps and nausea.

On a related note, *New Scientist* reports that reindeer also liked to nosh on fly agaric, so the Koryak people of Siberia would tie up the wasted animals until they stopped tripping, butcher them, then eat them for a second-hand high.

12

xenon

The noble gas xenon—which you might remember from your days of studying the periodic table—can be inhaled for a high similar to nitrous oxide (laughing gas). In a trip report on the website Lyceaum, an anonymous user notices "an amazing ability to zero in on 'singularity' thoughts and memories and hold them in suspension for 'sentiment orgasms.'" This adventurous soul notes that, unlike laughing gas, there's no headachiness or "wa-wa" auditory hallucinations. "As with nitrous, I get the repeating themes of cycles as a major message. Probably because it is so connected with breathing; cycles of life / life-cycles / life is cycles: that's the message."

> **Drug Quote # 9**
> "I am a great believer in the value of being high. High states of consciousness show us the potentials of our nervous systems. They help us integrate mind and body. They promote health. And they feel good."
> –Andrew Weil, M.D.

Honorable Mention

old books

Okay, it's not the books themselves that can get you high but the fungus that sometimes grows on them. Damp, musty libraries with creaky, old volumes are breeding grounds for mold, including some types that can cause hallucinations and other effects, such as dizziness and vomiting. ⌂

Brand loyalty isn't just for soap and cigarettes. Heroin dealers often create their own "brand," signified by a name and/or logo. If a user likes a particular high, this "mark of quality" keeps them coming back for more of the same kind of skag. Some brands last for years; some are around literally for a single day. The National Drug Intelligence Center reported on a "cutting mill" found in New York: "On the walls of the apartment charts displayed several brand names of heroin along with different formulas for cutting each brand."

1. **america on-line**
2. **bart simpson**
3. **big doodig**
4. **big mac**
5. **bin laden**
6. **black angel**
7. **body bag**
8. **bone collector**
9. **chevrolet**
10. **cold water**
11. **colt 45**
12. **dead on arrival**
13. **dead president**
14. **dead.com**
15. **death certificate**
16. **devil's advocate**
17. **diesel**
18. **DMX**

LIST 11

82 Brands of Heroin

19. **Double UOGlobe**
    (a/k/a Double Globe)

    Created in the refinery of America's "ally" General Ouane Rattikone of Laos, this was the favorite brand among American GIs during the Vietnam War.

20. **doo-wop**

21. **fatal**

22. **fingers**

23. **G-money**

24. **Godzilla**

25. **godfather**

26. **holy terror**

27. **holyfield**

28. **homicide**

29. **I'll be back**

30. **jerry springer**

31. **john hinkley**

32. **kembra**

    Named after rock 'n' roll performance artist Kembra Pfahler.

33. **lexus**

34. **life**

35. **life after death**

36. **lucifer**

37. **m & m**

38. **maggie 2**

39. **magnum 357**

40. **mercedes**

41. **mike tyson**

42. **millennium 2000**

43. **monica lewinski**

44. **motorola**

45. **movada**

46. **murder one**

47. **nautica**

48. **new york**

49. **nike**

50. **octopus**

51. **old navy**

52. **one and done**

53. **opium**

54. **pacman**

55. **painkiller**

56. **playboy**

57. **plymouth**

58. **poison**

59. **purple haze**

60. **red rum**

    Reportedly, this was the brand that killed Smashing Pumpkins' touring keyboardist Jonathan Melvion in July 1996.

61. **Shark**

62. **skull and crossbones**

63. **son of sam**

64. **suicide**

65. **super AT&T**

66. **super buick**

67. **timberland**

68. **tommy hilfiger**

69. **toombstone** [sic]

70. **toyota**

71. **Tres pesos**

72. **UPS**

73. **USA**

74. **white house**

75. **WTC**

76. **7up**

77. **747**

78. **777**

79. **8-ball**

80. **9/11 world trade center**

81. **911**

82. **$**

When cannabis has enough THC to get you high, it's called marijuana. When cannabis has very little or no THC, it's called hemp. Perhaps the world's most useful plant, hemp has been put to work by the human race since before recorded history. Only relatively recently, because its sibling makes people feel good, has this answer to our environmental and industrial problems been outlawed.

1. **flags**

   Up to the 1820s, most US flags were made of hemp.

2. **paper**

   The first instance of printed text on paper—one million copies of Buddhist prayers for peace in Japan, 764 A.D.—involved pure hemp paper. The drafts of the Declaration of Independence and the Constitution were written on hemp paper. The Gutenberg Bible, the original King James Bible, and early editions of Mark Twain's works are among the important books printed on hemp. Hemp makes good specialty paper, for things like tea bags, coffee filters, paper currency, and archival paper. According to the North American Industrial Hemp Council: "Kimberly-Clark (a Fortune 500 company) has a mill in France which produces hemp paper preferred for bibles and cigarette paper because it lasts a long time and doesn't yellow."

3–4. **paints** and **varnish**

5–11. **rope, string, twine,** and **thread; parachute webbing; nets; rigging** for ships. The *USS Constitution* (a/k/a Old Ironsides) contained a minimum of 60 tons of hemp.

LIST 12

42+ Things That Have Been Made Out of Hemp

12. **clothes**

Including such Smithsonian-worthy garments as the uniforms of George Washington's Continental Army and the original Levi's jeans. Since at least 500 BC, hemp has been woven into cloth so fine it is all but indistinguishable from linen. Shirts, pants, coats, hats, dresses, lingerie, diapers, and more have been and currently are being fashioned from cannabis.

13. **sheets** and **quilts**

14. **rugs**

15. **sacks, bags, etc.**

16. **towels**

17. **canvas**

The US government film *Hemp for Victory* reminds us: "Indeed the very word *canvas* comes from the Arabic word for hemp." It has been woven into tents, sails, wagon covers, and more. Hemp was the canvas of choice for many of the world's greatest painters, including Monet, Delacroix, Ingres, Rembrandt, Van Gogh, and Miró.

18. **food** and **drink**

Humans noshed on hemp seeds in prehistoric times and continue to do so. Besides being eaten straight, they can be made into oatmeal, porridge, flour, pastries, ice cream, candy, veggie burgers, cookies, cereal, margarine, cheese, soda, beer, milk....

19. **gum**

20. **birdseed**

21. **pet food**

22. **animal bedding**

The Queen of England's horse sleeps in a nest of pure hemp.

23. **medicine**

24-25. **soap** and **shampoo**

26. **lip balm**

27. **body lotion**

28. **sexual lubricant**

29. **deodorant**

30. **oil**

31. **fuel** (ethanol)

32. **methanol**

Methanol is a key chemical in the production of plastics, resins, and vinyl.

33. **crayons**

34. **candles**

35. **cars and other vehicles**

In 1941, Henry Ford unveiled a lightweight, dent-resistant car that was made except for the frame from plastic created from the fibers of hemp, wheat, an sisal.

36. **building materials**

Pure hemp pulp can be pressed into boards, bricks, beams, paneling, posts, cabinetry, and other material used to construct buildings.

37. **insulation**

38. **furniture**

39. **fire hoses**

40. **fire**

Hemp can be burned like wood to create heat.

41. **burning oil**

Used instead of kerosene in lamps.

42. **dynamite**

Tommy Chong—the comedian best known for his stoner movies with Cheech Marin—was the impresario of Chong Glass, a small outfit that made beautiful smoking paraphernalia (bongs and various pipes). As part of the Drug Enforcement Administration's spring 2003 crackdown on Web-based sellers of toking equipment—Operation Pipe Dreams and Operation Headhunter—Chong's home was raided, and the feds seized all the goods from his business. Around three months later, Chong pled guilty to conspiring to sell drug paraphernalia and was sentenced to nine months in the clink, plus one year probation. Below are the names of the bong models that were stolen and destroyed by the feds.

1. **Babe**

2. **Big Bamboo**

3. **Bombay**

4. **Cheech**

5. **Malibu**

6. **Marbelized**

7. **Nectar**

8. **Strawberry**

9. **Tijuana**

10. **Topanga**

☿

Tommy Chong's Strawberry bong

LIST 13

10 of Chong's Bongs

Drugs are one of the most obvious—and, in some ways at least, the easiest—ways to induce altered states of mind, but there are many paths you can take. Alternative health guru Dr. Andrew Weil explains: "I believe strongly that psychedelics merely trigger or release certain experiences that originate in the human nervous system and that one can learn to have these experiences without drugs. That so many different methods lead to the same experiences suggests that the experiences come from inside us, that they are latent in the human nervous system, waiting to be released."

breathing

Little kids learn the hyperventilation trick, where lack of oxygen causes brief, basically uncontrollable altered states. In a more sophisticated approach, proper breathing technique is crucial to all forms of meditation, but sometimes respiration is the *complete* focus of the technique. In fact, "breathwork" is an entire field within holistic health and alternative healing.

eclipses

Dr. Weil is apparently the first, perhaps the only, person to suggest that being outside during a solar eclipse leads to altered states. A self-described "overt eclipse freak" who tries to view as many as possible, Weil has felt this "high" himself and heard the feeling described similarly by others who watch the Moon cover the Sun. He postulates that it has something to do with the unearthly light, the feelings of unreality and dreaminess, and the complete unique-

12 Ways to Alter Your Consciousness Without Drugs

ness and majesty of the event. "Time did not flow," he writes. "I have no way of comparing those three and a half minutes of clock time to any other three-and-a-half minute interval I have experienced."

3

Finnegans Wake

Guerrilla philosopher and reality hacker Robert Anton Wilson believes that reading aloud James Joyce's experimental novel *Finnegans Wake* triggers altered states.

4

flickering lights

Not only does strobing light create a feeling of unreality, but it has concrete physical effects on the brain, as evidenced by the fact that it triggers seizures in people with epilepsy. The rotating "Dreamachine"—created by Brion Gysin and Ian Sommerville—is a sophisticated use of flashing light to send consciousness to new heights.

5 6

laughing and crying

Not just any laughing will do the trick, but a gut-busting, eye-watering fit of hysteria is likely to invoke a cleansed sense of well-being that feels like a pleasant high. Andrew Weil believes this results from the fact that during laughter, our logical, uptight cerebral cortex is no longer in control, having given over to the primitive brainstem. This is evidenced by the creation of tears, the spasming of the

diaphragm, and "the loss of upright posture" that occur when you laugh your ass off. All are signs that the autonomic nervous system has taken over. Weil writes, "In a fit of laughter there is no ego—no censorship of messages flowing back and forth in the brain." Research has shown that laughter reduces stress hormones (such as dopamine) and stimulates the release of endorphins, the body's own opiates.

As with laughing, a good crying jag can lead to a transcendent sense of lightness and well-being, a cleansed feeling due partially to endorphins, deeper respiration, and other effects of the limbic system.

7

music

Whether it's loud, crunching rock and roll that makes you feel like you've taken speed, or ethereal chanting that lifts you out of your body, music has myriad ways of changing your state of being. And that's just from listening to it. Playing it can take you into a zone where nothing exists but you and the music. Performing chant is often cited as particularly transcendent, presumably because of the vibrations it sends throughout your body and the way it focuses and slows breathing.

8

pain, extreme discomfort, exhaustion

When applied in correct ways and settings, pain leads many people to altered states. This is a recurring theme in the literature of

SM, in which practitioners routinely describe transcendent, ecstatic experiences. Many ancient body-oriented rituals—such as the Sun Dance performed by many Native American tribes—apparently involve the same mechanisms. The pseudonymous Fakir Musafar has become legendary in alternative circles for having performed almost every type of body modification, adornment, and ritual known to the human race, starting with giving himself tattoos and piercings when he was a preteen. He says of his experiences:

> One of the first altered states you can learn is to separate your consciousness from your body. You don't walk away from your body, you don't separate from your body, but the part of you that feels and thinks can separate from the feelings in the body itself. So that makes it possible for you to push a needle through. You don't feel the pain; the body feels the pain, and you observe the body recording or feeling sensation. Then it's not pain. If you can learn to separate your consciousness and your attention from your body, you can do almost anything to it and you don't feel pain! If all your attention is locked in your body, and not focused outside the body or on a specific body point, you'll feel pain. That's one of the first lessons I learned. That's an altered state. And there are hundreds of different kinds of altered states.

Musafar also says:

> The negativity of pain (strong, unexpected sensation) only exists for people who are relatively undeveloped. If you have enough training, instruction and practice, you can transcend, transmute or change a sensation to anything you wish.... That's what I do when I hang by fleshhooks. People say, "That's incredibly painful!" I say, "No, it's ecstatic, it's beautiful!"

Writer Patrick Califia has been exploring and expounding on SM for around three decades now. In his essay "Shiny Sharp Things," he writes: "There is a whole other reality beyond our flesh. But in this world, our flesh is our only way to gather information and to experience what is within and outside of ourselves. So we have to use flesh to get to that other place. These practices have become taboo."

Of course, you don't need to do something as extreme as hanging by hooks to experience this transcendence (although it does seem that the more extreme the ritual, the more ecstatic the experience). The sweat lodge used by Native American tribes works on a similar principle, with the intense heat of the steam (created when water is thrown on a pit full of red-hot stones) in a small, enclosed area triggering altered states. Andrew Weil suggests that eating chili peppers is another way to use (mild) pain to invoke (mild) altered states.

Physical exhaustion can also act as a trigger, the "runner's high" being the most famous example. It has long been thought to spark the release of the body's own opioids, but recent studies are pointing toward the body's natural cannabis analogues as the biochemical that gets released. Similarly, not all instances of the Sun Dance involved suspension by flesh; sometimes the participants achieved altered states by dancing until they literally dropped from overexertion.

rapid blinking

In her autobiography, autistic Donna Williams writes: "One of the ways of making things seem to slow down was to blink or to turn the light on and off really fast. If you blinked really fast, people behaved like in old frame-by-frame movies; you got the effect of strobe lights without the control being taken out of your hands." By seeming to slow down the world around her, the rapid blinking gave Williams a sense of detachment, as if she were watching reality instead of being a part of it—a sure sign of an altered state. Since, as she points out, this technique simulates a strobe light, it might also have the physiological effects of strobe lights, triggering certain pulses in the brain.

10

spinning

From kids on playgrounds to Sufi mystics ("whirling dervishes"), spinning is a quick, easy way to instigate an undeniable trip, in the physical and mental senses.

11

touching, sex, orgasm

Physical contact with other people releases endorphins, which explains some of the pleasurable sensations of massage, cuddling, and sex. Orgasm releases a cascade of endorphins all by itself, as well as the hormone oxytocin. Not a whole lot is known about the effects of oxytocin, but it seems to increase interpersonal bonding and feelings of closeness.

Besides inciting the release of these hormones, the orgasm itself is simply a transcendent experience. If you give yourself over to it completely, it transports you to another state of consciousness where the ego can-

not tread. There's a reason that the French call it *petit mort*, "little death." Hinduism, Buddhism, and Taoism all have branches that seek to use orgasm (or withholding of orgasm) as a means of channeling life-force energy into heightened spirituality.

12

vomiting

Yacking your guts up is usually considered a miserable experience, but Andrew Weil argues that it may be a way of experiencing an altered state. He highlights yogic and Native American rituals involving the act, and he points out that barfing massively invokes the parasympathetic nervous system, which can have pleasing effects on respiration, heart rate, and lacrimation (production of tears). It might also be a way to rid yourself of unwanted emotions and patterns. Weil reports on his self-induced vomiting: "From the successes I have had, I can testify that the result is indeed a feeling of well-being."

Others: **falling in love, fasting, hypnosis, meditation, sensory deprivation, sensory overload,** and **sleeping and dreaming.**

+ Crime and Punishment

At press time, the Innocence Project had secured the release of 141 people who were rotting in prison for crimes they didn't commit. Using DNA testing, the nonprofit group proves that the wrongfully convicted are not the ones who committed the crimes in question.

1

Steven Avery

Avery was sent up in 1986 on convictions for first-degree sexual assault, attempted murder, and false imprisonment. After serving eighteen years in hell, DNA uncovered the real perp.

2

Terry Chalmers

Chalmers is one of many poor saps who went to prison based solely on identification by the victim. The woman who was raped was unable to pick Chalmers out of a photo line-up the first time around. A month and a half later, she was shown another group of six photos. Chalmers was the only one whose picture was in both line-ups, and the victim chose him. In court, she reaffirmed that he was the one who raped and robbed her. Chalmers was sentenced to twelve to 24 years for rape, sodomy, robbery, and two counts of grand larceny. DNA tests performed in summer 1994 showed that he didn't do it, and he was released after spending seven and a half years in prison.

LIST 15 | 13 Innocent People Who Went to Prison

3

Lonnie Erby

In 1985, a series of rapes and attempted rapes of teenage girls in St. Louis had the city on edge. Police picked up Erby in the vicinity where a peeping tom had been reported, and prosecutors considered him a suspect in the attacks. All of the victims fingered him as their assailant. Even though he had alibi witnesses for the times of the attacks, he was sentenced to 115 years on multiple counts: kidnapping, armed criminal action, forcible rape, forcible sodomy, and stealing. The Innocence Project started working on his case in 1995 but wasn't able to force DNA testing until eight years later. The results showed that Erby could not possibly have committed any of the crimes.

4

Richard Johnson

Johnson was charged with raping and robbing a woman who later picked him out of a photo line-up and a live line-up. No other evidence was presented, and, unbelievably, his own attorney failed to submit evidence that would've immediately cleared Johnson (tests showed the victim had been raped by someone who secretes H antigens; Johnson does not secrete them). After four years in the clink, he was given his life back in 1996, thanks to DNA testing and the Innocence Project.

5

Larry Maze

In 2001, Maze became the one-hundredth innocent person to be released from prison based on DNA tests. A rape victim hadn't picked him out of two live line-ups but fingered him in a photo line-up. Based completely on this less-than-reassuring identification, Maze was given 80 years in the slammer. After the Innocence Project got involved, authorities said that the rape kit had been lost. When pressed, they finally located it, and it showed that Maze was not the rapist. He had served *21 years*. The Project reports: "Shockingly, after the new prosecutors on the case contacted the victim, she revealed that the police had hypnotized her prior to her identification of Mayes from the photographic lineup."

6

Calvin Lee Scott

Scott was convicted of a rape that occurred in 1982. He started serving his sentence the next year, and it wasn't until 20 years later the real rapist was uncovered and Scott was freed.

7

Earl Washington

Police thought Washington had raped and killed a young mother in Culpeper, Virginia.

When they picked him up for an alleged assault, Washington—whose IQ is in the neighborhood of 69—rapidly agreed with police that he was responsible for five different crimes, including the sexual assault/murder. The courts threw out four of those confessions when it became obvious that Washington had just told the cops what they wanted to hear. Yet the district attorney apparently was convinced that the fifth confession was genuine, even though Washington didn't know any of the details (for example, he said he knifed the victim two or three times when she had actually been stabbed 38 times). This obviously bogus confession was literally the only evidence against Washington, but it was enough to get him sentenced to death. After seventeen years, he was sprung when DNA showed the perp was someone else.

8

Bernard Webster

Three eyewitnesses (including the victim) and misleading scientific testimony were enough to get Webster sentenced to 30 years for rape and housebreaking. He went in as a 20-year-old and came out as a 40-year-old after DNA testing showed he could not have been the one who committed the 1982 crime.

9 **10** **11** **12** **13**

The Central Park Five

In a crime that became seared into our collective psyche, Trisha Meili was viciously raped and beaten almost to death while jogging in Central Park on April 19, 1989. Through intense, marathon interrogations, police obtained conflicting confessions from five teenagers: Yusef Salaam, Kevin Richardson, Antron McCray, Raymond Santana, and Kharey Wise. After they had served eight years, Matias Reyes—already in prison for rape and murder—said that he had committed the crime. DNA from hair and semen on the victim were tested and matched to Wise. A hair found on one of the boys, which had "matched and resembled" the victim's hair, was shown through mitochondrial DNA testing not to be hers. The five young men were freed in December 2002. ◘

Law Quote #1
"Law never made men a whit more just; and, by means of their respect for it, even the well-disposed are daily made the agents of injustice."
–Henry David Thoreau

1

Frank J. Coppola

August 10, 1982; Virginia; electrocution. Although no media representatives witnessed the execution and no details were ever released by the Virginia Department of Corrections, an attorney who was present later stated that it took two 55-second jolts of electricity to kill Coppola. The second jolt produced the odor and sizzling sound of burning flesh, and Coppola's head and leg caught on fire. Smoke filled the death chamber from floor to ceiling.

2

John Evans

April 22, 1983; Alabama; electrocution. After the first jolt of electricity, sparks and flames erupted from the electrode attached to Evans' leg. The electrode burst from the strap holding it in place and caught on fire. Smoke and sparks also came out from under the hood in the vicinity of Evans' left temple. Two physicians entered the chamber and found a heartbeat. The electrode was reattached to his leg, and another jolt of electricity was applied. This resulted in more smoke and burning flesh. Again the doctors found a heartbeat. Ignoring the pleas of Evans' lawyer, a third jolt of electricity was applied. The execution took fourteen minutes and left Evans' body charred and smoldering.

3

Jimmy Lee Gray

September 2, 1983; Mississippi; asphyxiation. Officials had to clear the room eight minutes after the gas was released when Gray's desperate gasps for air repulsed witnesses. His attorney, Dennis Balske of Montgomery, Alabama, criticized state officials for clearing the room when the inmate was still alive. Said noted death penalty defense attorney David Bruck: "Jimmy Lee Gray died banging his head against a steel pole in the gas chamber while the reporters counted his moans (eleven, according to the Associated Press)." Later it was revealed that the executioner, Barry Bruce, was drunk.

LIST 16 | 36 Botched Executions
Michael L. Radelet, Ph.D.

Alpha Otis Stephens

December 12, 1984; Georgia; electrocution.
"The first charge of electricity...failed to kill him, and he struggled to breathe for eight minutes before a second charge carried out his death sentence..." After the first two-minute power surge, there was a six-minute pause so his body could cool before physicians could examine him (and declare that another jolt was needed). During that six-minute interval, Stephens took 23 breaths. A Georgia prison official said, "Stephens was just not a conductor" of electricity.

Stephen Peter Morin

March 13, 1985; Texas; lethal injection.
Because of Morin's history of drug abuse, the execution technicians were forced to probe both of Morin's arms and one of his legs with needles for nearly 45 minutes before they found a suitable vein.

6

William E. Vandiver

October 16, 1985; Indiana; electrocution.
After the first administration of 2,300 volts, Vandiver was still breathing. The execution eventually took seventeen minutes and five jolts of electricity. Vandiver's attorney, Herbert Shaps, witnessed the execution and observed smoke and a burning smell. He called the execution "outrageous." The Department of Corrections admitted the execution "did not go according to plan."

Randy Woolls

August 20, 1986; Texas; lethal injection. A drug addict, Woolls helped the execution technicians find a useable vein for the execution.

Elliot Rod Johnson

June 24, 1987; Texas; lethal injection.
Because of collapsed veins, it took nearly an hour to complete the execution.

9

Raymond Landry

December 13, 1988; Texas; lethal injection.
Pronounced dead 40 minutes after being strapped to the execution gurney and 24 minutes after the drugs first started flowing into his arms. Two minutes after the drugs were administered, the syringe came out of Landry's vein, spraying the deadly chemicals across the room toward witnesses. The curtain separating the witnesses from the inmate was then pulled and not reopened for fourteen minutes, while the execution team reinserted the catheter into the vein. Witnesses reported "at least one groan." A spokesman for the Texas Department of Correction, Charles Brown, said: "There was something of a delay in the execution because of what officials called a 'blowout.' The syringe came out of the vein, and the warden ordered the (execution) team to reinsert the catheter into the vein."

10

Stephen McCoy

May 24, 1989; Texas; lethal injection. McCoy had such a violent physical reaction to the drugs (heaving chest, gasping, choking, back arching off the gurney, etc.) that one of the witnesses (a male) fainted, crashing into and knocking over another witness. Houston attorney Karen Zellars, who represented McCoy and witnessed the execution, thought the fainting would catalyze a chain reaction. The Texas Attorney General admitted the inmate "seemed to have a somewhat stronger reaction," adding: "The drugs might have been administered in a heavier dose or more rapidly."

11

Horace Franklin Dunkins, Jr.

July 14, 1989; Alabama; electrocution. It took two jolts of electricity, nine minutes apart, to complete the execution. After the first jolt failed to kill the prisoner (who was mildly retarded), the captain of the prison guard opened the door to the witness room and stated: "I believe we've got the jacks on wrong." Because the cables had been connected improperly, it was impossible to dispense sufficient current to cause death. The cables were reconnected before a second jolt was administered. Death was pronounced nineteen minutes after the first electric charge. At a post-execution news conference, Alabama Prison Commissioner Morris Thigpen said, "I regret very, very much what happened. [The cause] was human error."

12

Jesse Joseph Tafero

May 4, 1990; Florida; electrocution. During the execution, six-inch flames erupted from Tafero's head, and three jolts of power were required to stop his breathing. State officials claimed that the botched execution was caused by "inadvertent human error"—the inappropriate substitution of a synthetic sponge for a natural sponge that had been used in previous executions. They attempted to support this theory by sticking a part of a synthetic sponge into a "common household toaster" and observing that it smoldered and caught fire.

13

Charles Walker

September 12, 1990; Illinois; lethal injection. Because of equipment failure and human error, Walker suffered excruciating pain during his execution. According to Gary Sutterfield, an engineer from the Missouri State Prison who was retained by the State of Illinois to assist the execution, a kink in the plastic tubing going into Walker's arm stopped the deadly chemicals from reaching Walker. In addition, the intravenous needle was inserted pointing at Walker's fingers instead of his heart, prolonging the execution.

14

Wilbert Lee Evans

October 17, 1990; Virginia; electrocution. When Evans was hit with the first burst of electricity, blood spewed from the right side of the mask on his face, drenching his shirt and causing a sizzling sound as blood dripped from his lips. Evans continued to moan before a second jolt of electricity was applied. The autopsy concluded that Evans suffered a bloody nose after the voltage surge elevated his high blood pressure.

15

Derick Lynn Peterson

August 22, 1991; Virginia; electrocution. After the first cycle of electricity was applied, and again four minutes later, prison physician David Barnes inspected Peterson's neck and checked him with a stethoscope, announcing each time: "He has not expired." Seven and one-half minutes after the first attempt to kill the inmate, a second cycle of electricity was applied. Prison officials later announced that in the future they would routinely administer two cycles before checking for a heartbeat.

16

Rickey Ray Rector

January 24, 1992; Arkansas; lethal injection. It took medical staff more than 50 minutes to find a suitable vein in Rector's arm. Witnesses were kept behind a drawn curtain and not permitted to view this scene, but they reported hearing Rector's eight loud moans throughout the process. During the ordeal, Rector (who suffered from serious brain damage) helped the medical personnel find a vein. The administrator of the state's Department of Corrections medical programs said (paraphrased by a newspaper reporter): "The moans did come as a team of two medical people that had grown to five worked on both sides of his body to find a vein." The administrator said: "That may have contributed to his occasional outbursts." The difficulty in finding a suitable vein was later attributed to Rector's bulk and his regular use of antipsychotic medication.

17

Donald Eugene Harding

April 6, 1992; Arizona; asphyxiation. Death was not pronounced until ten and a half minutes after the cyanide tablets were dropped. During the execution, Harding thrashed and struggled violently against the restraining straps. A television journalist who witnessed the execution, Cameron Harper, said that Harding's spasms and jerks lasted six minutes and 37 seconds. "Obviously, this man was suffering. This was a violent death...an ugly event. We put animals to death more humanely." Another witness, newspaper reporter Carla McClain, said: "Harding's death was extremely violent. He was in great pain. I heard him gasp and moan. I saw his body turn from red to purple." One reporter who witnessed the execution suffered from insomnia and assorted illnesses for several weeks; two others were "walking vegetables" for several days.

18

Robyn Lee Parks

March 10, 1992; Oklahoma; lethal injection. Parks had a violent reaction to the drugs used in the lethal injection. Two minutes after the drugs were dispensed, the muscles in his jaw, neck, and abdomen reacted spasmodically for approximately 45 seconds. Parks continued to gasp and violently gag until death came, some eleven minutes after the drugs were first administered. *Tulsa World* reporter Wayne Greene wrote that the execution looked "painful and ugly [and] scary." "It was overwhelming, stunning, disturbing—an intrusion into a moment so personal that reporters, taught for years that intrusion is their business, had trouble looking each other in the eyes after it was over."

19

Billy Wayne White

April 23, 1992; Texas; lethal injection. White was pronounced dead some 47 minutes after being strapped to the execution gurney. The delay was caused by difficulty finding a vein; White had a long history of heroin abuse. During the execution, White attempted to assist the authorities in finding a suitable vein.

20

Justin Lee May

May 7, 1992; Texas; lethal injection. May had an unusually violent reaction to the lethal drugs. According to one reporter who witnessed the execution, May "gasped, coughed and reared against his heavy leather restraints, coughing once again before his body froze..." Associated Press reporter Michael Graczyk wrote: "Compared to other recent executions in Texas, May's reaction was more violent. He went into a coughing spasm, groaned and gasped, lifted his head from the death chamber gurney and would have arched his back if he had not been belted down. After he stopped breathing, his eyes and mouth remained open."

21

John Wayne Gacy

May 10, 1994; Illinois; lethal injection. After the execution began, the lethal chemicals unexpectedly solidified, clogging the IV tube that lead into Gacy's arm and prohibiting any further passage. Blinds covering the window through which witnesses observed the execution were drawn, and the execution team replaced the clogged tube with a new one. Ten minutes later, the blinds were then reopened and the execution process resumed. It took eighteen minutes to complete. Anesthesiologists blamed the problem on the inexperience of prison officials who were conducting the execution, saying that proper procedures taught in "IV 101" would have prevented the error.

22

Emmitt Foster

May 3, 1995; Missouri; lethal injection.
Seven minutes after the lethal chemicals began to flow into Foster's arm, the execution was halted when the chemicals stopped circulating. With Foster gasping and convulsing, the blinds were drawn so the witnesses could not view the scene. Death was pronounced 30 minutes after the execution began, and three minutes later the blinds were reopened so the witnesses could view the corpse.

According to William "Mal" Gum, the Washington County Coroner who pronounced death, the problem was caused by the tightness of the leather straps that bound Foster to the execution gurney; they were so tight that the flow of chemicals into the veins was restricted. Foster did not die until several minutes after a prison worker finally loosened the straps. The coroner entered the death chamber 20 minutes after the execution began, diagnosed the problem, and told the officials to loosen the strap so the execution could proceed. In an editorial, the *St. Louis Post-Dispatch* called the execution "a particularly sordid chapter in Missouri's capital punishment experience."

23

Richard Townes, Jr.

January 23, 1996; Virginia; lethal injection.
This execution was delayed for 22 minutes while medical personnel struggled to find a vein large enough for the needle. After unsuccessful attempts to insert the needle through the arms, the needle was finally inserted through the top of Townes' right foot.

24

Tommie J. Smith

July 18, 1996; Indiana; lethal injection.
Because of unusually small veins, it took one hour and nine minutes for Smith to be pronounced dead after the execution team began sticking needles into his body. For sixteen minutes, the execution team failed to find adequate veins, so a physician was called. Smith was given a local anesthetic and the physician twice attempted to insert the tube into Smith's neck. When that failed, an angio-catheter was inserted in Smith's foot. Only then were witnesses permitted to view the process. The lethal drugs were finally injected into Smith 49 minutes after the first attempts, and it took another 20 minutes before death was pronounced.

25

Pedro Medina

March 25, 1997; Florida; electrocution. A crown of foot-high flames shot from the headpiece during the execution, filling the execution chamber with a stench of thick smoke and gagging the two-dozen official witnesses. An official then threw a switch to manually cut off the power and prematurely end the two-minute cycle of 2,000 volts. Medina's chest continued to heave until the flames stopped and death came. After the execution, prison officials blamed the fire on a corroded copper screen in the head-piece of the electric chair, but two experts hired by the governor later concluded that the fire was caused by the improper application of a sponge (designed to conduct electricity) to Medina's head.

26

Scott Dawn Carpenter

May 8, 1997; Oklahoma; lethal injection. Carpenter was pronounced dead some eleven minutes after the lethal injection was administered. As the drugs took effect, Carpenter began to gasp and shake. "This was followed by a guttural sound, multiple spasms and gasping for air" until his body stopped moving, three minutes later.

27

Michael Eugene Elkins

June 13, 1997; South Carolina; lethal injection. Because Elkins' body had become swollen from liver and spleen problems, it took nearly an hour to find a suitable vein for the insertion of the catheter. Elkins tried to assist the executioners, asking: "Should I lean my head down a little bit?" as they probed for a vein. After numerous failures, a usable vein was finally found in Elkins' neck.

28

Joseph Cannon

April 23, 1998; Texas; lethal injection. It took two attempts to complete the execution. After Cannon made his final statement, the process began. A vein in Cannon's arm collapsed and the needle popped out. Seeing this, Cannon lay back, closed his eyes, and exclaimed to the witnesses, "It's come undone." Officials then pulled a curtain to block the view of the witnesses, reopening it fifteen minutes later when a weeping Cannon made a second final statement and the execution process resumed.

29

Genaro Ruiz Camacho

August 26, 1998; Texas; lethal injection. The execution was delayed approximately two hours due, in part, to problems finding suitable veins in Camacho's arms.

30

Roderick Abeyta

October 5, 1998; Nevada; lethal injection. It took 25 minutes for the execution team to find a vein suitable for the lethal injection.

31

Allen Lee Davis

July 8, 1999; Florida; electrocution. "Before he was pronounced dead...the blood from his mouth had poured onto the collar of his white shirt," reported the *Gainesville Sun*, "and the blood on his chest had spread to about the size of a dinner plate, even oozing through the buckle holes on the leather chest strap holding him to the chair." The execution was the first in Florida's new electric chair, built especially so it could accommodate a man Davis' size (approximately 350 pounds).

Later, when another Florida death row inmate challenged the constitutionality of the electric chair, Florida Supreme Court Justice Leander Shaw commented that "the color photos of Davis depict a man who—for all appearances—was brutally tortured to death by the citizens of Florida." Justice Shaw also described the botched executions of Jesse Tafero and Pedro Medina, calling the three executions "barbaric spectacles" and "acts more befitting a violent murderer than a civilized state." Justice Shaw included pictures of Davis' dead body in his opinion. The execution was witnessed by a Florida State Senator, Ginny Brown-Waite, who at first was "shocked" to see the blood, until she realized that the blood was forming the shape of a cross and that it was a message from God saying he supported the execution.

32

Christina Marie Riggs

May 3, 2000; Arkansas; lethal injection. Riggs dropped her appeals and asked to be executed. However, the execution was delayed for eighteen minutes when prison staff couldn't find a suitable vein in her elbows. Finally, Riggs agreed to the executioners' requests to have the needles inserted into her wrists.

33

Bennie Demps

June 8, 2000; Florida; lethal injection. It took execution technicians 33 minutes to find suitable veins for the execution. "They butchered me back there," said Demps in his final statement. "I was in a lot of pain. They cut me in the groin; they cut me in the leg. I was bleeding profusely. This is not an execution; it is murder." The executioners had no unusual problems finding one vein, but because Florida protocol requires a second alternate intravenous drip, they continued to work to insert another needle, finally abandoning the effort after their prolonged failures.

34

Claude Jones

December 7, 2000; Texas; lethal injection. Jones' execution was delayed 30 minutes while the execution "team" struggled to insert an I.V. into a vein. He had been a long-time intravenous drug user. One member of the execution team commented, "They had to stick him about five times. They finally put it in his leg." Wrote Jim Willett, the warden of the Walls Unit and the man responsible for conducting the execution:

> The medical team could not find a vein. Now I was really beginning to worry. If you can't stick a vein then a cut-down has to be performed. I have never seen one and would just as soon go through the rest of my career the same way. Just when I was really getting worried, one of the medical people hit a vein in the left leg. Inside calf to be exact. The executioner had warned me not to panic as it was going to take a while to get the fluids in the body of the inmate tonight because he was going to push the drugs through very slowly. Finally, the drug took effect and Jones took his last breath.

35

Bert Leroy Hunter

June 28, 2000; Missouri; lethal injection. Hunter had an unusual reaction to the lethal drugs, repeatedly coughing and gasping for air before he lapsed into unconsciousness. An attorney who witnessed the execution reported that Hunter had "violent convulsions. His head and chest jerked rapidly upward as far as the gurney restraints would allow, and then he fell quickly down upon the gurney. His body convulsed back and forth like this repeatedly.... He suffered a violent and agonizing death."

36

José High

November 7, 2001; Georgia; lethal injection. High was pronounced dead some one hour and nine minutes after the execution began. After attempting to find a useable vein for 39 minutes, the emergency medical technicians under contract to do the execution abandoned their efforts. Eventually, one needle was stuck into High's hand, and a physician was called in to insert a second needle between his shoulder and neck. ◻

> *Law Quote #2*
> "The law in its majestic equality, forbids the rich as well as the poor to sleep under bridges, to beg in the streets, and to steal bread."
> —Anatole France

Taken verbatim from a now-deleted page on the Texas Department of Criminal Justice website.

3

John Baltazar

Executed January 15, 2003. "Cool Whip and cherries."

1

Stanley Baker, Jr.

Executed May 30, 2002. "Two 16 oz. ribeyes, one lb. turkey breast (sliced thin), twelve strips of bacon, two large hamburgers with mayo, onion, and lettuce, two large baked potatoes with butter, sour cream, cheese, and chives, four slices of cheese or one-half pound of grated cheddar cheese, chef salad with blue cheese dressing, two ears of corn on the cob, one pint of mint chocolate chip ice cream, and four vanilla Cokes or Mr. Pibb."

4

Henry Dunn, Jr.

Executed February 6, 2003. "Cheeseburger (extra cheese, pickles, onion, lettuce, and salad dressing), tray of French fries, bottle of ketchup, 25 breaded fried shrimp, four cans of pineapple juice, two banana splits, bottle of Hershey's syrup, and one jar of apple butter jam."

5

Cornelius Goss

Executed February 23, 2000. "One apple, one orange, one banana, coconut, and peaches."

2

Odell Barnes, Jr.

Executed March 1, 2000. For his last meal request, Barnes wrote: "Justice, Equality, World Peace."

LIST **17** | **13 Last Meals Requested by Executed Texas Prisoners**

6

Danny Harris

Executed July 30, 1993. "God's saving grace, love, truth, peace and freedom."

7

Stacey Lawton

Executed November 14, 2000. "One jar of dill pickles."

8

Robert Madden

Executed May 28, 1997. "Asked that final meal be provided to a homeless person."

9

Gerald Mitchell

Executed October 22, 2001. "One bag of assorted Jolly Ranchers."

10

James Powell

Executed October 1, 2002. "One pot of coffee."

11

Miguel Richardson

Executed June 26, 2001. "Chocolate birthday cake with '2/23/90' written on top, seven pink candles, one coconut, kiwi fruit juice, pineapple juice, one mango, grapes, lettuce, cottage cheese, peaches, one banana, one delicious apple, chef salad without meat and with thousand island dressing, fruit salad, cheese, and tomato slices."

12

Juan Soria

Executed July 26, 2000. "Chicken, three pieces of fish, burgers, pizza, fruit (grapes, plums, peaches, apples, tangerines), doughnuts, walnuts, chocolate candy bar, plain potato chips, picante sauce, hot sauce, salad with ranch dressing, Coke, and Sprite."

13

Delbert Teague, Jr.

Executed September 9, 1998. The Texas Department of Criminal Justice notes: "Last minute he decided to eat a hamburger at his Mother's request." ⌻

Law Quote #3
"The more corrupt the state, the more laws."
—Tacitus

1

hanger

In order to keep prison garb looking nice, a prisoner named Angelo—author of *Prisoners' Inventions*—says that inmates will roll up a newspaper until its fairly stiff, then run a thin strip of bedsheet through the hollow center. Tying the ends together with plenty of extra length creates a triangle with the paper as the sturdy base. The contraption is then hung on an improvised hook made out of a paperclip and a wooden domino glued to the wall with contact cement.

2

immersion heater

Familiar to many campers, the immersion heater has a metal projection that gets hot and is used to warm up beverages. It's used this way in prison, where it's called a "stinger," though it's also handy for branding, either for purposes of voluntary body modification or torture. One way prisoners make their own is to use metal tabs from paper binders attached to handles of toothbrushes. The two tabs at one end are inserted into a wall socket, heating the tabs at the other end, which are lowered into the drink.

3

condom

Presumably to prevent catching diseases, some jailhouse Romeos fashion condoms out of plastic wrap or sandwich bags fastened in place with thread or a rubberband.

4

muff bag

If you'd rather not have to worry about diseases at all, you can whip up a homemade blow-up doll of sorts. Although known as a muff bag, this contraption simulates a bountiful booty. According to Angelo, you tie together the corners of two plastic bags used to line small wastebaskets, fill with water, and tie off the openings. "Add rolled-up blankets to simulate the torso and legs and supply support, and you're ready to slip it to her."

5

toilet paper maché

Wet toilet paper can me molded into almost any shape, which it retains after drying. Because of this, toilet paper maché has been made into dice, dominos, chess pieces, cups

LIST 18 | 8 Handmade Prison Objects

(lined with Saran wrap), and even sculpted works of art.

tattoo gun

Tattoos are common among inmates, but how do you get one behind bars? With devices made from a sharpened piece of wire, guitar string, pens, paperclips, rubber bands, and a motor from a portable cassette player (i.e., a Walkman), a slot car, an electric razor, etc.

pruno

Pruno, also called cellblock wine, is alcohol "brewed" in prison. The basic idea is to crudely ferment anything containing sugar by mashing it up with water in a bag, letting the contents stew for around a week while occasionally heating the concoction by running warm water over the bag. Pruno has been made from oranges, raisins, tabletop sugar, yams, Jello, honey, candy, cake frosting, ketchup, or combinations thereof. The guys behind the webzine *Black Table* made their own pruno as an experiment: "For lack of a better metaphor, pruno tastes like a bile flavored wine cooler. It tastes so bad, in fact, that it could very well be poisonous or psychedelic, which might explain the violence it induces in prisoners."

shank

Also known as a shiv, a shank is anything that can be used to slash or stab. Trying to get a knife smuggled into prison is riskier than simply making one yourself out of available material within the prison. Shanks can be created from plastic, Plexiglas, wood, metal scraps, toothbrushes, pens, nails and bolts, spoons, screwdrivers, bed springs, and pretty much any other material or object you can imagine.

Judge Lambasts Police for Abuse of Protesters

Circuit Court Judge Richard Margolius took to the street to observe demonstrations during the Free Trade Area of the Americas summit in Miami on November 20-21, 2003. While presiding over the case against two protestors who had been arrested, he declared that he witnessed "no less than 20 felonies committed by police officers." He also said: "Pretty disgraceful what I saw with my own eyes. And I have always supported the police during my entire career. This was a real eye-opener. A disgrace for the community."

He also engaged in the following exchange with an assistant state attorney:

Judge: "How many police officers have been charged by the State Attorney so far for what happened out there during the FTAA?"

Assistant state attorney: "None."

Judge: "None? Pretty sad commentary. At least from what I saw."

In the so-called sport of cockfighting, two roosters are put into a pit where they slash each other to pieces until one is dead or at least can no longer stand. The doomed birds are outfitted with either sharp metal blades or spikes (gaffs) and are given various drugs—such as caffeine and meth—to make them more aggressive and resistant to pain and injury. Cockfighting has been illegal in most states for over a century, and Oklahoma voters banned it in 2002. You might assume that it's illegal throughout the entire country, but it isn't. There's even a monthly magazine published out of South Carolina, *Grit & Steel*, devoted to this current equivalent of bearbaiting, in which the ancient Romans cheered as a pack of dogs ripped apart a chained bear.

1. **Louisiana**

2. **New Mexico**
   (in certain areas)

3. **Virginia**
   (gambling on this savagery is illegal, but the fights themselves aren't)

LIST **19** | 3 States Where Cockfighting is Legal

1

Crime: Officer Mark Bolger of Richmond, Virginia, forced a woman to blow him in exchange for not arresting her.

Outcome: Bolger was charged with forcible sodomy (a felony) but pled to the much lesser charge of simple assault (a misdemeanor).

Punishment: None. The *Richmond Times-Dispatch* reports: "He does not face jail time or a fine, but his guilty plea is admissible in future civil proceedings." After he was charged, Bolger had received four months of paid leave (also known as paid vacation). Upon pleading guilty, he resigned.

2

Crime: Sheriff's Deputy Jeremy Webb of Newton County, Georgia, had four kiddie porn videos on his computer.

Outcome: Pled guilty to five counts of sexual exploitation.

Punishment: Five years probation (first year in a halfway house), $3,000 in fines, mental therapy, no contact with children under sixteen, including his daughter.

3

Crime: Sheriff's Lieutenant Eric Douglass of Boone County, Indiana, was busted for driving drunk. He had a blood alcohol level of 0.17 percent (the legal limit is 0.08). Douglass was the county's DARE officer, teaching the children the evils of illegal drugs.

Outcome: Pled guilty.

Punishment: Suspended 180-day sentence, six months probation, 90 days suspended drivers license, $584.50 in fines and fees.

4 5 6 7 8 9

Crime: A gang of six cops in Vancouver, British Columbia, picked up three men with drug records, drove them to a remote location in a park, and physically and verbally assaulted them.

Outcome: All six pled guilty to assault.

Punishments: Duncan Gemmell: 60 days house arrest, 40 hours of community service, six months probation. Gabriel Kojima: 30 days house arrest. Christopher Cronmiller: conditional discharge, six months probation. Raymond Gardner: 50 hours community service, nine months probation. Sgt.

LIST 20

14 Criminal Cops and Their "Punishments"

James Kenney: absolute discharge without conditions. Brandon Steele: suspended sentence, 25 hours of community service, six months probation.

Comment from the judge: "Instead of a heat-of-the-moment situation it became, in my view, a situation of mob mentality."

10

Crime: Sheriff's Deputy Sean Davis in Utah County, Utah, molested two eleven-year-old boys, one of whom was an unspecified "relative."

Outcome: Pled guilty to four charges of attempted sodomy of a child.

Punishment: Amazingly, Davis asked for the maximum penalty, and, even more amazingly, the judge obliged: six and half years to life.

Quotes: Officials were filled with praise for the incestuous child-rapist. The presiding judge said: "The truth of the matter is you've done an unbelievable amount of good, and it's a shame that we're here today." The Utah County Sheriff enthused: "He was a hard worker with a good work ethic. [His work] was much appreciated."

11

Crime: New York City police Sgt. William T. Miley drove drunk and slammed into a stopped car at a red light, killing two men and injuring three other people. When other cops showed up at the scene, according to the website NY Finest's New & Views: "He pulled out a fistful of $20 bills and told cops, 'Please let me go home. I'm a New York City police sergeant. Please help me.'"

Outcome: A trial on charges of vehicular manslaughter resulted in a hung jury. In a later trial, Miley was convicted of two counts of criminally negligent homicide and driving under the influence.

Punishment: Prison term of one year and four months to four years.

12

Crime: Police officer David Mueller of New Vienna, Ohio, responded to a domestic violence call. The husband, Robert Cundiff, avoided being handcuffed and supposedly made a move at Mueller. The policeman hit Cundiff on the leg with his baton, then bashed his head so hard that the baton bent. Mueller pulled out his gun and shot Cundiff in the face, killing him. Later, he asked colleagues on the force to destroy his original report on the deadly incident.

Outcome: Pled guilty to voluntary manslaughter and evidence-tampering, admitting that he used "excessive force."

Punishment: Six-year prison sentence.

13

Crime: Police officer Garland Yancey of Fyffe, Alabama, sexually abused four girls under twelve and a fifth girl who was twelve years old.

Outcome: Pled guilty to five counts of child molestation (two counts of enticing a child for immoral purposes; three counts of first-degree sexual abuse).

Punishment: Two years in a state prison, five years probation.

14

Crime: Cpl. John R. Mason, a Pennsylvania State Trooper, downloaded over 500 images and several films of child pornography onto a police computer and his home computer.

Outcome: Convicted on 20 counts of sexual abuse of children and eighteen counts of criminal use of a communications facility.

Punishment: Sentenced to nine to eighteen *months* in county jail, $2,000 fine.

Note: Federal statute dictates a minimum of five years in prison for each kiddie porn offense, and many courts count every individual image as a separate offense. Mason could've been sentenced to over 2,500 years and, in any case, should've been sentenced to no less than five years.

Dishonorable Mentions

Incidents: The *Philadelphia Inquirer* summarizes three alleged incidents: "Kensington resident Michael Lugo is disabled from a broken neck. But that didn't stop a Philadelphia police officer, he says, from roughing him up, ridiculing him for being a 'cripple,' and arresting him on false charges. Schoolteacher Angelo DiBartolo's throat was slashed in a Northeast Philadelphia bar fight involving a bouncer. An officer helped the bouncer—her boyfriend—flee the scene. US Department of Agriculture inspector Sukhwinder Dhillon reported that her car was rear-ended by a police officer, who threatened to arrest her and lied to investigators."

Outcome: In each case, the police department's Internal Affairs Bureau concluded that the cops had engaged in the abuses. Though each alleged incident would appear to be a crime, no criminal charges were ever filed.

Punishments: Five-day suspension, one-day suspension, eighteen-day suspension (respectively). ◻

> **Law Quote # 4**
> "Laws are like cobwebs—strong enough to catch the weak, but insufficient to hold the strong."
> –Anacharis

+ Feds and Spooks

In January 1997, the public finally got to see "KUBARK COUNTERINTELLIGENCE INTERROGATION," the CIA's 1963 manual for getting information out of unwilling prisoners, typically enemy agents. The 128-page instruction book opens with the lines: "This manual cannot teach anyone how to be, or become, a good interrogator. At best it can help readers avoid the characteristic mistakes of a bad interrogator." All quotes—including the names of techniques that are in quotes—are taken directly from the declassified document.

1

Décor

"The room in which the interrogation is to be conducted should be free of distractions. The colors of the walls, ceiling, rugs, and furniture should not be startling. Pictures should be missing or dull." A plain table is a good idea, unless a fancy desk would send the message that the interrogator is a powerful authority figure.

2

The chair

"An overstuffed chair for the use of the interrogatee is sometime preferable to a straight-backed, wooden chair because if he is made to stand for a lengthy period or is otherwise deprived of physical comfort, the contrast is intensified and increased disorientation results."

LIST 21

25 Tips for Interrogating a Prisoner, From the CIA

3

The "do not disturb" sign

"The effect of someone wandering in because he forgot his pen or wants to invite the interrogator to lunch can be devastating."

4

Listening in on the interrogation

"If possible, audio equipment should also be used to transmit the proceedings to another room, used as a listening post. The main advantage of transmission is that it enables the person in charge of the interrogation to note crucial points and map further strategy, replacing one interrogator with another, timing a dramatic interruption correctly, etc."

5

Sincerity

"The interrogator who merely pretends, in his surface performance, to feel a given emotion or to hold a given attitude toward the source is likely to be unconvincing; the source quickly senses the deception. Even children are very quick to feel this kind of pretense. To be persuasive, the sympathy or anger must be genuine; but to be useful, it must not interfere with the deeper level of precise, unaffected observation."

6

Unpredictable schedule

"Interrogation sessions with a resistant source who is under detention should not be held on an unvarying schedule. The capacity for resistance is diminished by disorientation. The subject may be left alone for days; and he may be returned to his cell, allowed to sleep for five minutes, and brought back to an interrogation which is conducted as though eight hours had intervened. The principle is that sessions should be so planned as to disrupt the source's sense of chronological order."

Also, it's suggested that you make everything in the subject's life, such as his sleeping and eating schedules, random and unpredictable.

7

The "Nobody Loves You" technique

"An interrogatee who is withholding items of no grave consequence to himself may sometimes be persuaded to talk by the simple tactic of pointing out that to date all of the information about his case has come from persons other than himself. The interrogator wants to be fair. He recognizes that some of the denouncers may have been biased or malicious. In any case, there is bound to be some slanting of the facts unless the interrogatee redresses the balance. The source owes it to himself to be sure that the interrogator hears both sides of the story."

8

The "All-Seeing Eye (or Confession is Good for the Soul)" technique

"The interrogator who already knows part of the story explains to the source that the purpose of the questioning is not to gain information; the interrogator knows everything already. His real purpose is to test the sincerity (reliability, honor, etc.) of the source. The interrogator then asks a few questions to which he knows the answers. If the subject lies, he is informed firmly and dispassionately that he has lied. By skilled manipulation of the known, the questioner can convince a naive subject that all his secrets are out and that further resistance would be not only pointless but dangerous."

9

The double-informant technique

The manual notes that planting a snitch in the subject's cell is a ruse so obvious as to be useless. "Less well known is the trick of planting two informants in the cell. One of them, A, tries now and then to pry a little information from the source; B remains quiet. At the proper time, and during A's absence, B warns the source not to tell A anything because B suspects him of being an informant planted by the authorities. Suspicion against a single cellmate may sometimes be broken down if he shows the

source a hidden microphone that he has 'found' and suggests that they talk only in whispers at the other end of the room."

10

The "News from Home" technique

Letting the subject get some letters from the outside is a good way to gain trust and increase his longing to cooperate and, thus, get released. Conversely, letting him write letters can be profitable, since they can be read for useful information.

11

Playing two subjects against each other

If you have two suspects who are suspected of operating together, pretend that one is squealing on the other. Creatively edit audiotape of your interrogations of the first one. Doctor up a phony "signed" confession.

12

The "Ivan Is a Dope" technique

"It may be useful to point out to a hostile agent that the cover story was ill-contrived, that the other [intelligence] service botched the job, that it is typical of the other service to ignore the welfare of its agents. The interrogator may personalize this pitch by explaining that he has been impressed by the agent's courage and intelligence. He sells the agent the idea that the interrogator, not his old service, represents a true friend, who understands him and will look after his welfare."

13

The good-cop/bad-cop routine

In this age-old technique, one interrogator pretends to be an angry SOB who is restraining himself from getting medieval on the subject. The other interrogator pretends to be nice and reasonable, establishing false trust. The manual notes: "This routine works best with women, teenagers, and timid men."

14

Language games

"If the recalcitrant subject speaks more than one language, it is better to question him in the tongue with which he is least familiar as long as the purpose of interrogation is to obtain a confession. After the interrogatee admits hostile intent or activity, a switch to the better-known language will facilitate follow-up. An abrupt switch of languages may trick a resistant source. If an interrogatee has withstood a barrage of questions in German or Korean, for example, a sudden shift to 'Who is your case officer?' in Russian may trigger the answer before the source can stop himself."

15

The "Spinoza and Mortimer Snerd" technique

First you ask the subject questions about the high-level operations of his agency, questions that he is truly unable to answer. "His complaints that he knows nothing of such matters are met by flat insistence that he does know, he would have to know, that even the most stupid men in his position know." Suddenly, the interrogator switches to questions about low-level information, which the subject *does* know and may reveal. An American POW who was the victim of this tactic later said: "I know it seems strange now, but I was positively grateful to them when they switched to a topic I knew something about."

16

The "Wolf in Sheep's Clothing" technique

In this risky maneuver, a CIA decoy pretends to be a representative of an enemy agency, the same agency that employs the sap being interrogated. Thinking he's being debriefed by his side, he spills his guts.

17

The "Alice in Wonderland" technique

Simply put: Mess with the subject's head. You attempt "not only to obliterate the familiar but to replace it with the weird. Although this method can be employed by a single interrogator, it is better adapted to use by two or three. When the subject enters the room, the first interrogator asks a doubletalk question—one which seems straightforward but is essentially nonsensical. Whether the interrogatee tries to answer or not, the second interrogator follows up (interrupting any attempted response) with a wholly unrelated and equally illogical query. Sometimes two or more questions are asked simultaneously. Pitch, tone, and volume of the interrogators' voices are unrelated to the import of the questions. No pattern of questions and answers is permitted to develop, nor do the questions themselves relate logically to each other. In this strange atmosphere the subject finds that the pattern of speech and thought which he has learned to consider normal have been replaced by an eerie meaninglessness. The interrogatee may start laughing or refuse to take the situation seriously. But as the process continues, day after day if necessary, the subject begins to try to make sense of the situation, which becomes mentally intolerable. Now he is likely to make significant admissions, or even to pour out his story, just to stop the flow of babble which assails him."

18

The "Placebo" technique

Make the subject take a sugar pill, then tell him it was a truth serum. If he's consciously or subconsciously looking for an excuse to cooperate, he'll tell all.

19

Take away his clothes

Clothes provide a sense of identity, so get him into unfamiliar garb as soon as possible "If the interrogatee is especially proud or neat, it may be useful to give him an outfit that is one or two sizes too large and to fail to provide a belt, so that he must hold his pants up."

20

Sensory deprivation

"The more completely the place of confinement eliminates sensory stimuli, the more rapidly and deeply will the interrogatee be affected. Results produced only after weeks or months of imprisonment in an ordinary cell can be duplicated in hours or days in a cell which has no light (or weak artificial light which never varies), which is sound-proofed, in which odors are eliminated, etc. An environment still more subject to control, such as [a] water-tank or iron lung, is even more effective."

21

"Threats and Fear"

"The threat of coercion usually weakens or destroys resistance more effectively than coercion itself. The threat to inflict pain, for example, can trigger fears more damaging than the immediate sensation of pain. In fact, most people underestimate their capacity to withstand pain. The same principle holds for other fears: sustained long enough, a strong fear of anything vague or unknown induces regression, whereas the materialization of the fear, the infliction of some form of punishment, is likely to come as a relief. The subject finds that he can hold out, and his resistances are strengthened...."

"Threats delivered coldly are more effective than those shouted in rage."

However, the interrogator should never threaten death:

> The threat of death has often been found to be worse than useless. It "has the highest position in law as a defense, but in many interrogation situations it is a highly ineffective threat. Many prisoners, in fact, have refused to yield in the face of such threats who have subsequently been 'broken' by other procedures" [*A Study for Development of Improved Interrogation Techniques*, Albert D. Biderman]. The principal reason is that the ultimate threat is likely to induce sheer hopelessness if the interrogatee does not believe that it is a trick; he feels that he is as likely to be condemned after compliance as before. The threat of death is also ineffective when used against hard-headed types who realize that silencing them forever would defeat the interrogator's purpose. If the threat is recognized as a bluff, it will not only fail but also pave the way to failure for later coercive ruses used by the interrogator.

22

Inducing debility

The CIA mentions ancient techniques of physically weakening people: "prolonged constraint; prolonged exertion; extremes of heat, cold, or moisture; and deprivation or drastic reduction of food or sleep." It doesn't, however, recommend these approaches, since "experience" shows that they're pretty ineffective. In fact, the Agency says that you'll probably have better luck with threatening to do these things, rather than actually doing them.

23

Pain

The manual's section on pain (i.e., physical torture) argues against it on many grounds:

> Interrogatees who are withholding but who feel qualms of guilt and a secret desire to yield are likely to become intractable if made to endure pain. The reason is that they can then interpret the pain as punishment and hence as expiation. There are also persons who enjoy pain and its anticipation and who will keep back information that they might otherwise divulge if they are given reason to expect that withholding will result in the punishment that they want. Persons of considerable moral or intellectual stature often find in pain inflicted by others a confirmation of the belief

that they are in the hands of inferiors, and their resolve not to submit is strengthened.

Intense pain is quite likely to produce false confessions, concocted as a means of escaping from distress.

24

Hypnosis

The CIA heavily qualifies its recommendation of hypnosis, but at the right time and in the hands of a pro, it can be employed. "For example, a KUBARK [CIA] interrogator could tell a suspect double agent in trance that the KGB is conducting the questioning, and thus invert the whole frame of reference.... The value of hypnotic trance is not that it permits the interrogator to impose his will but rather that it can be used to convince the interrogatee that there is no valid reason not to be forthcoming."

25

Drugs

"The effect of most drugs depends more upon the personality of the subject than upon the physical characteristics of the drugs themselves. If the approval of Headquarters has been obtained and if a doctor is at hand for administration, one of the most important of the interrogator's functions is providing the doctor with a full and accurate description of the psychological make-up of the interrogatee, to facilitate the best possible choice of a drug."

"This discussion does not include a list of drugs that have been employed for interrogation purposes or a discussion of their properties because these are medical considerations within the province of a doctor rather than an interogator [*sic*]." ⬯

In May 1967, the Central Intelligence Agency's Inspector General issued "Report on Plots to Assassinate Fidel Castro," a detailed rundown of the CIA's attempts to kill Cuba's leader. Highly classified, it wasn't released to the public until 1993. All quotes below are taken directly from this official report.

1

Dosing

According to the report, there was "discussion of a scheme to contaminate the air of the radio station where Castro broadcasts his speeches with an aerosol spray of a chemical that produces reactions similar to those of lysergic acid (LSD)." The idea apparently was to get El Presidente to sound like a drug-addled flake on the air. "Nothing came of the idea. [redacted] said he had discouraged the scheme, because the chemical could not be relied upon to be effective."

2

Tainted cigars

A batch of cigars was cooked up with the intention of giving them to Castro. The effects that the cigars were supposed to have is hazy. Either they were treated with a chemical that would make him disoriented, thus causing him to act strangely in public, or they were treated with a depilatory to make his beard fall out, dealing a blow to the machismo of the now smooth-faced girly-man. The plot never got farther than that, and the stogies were destroyed.

3

Spiked shoes

Similarly, the Agency brewed "a scheme involving thallium salts, a chemical used by women as a depilatory—the thought being to destroy Castro's image as 'The Beard' by causing the beard to fall out.... The idea was to dust thallium powder into Castro's shoes when they were put out at night to be shined. The scheme progressed as far as procuring

LIST 22
7 CIA Plots to Kill Castro

the chemical and testing it on animals." Castro's shoes were to be spiked during a specific trip outside of Cuba, but the trip didn't happen and the plot fell through.

Poison pills

In the most elaborate, firm plan for assassination, a CIA agent—under orders from his superiors—offered mobsters in Cuba $150,000 to whack Castro. The spook, of course, didn't reveal his true affiliation, instead claiming to represent businessmen who saw the dictator as an impediment. As for the actual mechanism of death, "four possible approaches were considered: (1) something highly toxic, such as shellfish poison to be administered with a pin (which Roosevelt said was what was supplied to Gary Powers); (2) bacterial material in liquid form; (3) bacterial treatment of a cigarette or cigar; and (4) a handkerchief treated with bacteria." The focus was put on option two, with the idea being to dump the lethal liquid into Castro's drink or soup. Meanwhile, the CIA's Technical Services Division laced a box of Cuban cigars with botulism. "The cigars were so heavily contaminated that merely putting one in the mouth would do the job; the intended victim would not actually have to smoke it." In the end, however, the poison took the form of "small pills" containing botulism. The tablets were tested on monkeys, who keeled over.

In February-March 1961, the pills made their way from the CIA to the Mafia to a disaffected Cuban official close to Castro, Juan Orta, head of the Prime Minister's Office. But Orta lost his job around that time—apparently for skimming gambling profits—and couldn't deliver the poison. Orta suggested someone else for the job, who reportedly tried a few times but failed. The CIA then approached a prominent Cuban exile, who was set to do the job for $10,000 or $20,000. For reasons that remain unclear, the Agency canceled the operation.

By April 1962, the plan was back in full effect. More poison pills were given to Varona, who then requested (and was given) additional equipment that he claimed to need for the operation: "explosives, detonators, twenty .30 caliber rifles, twenty .45 caliber hand guns, two radios, and one boat radar." In June, Varona sent a three-man squad to Cuba. "They were to recruit others who might be used in such a scheme. If an opportunity to kill Castro presented itself, they or the persons they recruited were to make the attempt—perhaps using the pills." By February of the next year, it was apparent that the operation was going nowhere, so it was shut down.

Poison diving suit

"The technique involved dusting the inside of the suit with a fungus that would produce a disabling and chronic skin disease (Madura foot) and contaminating the breathing apparatus with tubercle bacilli." The suit was never given to Castro, although "this scheme progressed to the point of actually buying a diving suit and readying it for delivery."

6

Exploding conch

The idea was to take an unusually spectacular sea shell that would be certain to catch Castro's eye, load it with an explosive triggered to blow when the shell was lifted, and submerge it in an area where Castro often went skin diving....

The scheme was soon found to be impracticable. None of the shells that might conceivably be found in the Caribbean area was both spectacular enough to be sure of attracting attention and large enough to hold the needed volume of explosive. The midget submarine that would have had to be used in emplacement of the shell has too short an operating range for such an operation.

"He said that the needle was so fine that the victim would hardly feel it when it was inserted—he compared it with the scratch from a shirt with too much starch." On the 21st, at the exact moment that President Kennedy was being assassinated, a CIA agent was giving Cubela the pen-needle to kill Castro. Cubelo dicked around for a year and a half; finally, CIA headquarters put out the word to stop all association with him in June 1965. His CIA support had become too well known.

This is the last reported attempt to put Castro's lights out. 🗖

7

Poison pen

In March 1961, the Agency approached Rolando Cubela, Cuba's disaffected Military Attaché to Spain, about icing Castro. By November 1963, Cubela was ready to do the deed and asked the CIA to supply him with the means. "What they settled upon was Black Leaf 40, a common, easily-obtainable insecticide containing about 40% nicotine sulphate. Nicotine is a deadly poison that may be administered orally, by injection, or by absorption through the skin."

The CIA decided not give Cubela the poison, telling him to obtain it himself, but they did hand him the method of delivery: "a ball-point pen rigged as a hypodermic syringe" that the CIA's Dr. Gunn created overnight.

> **Classified Quote #1**
> "A lot of documents are classified for the wrong reason—because they're embarrassing, or perhaps because of a coverup."
> –Senator Richard Shelby (Republican - Alabama), former Chair of the Senate Intelligence Committee

The CIA uses cryptonyms (code names) extensively in its communications and other internal documents. Over the years, many of them have been decoded.

1. **AMQUACK**
   Ernesto "Che" Guevara

2. **AMTHUG**
   Fidel Castro

3. **BGGYPSY**
   Russia or a Russian

4. **DTFROGS**
   El Salvador

5. **FJHOPEFUL**
   a military base

6. **GPFLOOR**
   Lee Harvey Oswald

7. **HTKEEPER**
   Mexico City

8. **HTPLUME**
   Panama

9. **ISOLATION**
   Camp Peary, the CIA's spook-training school near Williamsburg Virginia.

10. **KMFLUSH**
    Nicaragua

LIST 23 | 34 CIA Cryptonyms

11. **KMPAJAMA**
Mexico

12. **KMPLEBE**
Peru

13. **KUBARK**
Central Intelligence Agency

14. **KUCLUB**
CIA Office of Communications

15. **KUDOVE**
Office of the Director of Central Intelligence

16. **KUFIRE**
intelligence

17. **KUGOWN**
propaganda

18. **KUSODA**
CIA interrogators

19. **LCFLUTTER**
Polygraph, or possibly truth serum

20. **LCPANGS**
Costa Rica

21. **ODACID**
US Embassy

22. **ODEARL**
Department of Defense

23. **ODENVY**
Federal Bureau of Investigation (FBI)

24. **ODOATH**
US Navy

25. **ODUNIT**
US Air Force

26. **ODYOKE**
US government

27. **PBPRIME**
United States

28. **QKFLOWAGE**
United States Information Agency

29. **RNMAKER**
Franklin Delano Roosevelt

30. **RTACTION**
CIA

31. **SGSWIRL**
polygraph

32. **SGUAT**
CIA station in Guatemala

33. **WSBURNT**
Guatemala

34. **WSHOOFS**
Honduras

Intelligence-related communications from CIA agents and stations to CIA headquarters are labeled with a word that indicates the urgency of the message. In descending order of urgency, they are:

1. **critic**

2. **flash**

3. **immediate**

4. **priority**

5. **routine**

ὅ

LIST 24 | 5 Designations of Importance Used by the CIA

1. **Gibraltar Steamship Company**

   Used to cover activities related to the Bay of Pigs invasion.

2. **Air America**

   Supposedly a civilian air service whose planes were allowed to buzz all over Southeast Asia during the Vietnam War, this was a huge CIA operation that shuttled spooks, military brass, arms, drugs, and other people and contraband.

3. **Brewster Jennings & Associates**

   CIA operative Valerie Plame—whose cover was blown by two senior Bush Administration officials and conservative columnist Robert Novak—listed this nonexistent company on a public form. Its address is supposedly 101 Arch Street, Boston, Massachusetts, even though the office tower there has no such tenant. The *Boston Globe* reports:

   > A spokeswoman for Dun & Bradstreet Inc., a New Jersey operator of commercial databases, said Brewster Jennings was first entered into its records on May 22, 1994, but wouldn't discuss the source of the filing. Its records list the company at 101 Arch St. as a "legal services office," which could mean a law firm, with annual sales of $60,000, one employee, and a chief executive identified as "Victor Brewster, Partner." That person isn't listed elsewhere.

4. **Aroundworld Shipping, Inc.**

   This and the following companies were created for gun-running by Edwin Wilson, a former CIA officer who supposedly was kicked out of the Agency and then supplied arms to Libya.

5. **Consultants International, Inc.**

6. **Delex International Corporations**

7. **Egyptian-American Transport Service Company**

8. **Inter-Technology, Inc.**

9. **Scientific Communications, Inc.**

10. **Systems Services International**

Note: Some legitimate companies may also be using these names, so don't assume that any company with one of the names is a spook operation. ♄

10 CIA Front Companies

1. **Bud Abbot**

   According to a snitch for the Los Angeles Police Department, funnyman Bud Abbot "is a collector of pornography and allegedly has 1,500 reels of obscene motion pictures which he shows in his home where he has a projector of his own."

2. **Gracie Allen**

   Comedian Gracie Allen and her friend Mary Livingston were said to have smuggled clothes and jewelry into the US without paying duty tax. Their husbands- George Burns and Jack Benny (respectively) ended up paying fines.

3. **Desi Arnaz**

   The feds wanted to make sure that Arnaz wasn't a Cuban commie, and they kept tabs on some of his TV productions. In an ass-kissing letter in 1959, Arnaz says that he's considering buying a script called *The FBI Story* and asks FBI Director J. Edgar Hoover, "would there be any objection on your part?" Arnaz curtsies: "One can never be sure as to the type of organization that would buy this property and develop it into a series without taking into account the requirements and interests of your department."

4. **Josephine Baker**

   The legendary banana-dancer was investigated on suspicion of being a commie.

5. **James Baldwin**

6. **Lucille Ball**

   "Oh, Lucy, you got some 'splaining to do about registering to vote as a Communist!" "Wah, Ricky, I only did it because my granddad made me!" Despite this explanation, the FBI claimed that Ball also donated to the Communist Party.

7. **Harry Belafonte**

8 **Lennie Bruce**

9. **James Cagney**

10. **Truman Capote**

11. **Billy Carter**

12. **Wilt Chamberlain**

LIST 26

111 People Who Are the Subjects of FBI Files

The file of Wilt "The Stilt" contains numerous allegations that he bet on and against his team, the Philadelphia 76ers, between 1966 and 1969, perhaps even shaving points. Indications are the FBI never launched a formal investigation, and no charges were ever brought.

13. Charlie Chaplin

The Little Tramp spoke glowingly of communism and the Soviet Union. This, plus the progressive themes of his films and his fondness for jailbait, led the FBI to intensely surveil the silent-movie actor. They also worked with US Attorney Charles Carr to nail Chaplin for transporting a 23-year-old woman to New York for "immoral" purposes, but he beat the rap.

14. Nat King Cole

15. Gary Cooper

16. Noel Coward

17. Bing Crosby

The FBI's main interest in the crooner was for his association with mobsters, which was basically deemed social and inconsequential.

18. E.E. Cummings

19. Sammy Davis, Jr.

Hoover wanted info on the Candy Man's alleged mob ties, his marriage to a white woman, and his involvement with civil rights. It's hard to say which Hoover thought was worst.

20. John Denver

The folksy singer's file contains tantalizing but mostly redacted references to La Cosa Nostra.

21. Marlene Dietrich

The Berlin-born movie idol was rumored to be secretly aiding the Nazis, so Hoover launched an investigation that included opening her mail and tapping her phone. The Agency dug up her lesbian affairs but nothing indicating a tie to the Third Reich.

22. Joe DiMaggio

23. Walt Disney

The now-defunct website APBNews writes:

There has been much speculation on just what Disney's FBI file means. A 1993 book by celebrity biographer Marc Eliot claimed Disney was an informant for the bureau, and, in return, agents helped search for his biological mother. *The New York Times* confirmed some of this, though other articles condemned Eliot's book and his conclusions. Did the FBI use Disney in any active investigations? Was he feeding the bureau secrets on Hollywood subversives? These files show Disney was very close to the FBI and on at least one occasion changed movie scripts to appease the bureau. "Mr. Disney has volunteered representatives of this office complete access to the facilities of Disneyland for use in connection with official matters and for recreational purposes," states one memo. Several heavily redacted files show the FBI was monitoring prospective Disney employees with the studio's consent.

24. **Jean Dixon**

Among other things, the tabloid psychic's file reveals that from 1966 to 1968, she was a "mouthpiece for the FBI." At her request, the agency fed her information (disinformation?) about the New Left, which she then worked into interviews and articles, claiming, for example, that the Soviet Union was behind student protests.

25. **W.E.B. Du Bois**

26. **Jimmy Durante**

27. **Albert Einstein**

According to the FBI: "Einstein was a member, sponsor, or affiliated with thirty-four communist fronts between 1937-1954. He also served as honorary chairman for three communist organizations."

28. **Hanns Eisler**

29. **Edward "Duke" Ellington**

30. **Medgar Evers**

31. **Douglas Fairbanks, Jr.**

32. **William Faulkner**

33. **Ella Fitzgerald**

34. **Ian Fleming**

35 **Errol Flynn**

The swashbuckling actor got on the FBI's radar for supposed communist sympathies and for two sex-related court cases one claiming that Flynn boinked two 15-year-old girls and the other charging that he pimped a woman he brought into the country from Mexico. He was found not guilty on all counts.

36. **Henry Ford**

37. **Eric Fromm**

38. **Clark Gable**

39. **Marcus Garvey**

40. **Allen Ginsberg**

The Beat poet's file is over 900 pages, and that's just for starters. *In Alien Ink: The FBI's War on Freedom of Expression*, Natalie Robins writes: "Ginsberg not only has an FBI file, but a record at fifteen other agencies, including the CIA, Defense Department, the US Postal Service, the Treasury Department, and the Drug Enforcement Agency."

41. **Woody Guthrie**

42. **Ernest Hemingway**

For a little while, Papa was an FBI operative, reporting on Spanish Fascists in Havana and looking for German submarines off the Cuban coast.

43. **Jimi Hendrix**

44. **Abbie Hoffman**

The radical's radical, Hoffman is the subject of an FBI file over 13,200 pages long.

45. **Billie Holliday**

46. **Lena Horne**

47. **L. Ron Hubbard**

48. **Rock Hudson**

49. **Howard Hughes**

50. **Langston Hughes**

51. **Aldous Huxley**

52. **Helen Keller**

There's no word on why Keller has a file, but it undoubtedly includes her effusive praise of the newly formed Soviet Union and its leader, Lenin.

53. **Gene Kelly**

54. **Joseph P. Kennedy**

55. **Martin Luther King, Jr.**

56. **Alfred Kinsey**

Kinsey's earth-shattering report *Sexual Behavior of the Human Male* upset the prudes at the FBI, as did the sexologist's acceptance of homosexuality. They kept tabs on Kinsey and his Institute for the Study of Human Sexuality, though nothing came of it.

57. **Paul Krassner**

Upon receiving his FBI file, Paul Krassner discovered that the Bureau was behind a poison-pen letter sent to *Life* magazine, calling the counterculture trickster "a raving, unconfined nut." This phrase became the title of Krassner's autobiography.

58. **Ray Kroc**

59. **Veronica Lake**

60. **Burt Lancaster**

Manly man Burt Lancaster ignited the FBI's wrath by speaking out against the House Un-American Activities Committee and working with blacklisted movie figures. When he needed a passport to France to work on his film *Trapeze*, the State Department refused until he sent them an affidavit praising the HUAC and declaring he would rat out anyone with communist sympathies.

The file also says that Lancaster and other celebrities attended a gay party with 250 Marines. This rumor was taken so seriously that the Office of Naval Intelligence raided the mansion where the giant orgy supposedly took place.

61. **Anton LaVey**

62. **John Lennon**

63. **Sinclair Lewis**

64. **Guy Lombardo**

65. **Jack London**

66. **Thomas Mann**

67. **Mickey Mantle**

Among other things, the FBI's file on Mantle looks at his alleged ties to professional gamblers.

68. **Bob Marley**

69. **Billy Martin**

70. **Dean Martin**

As with the rest of the Rat Pack, the FBI watched Dino's interactions with mobsters, Teamsters, and hookers.

71. **The Marx Brothers**

The Marx Brothers—Groucho, Harpo, Zeppo, and Chico are each the subject of an FBI file. A liberal, Groucho was investigated to see if he had commie affiliations, but despite his last name he was no follower of Karl. His comedy was monitored, however, because he occasionally was critical of the United States (which, according to his file, he once referred to as "the United Snakes").

72. **Carson McCullers**

73. **Marshall McLuhan**

74. **Steve McQueen**

75. **Arthur Miller**

76. **Thelonious Monk**

77. **Marilyn Monroe**

In describing Monroe's file, APBNews implies the G-Men's hard-on for the archetypal blonde bombshell: "The FBI collected intelligence on all aspects of the star's life, from a telegram announcing her marriage and a report on her husband's rumored Communist Party ties to risqué quotes she gave about herself to magazines."

78. **Georgia O'Keeffe**

79. **George Orwell**

80. **Jesse Owens**

81. **Linus Pauling**

82. **Pablo Picasso**

83. **Mary Pickford**

84. **Ezra Pound**

85. **Elvis Presley**

The King's file doesn't contain anything investigational toward him. Instead, it looks at attempts to extort him and collects letters of complaint from outraged bluenoses.

86. **Vincent Price**

87. **Ayn Rand**

88. **Diego Rivera**

89. **Norman Rockwell**

90. **Gene Roddenberry**

91. **Eleanor Roosevelt**

J. Edgar Hoover kept one of his notorious "secret and confidential" files on a socialist named Joseph Lash who joined the US Army. In the most explosive portion of the file, an agent reports that the Army Counterintelligence Corps, while surveilling Lash, recorded him having sex with First Lady Eleanor Roosevelt in a hotel room. This tape was then reportedly played for FDR, who ordered Lash transferred to combat and angrily confronted his wife. Although Ms. Roosevelt did have affairs, it's generally believed that this wasn't one of them. Given the timing, it seems likely that the sex tape, if it exists, captured Lash and his fiancée getting it on.

92. **Carl Sagan**

93. **Jonas Salk**

94. **Charles Schulz**

95. **Tupac Shakur**

96. **Frank Sinatra**

The FBI kept an ten-inch thick file on Old Blue Eyes that examined his alleged communist leanings (doubtful), his supposed attempt at extortion (case dropped when the victim wouldn't cooperate), his reported draft-dodging (found to be baseless), and his friendships with Mafiosi (suspicious but never enough to prosecute). Interestingly, in 1950, the Chairman of the Board volunteered to become an FBI rat by infiltrating the Communist Party. Associate Director Clyde Tolson sniffed: "We want nothing to do with him."

97. **Benjamin Spock**

98. **John Steinbeck**
Given Steinbeck's pro-labor views, it was inevitable that the FBI

would compile a dossier on him, focusing on the supposed communist connections of the writer and his wives. The attention was so notice-able that Steinbeck wrote to the Attorney General: "Do you sup-pose you could ask Edgar's boys to stop stepping on my heels? It's getting tiresome."

99. **Jimmy Stewart**

100. **Ed Sullivan**

101. **Rip Torn**

102. **Spencer Tracy**

103. **Lana Turner**

104. **Andy Warhol**

For about a decade starting in the late 1960s, the FBI investi-gated Pop artist Warhol for interstate transporta-tion of obscene material (i.e., his own films). Although some of his movies were banned in some areas (such as New York), Drella was never prosecuted.

105. **John Wayne**

Obviously, there was no need to monitor the Duke for communist activities. He was such

a fervent anti-Red that Stalin sent a KGB assassination squad to snuff him. The most interesting thing in Wayne's file is a memo relaying reports that the actor financially supported a plot to overthrow the govern-ment of Panama.

106. **Orson Welles**

107. **Mae West**

108. **Tennessee Williams**

109. **Frank Lloyd Wright**

110. **Richard Nathaniel Wright**

111. **Malcolm X**

Note: You can attempt to get these files for yourself. Some are posted at [foia.fbi.gov], but most will require a formal request. In your letter, men-tion the Freedom of Informa-tion Act, name the file(s) you're interested in, and cite the amount you're willing to pay. Send the letter to:

Record/Information Dissemination Section

Records Management Division

Federal Bureau of Investigation

Department of Justice

935 Pennsylvania Avenue, NW Washington DC 20535-0001 ◻

1. **The Doors**

2. **The Grateful Dead**

3. **The Jefferson Airplane**

4. **The Kingsmen**

   Somewhat famously, the FBI was obsessed with the Kingsmen's version of "Louie, Louie," which they turned into a garage rock classic with nearly unintelligible lyrics. Hoover's boys were convinced that it was a filthy song subverting America's youth. In fact, the FBI Laboratory was tasked with deciphering the words, never mind the unimportant stuff like solving murders and kidnappings. They never were able to break the code, but they took several hilarious stabs at it. In every instance, they thought the second line of the second verse contained the phrase "fuck you girl" or "fuck your girl." The actual line is, "Me think of girl constantly." The FBI's finest minds also heard lines like, "She's never a girl I'd lay at home," "She had a rag on, I moved above," "Every night and day I play with my thing," and, "Hey, you bitch." (That last line is really, "Me see Jamaica.")

   Here in reality, "Louie Louie"—written and originally performed by rhythm and bluesman Richard Berry is sung from the point of view of a Jamaican guy telling a bartender named Louie how he wants to get back to his girl. It's so tame that you could literally play it to a five-year-old without worrying. Whether or not the Kingsmen added their own off-color lyrics is debatable, but listening closely to their version while reading the original lyrics indicates that they were faithful to Berry's creation.

5. **Kiss**

6. **The Monkees**

6 Bands That Are the Subjects of FBI Files

All list items are taken verbatim from FBI form FD-140: "Application for Employment, Federal Bureau of Investigation."

1

used marijuana during the last 3 years

2

used marijuana more than 15 times

3

used an illegal drug or combination of illegal drugs, other than marijuana, more than 5 times

4

used an illegal drug or combination of illegal drugs, other than marijuana, during the last 10 years

5

sold an illegal drug for profit

6

used an illegal drug while employed in a law enforcement or prosecutorial position or while in a position of high-level responsibility of public trust

7

failed an FBI polygraph examination regarding prior drug use, even if the extent of use would not have been disqualifying

8

failed an FBI polygraph examination regarding truthfulness/candor on an FBI employment application

9

failed an FBI polygraph examination regarding contact with non-US Intelligence Services ◻

LIST 28
9 Things That Will Disqualify You From Employment with the FBI

1

Have you ever been fired from a job?

2

Have you ever left a job by mutual agreement following allegations of misconduct?

3

Did you register with the Selective Service System as required?

4

What foreign countries have you visited?

5

Have you or members of your immediate family, including in-laws, been employed by or acted as a consultant for a foreign government, firm, or agency?

6

Have you engaged in acts or activities designed to overthrow the United States Government by force?

LIST 29

17 Questions You'll be Asked When Applying to Become an FBI Agent

7

Have you ever been over 120 days delinquent on any debt(s) or had any debt placed for collection?

8

Are you a licensed motorcycle driver?

9

Where was your sister's spouse born?

10

Are you now of have you ever been a member of a foreign or domestic organization, association, movement, group, or combination of persons that is totalitarian, fascist, communist, or subversive?

11

Are you aware of any information about yourself or anyone with whom you are or have been closely associated (including relatives and roommates) that tends to reflect unfavorably on your reputation, morals, character, abilities, or loyalty to the United States?

12

If appointed as a Special Agent, do you agree to serve a minimum of three years, and do you clearly understand that you must be available for an assignment wherever your services are needed?

13

Do you use alcohol? To what extent?

14

Have you or any member of your family ever suffered from, or been treated for, any form of mental illness, insanity, epilepsy, been mentally retarded, or had psychiatric consultation of any kind?

15

Do you have any physical defects, including any which would preclude unrestricted, regular participation in all phases of the Bureau's firearms training, physical training, and defensive tactics?

16

Have you ever been declared bankrupt?

17

How did you become interested in Bureau employment? ◨

As of the beginning of 2004, these are the oldest classified documents in possession of the National Archives and Records Administration. If you're wondering how 85-year-old information on naval mines and German invisible ink can still represent such a threat to the republic that it must remain top-secret, you're not alone.

10 Oldest Still-Classified Documents at the National Archives

1

memo: Heingelman to Marlenck (October 30, 1917)

2

report: "Detection of Secret Ink" (January 1, 1918)

3

pamphlet on invisible photography and writing, synthetic ink, and other topics (January 1, 1918)

4

"US Naval Mines, Mine Anchor, Mark VI" (January 26, 1918)

5

report: "Secret Inks" (March 16, 1918)

6

"US Naval Mines, Mine Anchor, Mark VI" (May 1, 1918)

7

Ordnance Pamphlet 575: "Enemy Mines" (June 1, 1918)

8 **9**

report: "German Secret Ink Formula" (June 14, 1918) (one-page and three-page versions)

10

Ordnance Pamphlet 643: "Mine Mark VI and Mods., Description and Operation" (January 1, 1938) ⊓

Thanks to Michael Ravnitzky

+ War ~~and Peace~~

1

"He has not developed any significant capability with respect to weapons of mass destruction. He is unable to project conventional power against his neighbors."

–Secretary of State Colin Powell, referring to Saddam Hussein, February 24, 2001

2

"But in terms of Saddam Hussein being there, let's remember that his country is divided, in effect. He does not control the northern part of his country. We are able to keep arms from him. His military forces have not been rebuilt."

–National Security Advisor Condoleezza Rice, explaining why Hussein's Iraq is not a threat, July 29, 2001

3

"Fuck Saddam. We're taking him out."

–President George W. Bush, in March 2002, a year before the Iraq invasion (a period when he claims he hadn't yet decided how to handle Hussein)

4

"Simply stated, there is no doubt that Saddam Hussein now has weapons of mass destruction."

–Vice President Dick Cheney, August 26, 2002

5

"From a marketing point of view, you don't introduce new products in August."

–White House Chief of Staff Andy Card, on why the Bush Administration waited until September 2002 to start selling the public on an Iraq attack, September 7, 2002

6

"There is no doubt that he has chemical weapons stocks. We destroyed some after the Gulf War with the inspection regime, but there is no doubt in our mind that he still has chemical weapons stocks and he has the capacity to produce more chemical weapons. With respect to biological weapons, we are confident that he has some stocks of those weapons and he is probably continuing to try to develop more."

–Secretary of State Powell, referring to Hussein, September 8, 2002.

7

"Iraq probably has stocked at least 100 metric tons and possibly as much as 500 metric tons of CW [chemical warfare] agents."

–Central Intelligence Agency, October 2002

LIST **31** | **23 Quotes Regarding the 2003 Invasion of Iraq**

8

"In defiance of pledges to the UN it has stockpiled biological and chemical weapons. It is rebuilding the facilities used to make those weapons. UN inspectors believe that Iraq could have produced enough biological and chemical agent to kill millions of people."

–President Bush, October 2, 2002

9

"Intelligence gathered by this and other governments leaves no doubt that the Iraq regime continues to possess and conceal some of the most lethal weapons ever devised."

–President Bush, March 17, 2003

10

"I have always said to people throughout that...our aim has been the elimination of weapons of mass destruction."

–UK Prime Minister Tony Blair, March 25, 2003

11

"The president has made very clear that the reason why we are in Iraq is to find weapons of mass destruction. The fact that we haven't found them in seven or eight days doesn't faze me one little bit. Very clearly, we need to find this stuff or people are going to be asking questions."

–Assistant Secretary of State for Nonproliferation John Wolf, March 30, 2003

12

"We know where they are. They're in the area around Tikrit and Baghdad and east, west, south and north somewhat."

–Secretary of Defense Donald Rumsfeld, referring to Iraq's alleged WMD, March 30, 2003

13

"There is evidence that this war was planned well in advance."

–Hans Blix, UN Chief Weapons Inspector, April 9, 2003

14

"We have high confidence that they have weapons of mass destruction. This is what this war was about and is about. And we have high confidence it will be found."

–White House Press Secretary Ari Fleischer, April 14, 2003

15

"We found the weapons of mass destruction. We found biological laboratories... They're illegal. They're against the United Nations resolutions, and we've so far discovered two. And we'll find more weapons as time goes on. But for those who say we haven't found the banned manufacturing devices or banned weapons, they're wrong. We found them."

–President Bush, lying about two weather balloon-inflating stations found in Iraq, May 29, 2003 (he never made this claim again)

16

"I feel like I've died and gone to hell.... On my good days, I feel like maybe we're at least doing something worthwhile for these people. There aren't many good days. On my bad days, I feel like getting my machine gun and opening up on every one of them."

–Lori, a US Army private stationed in Baghdad, August 2003

17

"Please refrain from writing press releases highlighting killing the enemy."

–Capt. Perry Jarmon, of the Combined Joint Task Force, in an email to a military public relations flak in Iraq, circa October 15, 2003. (Jarmon accidentally sent his email to several prominent media outlets.)

18

"They used me as a way to symbolize all this stuff. It hurt in a way that people would make up stories that they had no truth about."

–Private Jessica Lynch, on the myths about her capture and rescue spun by the military and media, November 7, 2003

19

"I think in this case international law stood in the way of doing the right thing."

–Defense Policy Board member Richard Perle, admitting that the Iraq invasion was illegal, November 19, 2003. (Perle is a leading neoconservative hawk who loudly beat the drum for an Iraq attack.)

20

"With a heavy dose of fear and violence, and a lot of money for projects, I think we can convince these people that we are here to help them."

–Lt. Colonel Nathan Sassaman, stationed in Abu Hishma, Iraq, December 7, 2003

21

"Any indication that something like that happened would be a very serious matter. But I want to be very clear: we don't, at this point, have any indications that I would consider credible and firm that that has taken place, but we will tie down every lead."

–National Security Advisor Condoleezza Rice, squelching the silly theory that Iraq shipped its WMD to Syria right before the invasion, January 9, 2004

22

"There's plenty of blame to go around. The main problem was that the senior administration officials have what I call faith-based intelligence. They knew what they wanted the intelligence to show. They were really blind and deaf to any kind of countervailing information the intelligence community would produce. I would assign some blame to the intelligence community and most of the blame to the senior administration officials."

–Greg Thielmann, former director of the Office of Strategic Proliferation and Military Affairs in the State Department, February 4, 2004

23

"There was never a clear and present danger. There was never an imminent threat. Iraq—and we have very good intelligence on this—was never part of the picture of terrorism."

–Mel Goodman, a veteran CIA analyst who now teaches at the National War College ☐

The 660 or so people being held at the naval base in Guantanamo Bay, Cuba, have never been tried or even charged with crimes. They can be held for the rest of their lives at the whim of the government, and the military has floated the possibility of executing some of them. In an effort to remedy this disgraceful destruction of rights and the law, the Center for Constitutional Rights filed a petition seeking *habeas corpus*, which would force the government to Constitutionally process the prisoners (i.e., quick and speedy trials, jury of peers, right to confront accusers, etc.).

A district court refused, buying the feds' ridiculous argument that because the US military base is located on the island of Cuba, it isn't subject to US law, though it also is most definitely *not* subject to Cuban law. Following this line of argument, no law applies there, making it an autonomous zone, as devised by Hakim Bey, or an inter-zone, from the works of William Burroughs. I'm sure that the men and women stationed at Guantanamo Bay would be surprised to know that they can apparently steal, rape, and kill with impunity. Go ahead, snort coke off your commanding officer's desk. It's all right, because US law doesn't apply.

Seriously, it's hard to see how any court bought such a transparently stupid, self-serving argument. The Center for Constitutional Rights has appealed this boneheaded decision to the Supreme Court, which triggered a flood of *amicus curiae* (friend of the court) briefs from some powerful individuals and groups who used the chance to lambaste the concentration camp 90 miles off the coast of Florida.

12 Arguments Against the Police State at Guantanamo Bay

1

former US diplomats

Who: 23 former US diplomats, many of whom also served as Assistant Secretaries of State or in other high-level positions.

Excerpts: "This undermines what has long been one of our proudest diplomatic advantages—the nation's Constitutional guaranty, enforced by an independent judiciary, against arbitrary government."

"The world has taken due note of the fact that the United States has incarcerated these petitioners in Guantanamo and that there has been no effort to charge, try or judge them under law. This has generated international concern. The Inter-American Commission on Human Rights has undertaken precautionary measures. The UN High Commissioner for Human Rights has spoken out. The International Committee of the Red Cross has gone on record. The British Court of Appeal in the Abbasi case has expressed its displeasure. The Human Rights Chamber of Bosnia-Herzegovina, a court that the United States helped create, has issued its own protest. And Shirin Ebadi, the recipient of the most recent Nobel Peace Prize, referred specifically to Guantanamo in her acceptance remarks as an affront to universal human rights.

"Citizens of foreign countries cannot assume that what happened to the Guantanamo prisoners cannot happen to them. It will not be evident why, if the Executive Branch can detain prisoners in Guantanamo free of judicial inquiry, it cannot expand the practice to establish a global criminal justice system with other prison camps like Guantanamo, similarly subject to no legal oversight and in which any foreigner deemed a danger by some official might be detained indefinitely. Nor will it be evident why such a practice could not reach out to persons within the United States or even to American citizens."

2

former US government officials

Who: "[F]ormer US government officials who have exercised legal responsibility over matters concerning the US Naval Base at Guantanamo, the Panama Canal, or other US bases on foreign soil and those whose responsibilities substantially involved the scope of U.S. jurisdiction and activities abroad."

Excerpts: "Although Guantanamo is unusual, it is not *sui generis*. History records at least three other examples of territory outside US territorial borders and sovereignty, but still under the complete jurisdiction and control of the United States: the Canal Zone, the Trust Territory of the Pacific Islands, and the former American sector in Berlin. In each of these instances, US courts have, by extrapolation from the *Insular Cases*, found fundamental constitutional rights to be applicable to citizens and aliens within these territories. As in Guantanamo, the United States for strategic reasons gained full powers of jurisdiction and control over these territories, without ever possessing actual sovereignty."

"If the Government denies that foreign nationals have rights, then by confining them at Guantanamo, it is engaged not in legal detention, but in a lawless exercise of naked force."

"The Due Process Clause [of the Fourth Amendment] is phrased in universal terms, protecting any 'person' rather than 'citizens' or members of 'the people.' Nor does its wording suggest limitations as to place."

"Maintaining involuntary captives of the United States as rightless outlaws because of their captive status would revive the logic of slavery, a constitutional practice that this country has long abandoned.

"In any event, the Constitution undeniably protects involuntary subjects, such as children who may be too young to form voluntary connections."

"If the Due Process Clause does not apply to detainees at Guantanamo, the Government would have effective discretion to starve them, to beat them, and to kill them, with or without hearings and with or without evidence of any wrongdoing."

3

former American POWs

Who: "Leslie H. Jackson, Edward Jackfert, and Neal Harrington, former American prisoners of war detained by the German and Japanese governments during World War II."

Excerpt: "As these examples [occupied Germany, Vietnam, Grenada, Panama, Haiti, and the Persian Gulf] show, the use of tribunals traditionally has been an integral component of the United States' treatment of persons captured on enemy soil. The Government's current practice of imprisoning foreign citizens indefinitely without providing them with an individualized determination of their status represents a sharp break with this historical commitment. Allowing access to the courts is the only means for these detainees to achieve the narrow redress they seek—individualized determinations of their status as required by the Geneva Conventions and US military regulations."

retired US military officers

Who: "[T]hree retired military officers. Each one formerly served as the Judge Advocate General or the senior legal advisor for a branch of the United States military, and has extensive experience with US military regulations and the Laws of War."

Excerpts: "The United States has also demanded application of the principles codified in the Geneva Conventions to captured US service personnel, even when they were taken prisoner under circumstances when the Conventions, technically, did not apply. For example, following the capture of US Warrant Officer Michael Durant by forces under the control of Somali warlord Mohamed Farah Aideed in 1993, the United States demanded assurances that Durant's treatment would be consistent with the broad protections afforded under the Conventions, even though, '[u]nder a strict interpretation of the Third Geneva Convention's applicability, Durant's captors would not be bound to follow the convention because they were not a 'state.'"

"Invoking international human rights standards, the United States also has condemned foreign governments that have held detainees incommunicado, depriving them of the ability to seek judicial review of their confinements. The United States, for example, objected recently when the Liberian government arrested journalist Hassan Bility and held him incommunicado on the purported ground that he was an 'illegal combatant' involved in terrorist activity."

"Yet even as American officials condemn other nations for detaining people indefinitely without access to a court or tribunal, authoritarian regimes elsewhere are pointing to US treatment of the Guantanamo prisoners as justification for such actions. Eritrea's Ambassador to the United States defended his own government's roundup of journalists by claiming that their detention without charge was consistent with the United States' detention of material witnesses and aliens suspected by the United States of terrorist activities."

5

Fred Korematsu

Who: "More than sixty years ago, as a young man, Fred Korematsu challenged the constitutionality of President Franklin Roosevelt's 1942 Executive Order that authorized the internment of all persons of Japanese ancestry on the West Coast of the United States. He was convicted and sent to prison. In *Korematsu v. United States*, this Court upheld his conviction, explaining that because the United States was at war, the government could constitutionally intern Mr. Korematsu, without a hearing, and without any adjudicative determination that he had done anything wrong."

Excerpts: "Although certain aspects of the 'war against terrorism' may be unprecedented, the challenges to constitutional liberties these cases present are similar to those the nation has encountered throughout its history. The extreme nature of the Government's position here is all too familiar as well. When viewed in its historical context, the Government's position is part of a pattern whereby the executive branch curtails civil liberties much more than necessary during wartime and seeks to insulate the basis for its actions from any judicial scrutiny."

"In *Youngstown Sheet & Tube Co. v. Sawyer*, this Court invalidated President Truman's nationalization of the steel mills during the Korean Conflict, despite the Commander-in-Chief's insistence that his actions were necessary to maintain production of essential war material. During the Vietnam War, this Court rejected a Government request to enjoin publication of the Pentagon Papers, refusing to defer to executive branch claims that publication of this top-secret document would endanger our troops in the field and undermine ongoing military operations. *New York Times Co. v. United States*."

"During World War I, John Lord O'Brian served as Special Assistant Attorney General in charge of the War Emergency Division of the Department of Justice. In this capacity, he played a central role in enforcing the Espionage Act of 1917. Four decades later, reflecting on his own experience, O'Brian cautioned against the 'emotional excitement engendered...during a war,' and warned that 'the greatest danger to our institutions' may rest, not in the threat of subversion, but 'in our own weaknesses in yielding' to wartime anxiety and our 'readiness to...disregard the fundamental rights of the individual.' He expressed the hope that 'our judges will in the end establish principles reaffirming' our nation's commitment to civil liberties.

"As Chief Justice Rehnquist has written, '[i]t is all too easy to slide from a case of genuine military necessity...to one where the threat is not critical and the power [sought to be exercised is] either dubious or nonexistent.' It is, he added, 'both desirable and likely that more careful attention will be paid by the courts to the...government's claims of necessity as a basis for curtailing civil liberty.'"

6

UK Members of Parliament

Who: "175 Members of both Houses of the United Kingdom of Great Britain and Northern Ireland."

Excerpt: "There is no mechanism in place or being followed to ensure that the circumstances of these detentions meet even the most basic standards of due process or human rights. The rule of law requires reasonable due process to ascertain the bases asserted in support of prolonged detention as well as the veracity of the facts that support those bases. Indefinite detention without charge represents a violent departure from principles underlying our common legal heritage.

"The detention center at Guantanamo was designed, according to the US Administration, to house 'the worst of the worst' and 'hardest of the hardcore.' Yet, other statements by the administration suggest that Guantanamo holds no high ranking terrorist of any significance."

7

international law and jurisdiction professors

Who: Four law professors from the US. "All are academic international law experts who have devoted significant attention to the jurisdictional aspects of national and international law in areas such as international criminal law, international economic law, and human rights. Professors Barton and Carter are members of the bar of this Court."

Excerpts: "The prisoners held at the United States Naval Base at Guantanamo are not the only persons who will be affected by the Court's jurisdictional decision in this case. In the aftermath of September 11, 2001, it appears possible that the United States executive will establish its own special criminal court process, seeking to avoid the use of Article III judges and to use instead an executive form of review rather than an independent judicial review, such as that provided by this Court, *Military Order of Nov. 13, 2001: Detention, Treatment, and Trial of Certain Non-Citizens in the War Against Terrorism*. This new process may be applied far beyond those captured in connection with the Afghanistan or Iraq actions, for the war on terrorism is likely to last indefinitely."

"Moreover, precedents set in this terrorism conflict may end up being applied as well to international narcotics or money-laundering offenses."

8

legal historians

Who: A group of two-dozen legal historians from Harvard, Boston College, Columbia, Oxford, Stanford, Yale, Amherst, Princeton, Georgetown, and other universities.

Excerpt: "In sum, the historical evidence is not consistent with the government's claim that the writ of *habeas corpus* guaranteed by the Constitution is unavailable to test even the classification as 'alien enemies' of those detained at Guantánamo. Guantánamo lies a mere 90 miles from the United States and has been subject to the exclusive control and jurisdiction of the United States for the past century. No other law but US law operates there. The historical evidence suggests instead that the denial of all *habeas corpus* review in such a situation would contravene the fundamental principles that have governed the availability and operation of the Great Writ since well before the United States Constitution was adopted."

9

bipartisan coalition of national and international non-governmental organizations

Who: Amnesty International, Human Rights Watch, American Civil Liberties Union, Anti-Defamation League, Lawyers Committee for Human Rights, Association of the Bar of the City of New York, National Association of Social Workers (Legal Defense Fund), People For the American Way Foundation, National Council of the Churches of Christ in the USA, and seven other legal and religious groups.

Excerpts: "Were the Due Process Clause inapplicable to US actions in Guantanamo Bay, then the Constitution would allow the summary execution or torture of prisoners detained there. Indeed, the government has conceded this in open court. See *Gherebi v. Bush*, 2003. ('[A]t oral argument, the government advised us that its position would be the same even if the claims were that it was engaging in acts of torture or that it was summarily executing the detainees. To our knowledge, prior to the current detention of prisoners at Guantanamo, the US government has never before asserted such a grave and startling proposition.')"

"The US Department of Defense has asserted that the Guantanamo prisoners, nearly all of whose identities have not been officially disclosed, are 'battlefield' detainees who were engaged in combat when arrested. But in addition to Petitioners' claims of non-combatancy, it is clear that some detainees were apprehended far from battlefields. For instance, Guantanamo holds six Bosnians and Algerians who were arrested by Bosnian police in Bosnia and then handed over to US troops at the request of the United States. They were quickly transported to Guantanamo, despite a Bosnian court order that four of the men remain in Bosnia for further proceedings."

10

International Commission of Jurists

Who: "The ICJ is comprised of 60 jurists [judges, prosecutors, and attorneys] of high standing in their own country or at the international level."

Excerpts: "If the Court's interpretation of *Johnson v. Eisentrager* were correct, US officials could arrest foreign nationals and, by the simple device of transferring such prisoners to a place of detention outside the sovereign territory of the United States, defeat the jurisdiction of the United States Courts to review the legality of their detention. The US Executive could arbitrarily hold such individuals in detention with no accountability to any court of law."

"There are already disturbing signs that other nations have begun to use the example of the United States to justify arbitrary detention of their citizens. For example, Malaysia's Law Minister has justified the detention of militants without trial stating that its practice was 'just like the process at Guantanamo Bay.' The minister further indicated that he

'put the equation with Guantanamo Bay just to make it graphic to you that this is not simply a Malaysian style of doing things.'"

11

Human Rights Institute of the International Bar Association

Who: "The Human Rights Institute of the International Bar Association (the 'Institute') is an international body headquartered in London, England, that helps promote, protect and enforce human rights under a just rule of law, and works to preserve the independence of the judiciary and legal profession worldwide. Founded in 1995 under the Honorary Presidency of Nelson Mandela, the Institute now has more than 7,000 members worldwide."

Excerpt: "Even where the presumption of prisoner of war status is displaced, the [Geneva] Conventions afford due process protection to all detainees, ensuring that they are not held without justification and that any prosecution brought against them accords with fundamental justice. Combatants who are not members of any armed forces or volunteer corps belonging to a party to a conflict have been described as 'unlawful combatants,' although no such status is recognized in the Geneva Conventions. If they are not members of the armed forces, they fall within the scope of the Civilian Convention. Accordingly, while unlawful combatants (unlike prisoners of war) may be prosecuted for taking part in the conflict and for any crimes committed in that regard, they are entitled to the judicial guarantees set out within the Civilian Convention should they be prosecuted for their actions."

12

National Institute of Military Justice

Who: "[A] District of Columbia nonprofit corporation organized in 1991 to advance the fair administration of military justice and to foster improved public understanding of the military justice system."

Excerpts: "A well-developed body of law regarding individuals seized during hostilities has been enforced regularly by impartial tribunals in past conflicts, and is being applied today by United States armed forces in combat. The application of the rule of law to individuals seized during hostilities is not inconsistent with the Executive Branch's exercise of its war powers, either in theory or in the practice of the United States over the past fifty years. Nor is there anything novel about issuing a writ of *habeas corpus* on the application of an individual confined by the military at Guantanamo Bay, something the highest court of the military did in *Burtt v. Schick*, 23 M.J. 140 (1986)."

"Domestic law and practice thus make it clear that Guantanamo Bay has never been regarded by the United States as a 'law-free' zone. United States courts exercise criminal jurisdiction over both citizens and aliens at Guantanamo Bay. In connection with the detainees currently interned at Guantanamo Bay, the United States has already asserted jurisdiction over an Army chaplain, two translators, and an intelligence officer. Judicial resolution of charges against those individuals has not troubled the Government, which is according rights to everyone except the detainees themselves.

"While the Government devotes much attention to the supposed unavailability of *habeas corpus* in Guantanamo Bay, no such jurisdictional difficulty was found by the court with responsibility for the military justice system. In *Burtt v. Schick*, a Navy enlisted man confined at Guantanamo Bay sought a writ of *habeas corpus* after the prosecution had obtained a mistrial over his objection. Holding that the mistrial had been obtained without either 'manifest necessity,' or the consent of the accused, the Court of Military Appeals unanimously granted the writ against the officer-in-charge of the Guantanamo Bay brig. In doing so, it found no obstacle to asserting *habeas corpus* jurisdiction over individuals at Guantanamo Bay." ☐

Scorecard for the Domestic "War on Terror"

From 9/11 to Sept 30, 2003, number of federal prosecutions for "terrorism": 2,001
Number of convictions: 879
Number of prison sentences: 373
Number of those sentences that were for less than a year: 250
Number of those sentences that were for 20 years to life: 5

1

Around-the-corner gun

Guns with barrels that curve 90 degrees have been around since the late 1800s, according to the *How to Kill* series of books. The Kummlauf used by the Nazis is well-known, and the concept made headlines in 2003 when the Israeli Defense Force started using a modern version—the Corner Shot machine gun—for shooting Palestinians.

2

Bio-inoculator

A dartgun that looks like a pistol, used with shellfish poison and cobra venom. This puppy became public knowledge when, during the Church Committee's investigation into CIA crimes, Director William Casey displayed it before the startled Senators.

3

Bottle blowgun

Say you want to send a poison dart into your target's neck, but putting a blowgun to your mouth might tend to attract attention, especially in an urban environment. Well, just get an empty soda can and paint it the color of the beverage it once contained. Run a sawed-off blowgun from the lip to a hole cut in the button. While it looks like you're enjoying liquid refreshment, your actually dealing out horrible death!

4

Brow-beater

This specially-designed gun is built into a soldier's hard-helmet, with the trigger connected to the chin strap. When the soldier opens his mouth, the device fires out of the front of the helmet.

LIST 33 | 13 Exotic Guns and Knives

5

Duck's foot pistol

An uncommon design from the olden days, duck's foot pistols were flintlock derringers with two or more barrels that would simultaneous discharge with one pull of the trigger. Usually, the barrels pointed in different directions, so the ammo would fan out over a large area, making this gun good for handling grumbling crowds. One model was made with *eight* barrels, covering a 120-degree range!

6

Glass knife

Most obviously used for getting past metal detectors, these daggers are sharp but almost invisible.

7

Knuckle pistol

Around five inches long, this homemade number protrudes between your index and middle fingers when you make a fist. Punch someone in the skull or chest to activate the firing pin, which sends a single slug into the victim.

8

Lapel dagger

This flat blade—in the shape of either a long right triangle or a thin pyramid, is the perfect shape to slide into the lapel of a suit coat.

9

Liberator 9MM pistol

Probably the world's smallest gun, this steel and aluminum nine-milli from Stinger Manufacturing is the length and height of a credit card. And, with a width of nine-tenths of an inch, it's not very thick either.

10

Metal Storm

Australian inventor Mike O'Dwyer has created a gun that can fire *over one million rounds per minute*. The principle involves a unit that houses dozens of barrels, each lined with a row of bullets. Electronic pulses set off traditional gunpowder, launching all bullets in a barrel at once. The pulses are staggered so that each barrel fires a fraction of a second before or after any other barrel.

Wired News reported in 2001: "In a test firing of 36 barrels, lashed together and firing full bore, the gun reduced a series of 15 wooden doors to toothpicks in just two-tenths of a second." Since then, a protoype has been developed in which the 36 barrels are no longer tied together but are housed in one unit, called a pod.

The US and Australian militaries have granted O'Dwyer's Metal Storm company over $100 million for further development of this mega-gun.

11

Pen gun

Yes, Virginia, there really are guns disguised as pens. America's Office of Special Services and Britain's Special Operation Executive used them in WWII, and Stinger Manufacturing currently makes one, which it claims is the only legal model in the world. Their PenGun looks like a steel pen until you bend it in half, causing the trigger to pop out. You then have a .22 pistol with a single shot. In a related vein, the company's KnifeGun looks like a typical 3.7-inch buck knife, and it does indeed have a retractable blade. But it also has a retractable barrel, which fires a single .22 slug.

12

Rectal knife

Made to be smuggled into controlled settings, like prison, it looks like a slim, three-inch metal tube tucked far up your rear. Unscrew the top, which has a long spike attached, and screw it back on with spike facing outward. Also known as an "arse shiv."

13

Umbrella poison gun

The most famous victim of this weapon is Bulgarian dissident writer Georgi Markov, who had defected to the UK. In September 1979, he was walking across Waterloo Bridge when he felt a jab in the back of his thigh. A man carrying an umbrella apologized and quickly left the area. By the next morning, Markov was in dire straits, and in a few days he died. The umbrella had been rigged to fire a ricin-containing pellet the size of a pinhead. After Bulgaria's communist government fell, it was revealed that they were behind the assassination. ⌂

1. **belt buckle**

2. **bicycle pump**

3. **camera**

4. **car antenna** (zip gun)

5. **cellphone**

6. **flashbulb** (to ignite gunpowder)

7. **ground spike**

8. **table leg**

9. **toy gun**

10. **transistor radio**

11. **water piping**

LIST 34

11 Materials That Have Been Made Into Guns

Ever since the two adversaries in the Cold War, the USA and the USSR, realized that their nuclear arsenals were sufficient to do disastrous damage to both countries at short notice, the leaders and the military commanders have thought about the possibility of a nuclear war starting without their intention or as a result of a false alarm. Increasingly elaborate accessories have been incorporated in nuclear weapons and their delivery systems to minimize the risk of unauthorized or accidental launch or detonation. A most innovative action was the establishment of the "hotline" between Washington and Moscow in 1963 to reduce the risk of misunderstanding between the supreme commanders.

Despite all precautions, the possibility of an inadvertent war due to an unpredicted sequence of events remained as a deadly threat to both countries and to the world. That is the reason I am prepared to spend the rest of my life working for abolition of nuclear weapons.

One way a war could start is by a false alarm via one of the warning systems, followed by an increased level of nuclear forces readiness while the validity of the information was being checked. This action would be detected by the other side, and they would take appropriate action; detection of the response would tend to confirm the original false alarm, and so on to disaster. A similar sequence could result from an accidental nuclear explosion anywhere. The risk of such a sequence developing would be increased if it happened during a period of increased international tension.

On the American side, many "false alarms" and significant accidents have been listed, ranging from the trivial to the very serious, during the Cold War. Probably many remain unknown to the public and the research community because of individuals' desire to avoid blame and maintain the good reputation of their unit or command. No doubt there have been as many mishaps on the Soviet side.

Working with any new system, false alarms are more likely. The rising moon was misinterpreted as a missile attack during the early days of long-range radar. A fire at a broken gas pipeline was believed to be the enemy jamming by laser a satellite's infrared sensor when those sensors were first deployed.

The risks are illustrated by the following selection of mishaps. If the people involved had exercised less caution, or if some unfortu-

20 Mishaps That Might Have Started Nuclear War
Alan F. Philips, M.D.

nate coincidental event had occurred, escalation to nuclear war can easily be imagined. Details of some of the events differ in different sources; where there have been disagreements, I have chosen to quote those from the carefully researched book, *The Limits of Safety* by Scott D. Sagan. He gives references to original sources in all instances.

1

Suez Crisis coincidence

November 5, 1956. British and French Forces were attacking Egypt at the Suez Canal. The Soviet government had suggested to the US that they combine forces to stop this by a joint military action, and had warned the British and French governments that (non-nuclear) rocket attacks on London and Paris were being considered. That night NORAD HQ received messages that:

1. unidentified aircraft were flying over Turkey, and the Turkish air force was on alert;

2. 100 Soviet MIG-15's were flying over Syria;

3. a British Canberra bomber had been shot down over Syria;

4. the Soviet fleet was moving through the Dardanelles.

It is reported that in the US General Goodpaster himself was concerned that these events might trigger the NATO operations plan for nuclear strikes against the USSR. The four reports were all shown afterward to have innocent explanations. They were due, respectively, to:

1. a flight of swans;

2. a routine air force escort (much smaller than the number reported) for the President of Syria, who was returning from a visit to Moscow;

3. the Canberra bomber was forced down by mechanical problems;

4. the Soviet fleet was engaged in scheduled routine exercises.

2

BMEWS communication failure

November 24, 1961. On the night of November 24, 1961, all communication links went dead between Strategic Air Command Headquarters (SAC HQ) and North American Aerospace Defense Command (NORAD). The communication loss cut off SAC HQ from the three Ballistic Missile Early Warning Sites (BMEWS) at Thule (Greenland), Clear (Alaska), and Fillingdales (England). There were two possible explanations: either enemy action, or the coincidental failure of all the communication systems, which had redundant and ostensibly independent routes, including commercial telephone circuits. All SAC bases in the United States were therefore alerted, and B-52 bomber crews started their engines, with instructions not to take off without further orders. Radio communication was established with an orbiting B-52 on airborne alert near Thule. It contacted the BMEWS stations by radio and could report that no attack had taken place.

The reason for the "coincidental" failure was the redundant routes for telephone and telegraph communication between SAC HQ and NORAD all ran through one relay station in Colorado. At that relay station a motor had overheated and caused interruption of all the lines.

3

B-52 navigation error

August 23, 1962. SAC Chrome Dome airborne alert route included a leg from the northern tip of Ellesmore Island, southwest across the Arctic Ocean to Barter Island, Alaska. On August 23, 1962, a B-52 nuclear-armed bomber crew made a navigational error and flew 20 degrees too far north. They approached within 300 miles of Soviet airspace near Wrangel Island, where there was believed to be an interceptor base with aircraft having an operational radius of 400 miles.

Because of the risk of repetition of such an error, in this northern area where other checks on navigation are difficult to obtain, it was decided to fly a less provocative route in the future. However, the necessary orders had not been given by the time of the Cuban Missile Crisis in October 1962, so throughout that crisis the same northern route was being flown 24 hours a day.

4

U2 flights into Soviet airspace

August-October 1962. U2 high-altitude reconnaissance flights from Alaska occasionally strayed unintentionally into Soviet airspace. One such episode occurred in August 1962. During the Cuban Missile Crisis in October 1962, the U2 pilots were ordered not to fly within 100 miles of Soviet airspace.

On the night of October 26, for a reason irrelevant to the crisis, a U2 pilot was ordered to fly a new route, over the North Pole, where positional checks on navigation were by sextant only. That night the aurora prevented good sextant readings, and the plane strayed over the Chukotski Peninsula. Soviet MIG interceptors took off with orders to shoot down the U2. The pilot contacted his US command post and was ordered to fly due east toward Alaska. He ran out of fuel while still over Siberia. In response to his S.O.S., US F102-A fighters were launched to escort him on his glide to Alaska, with orders to prevent the MIGs from entering US airspace. The US interceptor aircraft were armed with nuclear missiles. These could have been used by any one of the F102-A pilots at his own discretion.

5

Cuban Missile Crisis: A Soviet satellite explodes

October 24, 1962. On October 24, a Soviet satellite entered its own parking orbit, and shortly afterward exploded. Sir Bernard Lovell, director of the Jodrell Bank observatory, wrote in 1968: "[T]he explosion of a Russian spacecraft in orbit during the Cuban missile crisis...led the US to believe that the USSR was launching a massive ICBM attack." The NORAD Command Post logs of the dates in question remain classified, possibly to conceal reaction to the event. Its occurrence is recorded, and US space tracking stations were informed on October 31 of debris resulting from the breakup of "62 BETA IOTA."

6

Cuban Missile Crisis: Intruder in Duluth

October 25, 1962. Around midnight on October 25, a guard at the Duluth Sector Direction Center saw a figure climbing the security fence. He shot at it and activated the "sabotage alarm." This automatically set off sabotage alarms at all bases in the area. At Volk Field, Wisconsin, the alarm was wrongly wired, and the Klaxon sounded, which ordered nuclear-armed F-106A interceptors to take off. The pilots knew there would be no practice alert drills while DEFCON 3 was in force, and they believed World War III had started.

Immediate communication with Duluth showed there was an error. By this time aircraft were starting down the runway. A car raced from command center and successfully signaled the aircraft to stop. The original intruder was a bear.

7

Cuban Missile Crisis: ICBM test launch

October 26, 1962. At Vandenburg Air Force Base, California, there was a program of routine ICBM test-flights. When DEFCON 3 was ordered, all the ICBMs were fitted with nuclear warheads, except one Titan missile that was scheduled for a test launch later that week. That one was launched for its test, without further orders from Washington, at 4 a.m. on the 26th.

It must be assumed that Russian observers were monitoring US missile activities as closely as US observers were monitoring Russian and Cuban activities. They would have known of the general changeover to nuclear warheads, but not that this was only a test launch.

8

Cuban Missile Crisis: Unannounced Titan missile launch

October 26, 1962. During the crisis, some radar warning stations that were under construction and near completion were brought into full operation as quickly as possible. The planned overlap of coverage was thus not always available.

A normal test launch of a Titan-II ICBM took place in the afternoon of October 26, from Florida to the South Pacific. It caused temporary concern at Moorestown radar site until its course could be plotted, showing no predicted impact within the United States. It was not until after this event that the potential for a serious false alarm was realized, and orders were given that radar warning sites must be notified in advance of test launches, and the countdown be relayed to them.

9

Cuban Missile Crisis: Malmstrom Air Force Base

October 26, 1962. When DEFCON 2 was declared on October 24, solid-fuel Minuteman-1 missiles at Malmstrom Air Force Base were being prepared for full deployment. The work was accelerated to ready the missiles for operation, without waiting for the normal handover procedures and safety checks. When one silo and missile were ready on October 26, no armed guards were available to cover transport from the separate storage, so the launch-enabling equipment and codes were all placed in the silo. It was thus physically possible for a single operator to launch a fully-armed missile at a target designated under SIOP (Single Integrated Operations Plan).

During the remaining period of the crisis, the several missiles at Malmstrom were repeatedly put on and off alert as errors and defects were found and corrected. Fortunately, no combination of errors caused or threatened an unauthorized launch, but in the extreme tension of the period, the danger can be well imagined.

10

Cuban Missile Crisis: NATO readiness

October 1962. It is recorded that on October 22, British Prime Minister Harold Macmillan and NATO Supreme Commander General Lauris Norstad agreed not to put NATO on alert in order to avoid provoking the USSR. When the US Joint Chiefs of Staff ordered DEFCON 3, Norstad was authorized to use his discretion in complying. Norstad did not order a NATO alert. However, several NATO subordinate commanders did order alerts to DEFCON 3 or equivalent levels of readiness at bases in West Germany, Italy, Turkey, and United Kingdom. This seems largely due to the action of General Truman Landon, Commander in Chief of US Air Forces Europe, who already had started alert procedures on October 17 in anticipation of a serious crisis over Cuba.

11

Cuban Missile Crisis: British alerts

October 1962. When the US Strategic Air Command went to DEFCON 2 on October 24, Bomber Command (the UK) was carrying out an unrelated readiness exercise. On October 26, Air Marshall Cross, Commander in Chief of Bomber Command, decided to prolong the exercise because of the Cuban Missile Crisis, and later increased the alert status of British nuclear forces, so that they could launch in fifteen minutes.

It seems likely that Soviet intelligence would perceive these moves as part of a coordinated plan in preparation for immediate war. They could not be expected to know that neither the British Minister of Defense nor Prime Minister Macmillian had authorized them.

It is disturbing to note how little was learned from these errors in Europe. National Security Advisor McGeorge Bundy wrote in *Danger and Survival* that "the risk [of nuclear war] was small, given the prudence and unchallenged final control of the two leaders."

12

Cuban Missile Crisis: Moorestown false alarm

October 28, 1962. Just before 9 a.m. on October 28, the Moorestown, New Jersey, radar operators informed the national command post that a nuclear attack was under way. A test tape simulating a missile launch from Cuba was being run, and simultaneously a satellite came over the horizon.

Operators became confused and reported by voice line to NORAD HQ that impact was expected eighteen miles west of Tampa at 9:02 a.m. The whole of NORAD was informed, but before irrevocable action had taken place, it was reported that no detonation had occurred at the predicted time, and Moorestown operators reported the reason for the false alarm.

During the incident, overlapping radars that should have confirmed or disagreed were not in operation. The radar post had not received routine information of satellite passage because the facility carrying out that task had been given other work for the duration of the crisis.

13

Cuban Missile Crisis: False warning due to satellite

October 28, 1962. At 5:26 p.m. on October 28, the Laredo radar warning site had just become operational. Operators misidentified a satellite in orbit as two possible missiles over Georgia and reported by voice line to NORAD HQ. NORAD was unable to identify that the warning came from the new station at Laredo and believed it to be from Moorestown, and therefore more reliable. Moorestown failed to intervene and contradict the false warning. By the time the Commander of NORAD had been informed, no impact had been reported and the warning was "given low credence."

14

The Penkovsky false warning

November 2, 1962. In the fall of 1962, Colonel Oleg Penkovsky was working with the Soviets as a double agent for the CIA. He had been given a code by which to warn the CIA if he was convinced that a Soviet attack on the United States was imminent. He was to call twice, one minute apart, and only blow into the receiver. Further information was then to be left at a "dead drop" in Moscow.

The pre-arranged code message was received by the CIA on November 2, 1962.

It was known at the CIA that Penkovsky had been arrested on October 22. Penkovsky knew he was going to be executed. It is not known whether he had told the KGB the meaning of the code signal or only how it would be given, nor is it known exactly why or with what authorization the KGB staff used it. When another CIA agent checked the dead drop, he was arrested.

15

Power failure and faulty bomb alarms

November 1965. Special bomb alarms were installed near military facilities and near cities in the US, so that the locations of nuclear bursts would be transmitted before the expected communication failure. The alarm circuits were set up to display a red signal at command posts the instant that the flash of a nuclear detonation reached the sensor and before the blast put it out of action. Normally the display would show a green signal, or yellow if the sensor was not operating or was out of communication for any other reason.

During the commercial power failure in the Northeastern United States in November 1965, displays from all the bomb alarms for the area should have shown yellow. In fact, two of them from different cities showed red because of circuit errors. The effect was consistent with the power failure being due to nuclear weapons explosions, and the Command Center of the Office of Emergency Planning went on full alert. Apparently the military did not.

16

B-52 crash near Thule

January 21, 1968. Communication between NORAD HQ and the BMEWS station at Thule, Greenland, had 3 elements:

1. direct radio communication;
2. a "bomb alarm," as described above;
3. radio communication relayed by a B-52 bomber on airborne alert.

On January 21, 1968, a fire broke out in the B-52 bomber on airborne alert near Thule. The pilot prepared for an emergency landing at the base. However, the situation deteriorated rapidly, and the crew had to bale out. There had been no time to communicate with SAC HQ, and the pilotless plane flew over the Thule base before crashing into the ice seven miles offshore. Its fuel and the high explosive component of its nuclear weapons exploded, but there was no nuclear detonation.

At that time, the "one point safe" condition of the nuclear weapons could not be guaranteed, and it is believed that a nuclear explosion could have resulted from accidental detonation of the high explosive trigger. Had there been a nuclear detonation even at seven miles distant, and certainly much nearer the base, all three communication methods would have given an indication consistent with a successful nuclear attack on both the base and the B-52 bomber. The bomb alarm would have shown red, and the other two communication paths would have gone dead. It would hardly have been anticipated that the combination could have been caused by accident, particularly as the map of the routes for B-52 airborne flights approved by the President showed no flight near Thule. The route had been apparently changed without informing the White House.

17

False alarm during Middle East crisis

October 24-25, 1973. On October 24, 1973, when the UN-sponsored cease-fire intended to end the Arab-Israeli war was in force, further fighting stared between Egyptian and Israeli troops in the Sinai desert. US intelligence reports and other sources suggested that the USSR was planning to intervene to protect the Egyptians. President Nixon was in the throes of Watergate and not available for a conference, so Kissinger and other US officials ordered DEFCON 3. The consequent movements of aircraft and troops were of course observed by Soviet intelligence. The purpose of the alert was not to prepare for war but to warn the USSR not to intervene in the Sinai. However, if the following accident had not been promptly corrected, the Soviet command might have had a more dangerous interpretation.

On October 25, while DEFCON 3 was in force, mechanics were repairing one of the Klaxons at Kinchole Air Force Base, Michigan, and accidentally activated the whole base alarm system. B-52 crews rushed to their aircraft and started the engines. The duty officer recognized the alarm as false and recalled the crews before any took off.

18

Computer exercise tape

November 9, 1979. At 8:50 a.m. on November 9, 1979, duty officers at four command centers (NORAD HQ, SAC Command Post, the Pentagon National Military Command Center, and the Alternate National Military Command Center) all saw on their displays a pattern showing a large number of Soviet missiles in a full-scale attack on the US. During the next six minutes, emergency preparations for retaliation were made. A number of Air Force planes were launched, including the President's National Emergency Airborne Command Post, though without the President! President Carter had not been informed, perhaps because he could not be found.

No attempt was made to use the hotline either to ascertain the Soviet intentions or to tell the Soviets the reasons for US actions. This seems to me to have been culpable negligence. The whole purpose of the hotline was to prevent exactly the type of disaster that was threatening at that moment.

With commendable speed, NORAD was able to contact the Air Force's PAVE PAWS early warning radar and learn that no missiles had been reported. Also, the sensors on the satellites were functioning that day and had detected no missiles. In only six minutes the threat assessment conference was terminated.

The reason for the false alarm was an exercise tape running on the computer system. US Senator Charles Percy happened to be in NORAD HQ at the time and is reported to

have said there was absolute panic. A question was asked in Congress, and the General Accounting Office conducted an investigation. An off-site testing facility was constructed so that test tapes did not in the future have to be run on a system that could be in military operation.

19

Faulty computer chip

June 1980. The warning displays at the Command Centers mentioned in the last episode included windows that normally showed:

0000 ICBMs detected 0000 SLBMs detected

At 2:25 a.m. on June 3, 1980, these displays started showing various numbers of missiles detected, represented by 2's in place of one or more 0's. Preparations for retaliation were instituted, including nuclear bomber crews starting their engines, the launching of Pacific Command's Airborne Command Post, and the readying of Minuteman missiles for launch. It was not difficult to assess that this was a false alarm because the numbers displayed were not rational.

While the cause of that false alarm was still being investigated three days later, the same thing happened, and again preparations were made for retaliation. The cause was a single faulty chip that was failing in a random fashion. The basic design of the system was flawed, allowing this single failure to cause a deceptive display at several command posts. The following incident is added to illustrate that even now, after the Cold War, errors can still cause for concern. This particular one could have hardly brought nuclear retaliation, but there are still 30,000 nuclear weapons deployed, and two nuclear weapon states could get into a hostile adversarial status again.

20

Russian false alarm

January 1995. On January 25, 1995, the Russian early warning radar detected an unexpected missile launch near Spitzbergen. The estimated flight time to Moscow was five minutes. The Russian President, the Defense Minister, and the Chief of Staff were informed. The early warning and the control and command center switched to combat mode. Within five minutes, radar determined that the missile's impact would be outside the Russian borders.

The missile was Norwegian, and was launched for scientific measurements. On January 16, Norway had notified 35 countries, including Russia, that the launch was planned. Information had apparently reached the Russian Defense Ministry, but failed to reach the on-duty personnel of the early warning system.

Comment and Note on Probability

The probability of actual progression to nuclear war on any one of the occasions listed may have been small, due to planned "fail-safe" features. However, the accumulation of small probabilities of disaster from a long sequence of risks add up to serious danger.

There is no way of telling what the actual level of risk was in these mishaps, but if the chance of disaster in every one of the 20 incidents had been only one in 100, it is a mathematical fact that the chance of surviving all 20 would have been 82% (i.e., about the same as the chance of surviving a single pull of the trigger at Russian roulette played with a six-shooter). With a similar series of mishaps on the Soviet side: another pull of the trigger. If the risk in some of the events had been as high as one in ten, then the chance of surviving just seven such events would have been less than 50-50. ◻

Nuclear Age Peace Foundation
1187 Coast Village Road, Suite 1, PMB 121
Santa Barbara CA 93108-2794

www.wagingpeace.org
voice: 805-965-3443
fax: 805-568-0466

From September 1961 to September 1992, the United States military conducted 824 nuclear tests. Of these, 433 released radioactive material into the area surrounding the immediate detonation site. In 52 such incidents, the atomic particles drifted outside of the entire testing area (usually the Nevada Test Range) and into civilian areas.

Antler

Date: September 15, 1961 (first known test in which radiation leaked offsite)
Location: Nevada Test Site
Bomb yield: 2.6 kilotons
Length of release: unknown
Farthest location radiation detected: "21.1 miles northeast of the junction of Highway 6 and Highway 25 (Nevada)"
Most radiation detected: 28 picocuries @ Diablo, Nevada

Gnome

Date: December 10, 1961
Location: Carlsbad, New Mexico
Bomb yield: 3.0 kilotons
Length of release: "Large flow" for 30 minutes; "small flow" until the following day
Farthest location radiation detected: Roswell, New Mexico
Most radiation detected: 160 picocuries @ IMCC Mine, New Mexico

Pampas

Date: March 1, 1962
Location: Nevada Test Site
Bomb yield: 9.5 kilotons
Length of release: 20 minutes
Farthest location radiation detected: Sand Springs Valley, Nevada
Most radiation detected: 1,700 picocuries @ Penoyer, Nevada

LIST 36

13 Nuclear Tests That Spread Radiation into Civilian Areas

4

Platte

Date: April 14, 1962
Location: Nevada Test Site
Bomb yield: 1.85 kilotons
Length of release: not specified
Farthest location radiation detected: "28.1 miles northeast of Currant, Nevada"
Most radiation detected: 34,000 picocuries @ Queen City Summit, Nevada

5

Sedan

Date: July 6, 1962
Location: Nevada Test Site
Bomb yield: 104 kilotons
Length of release: not specified
Farthest location radiation detected: near McGill, Nevada
Most radiation detected: 13,000 picocuries @ Diablo, Nevada

6

Johnnie Boy

Date: July 11, 1962
Location: Nevada Test Site
Bomb yield: 500 tons
Length of release: not specified
Farthest location radiation detected: 11 miles northeast of Lockes, Nevada
Most radiation detected: 23,000 picocuries @ Twin Springs Ranch, Nevada

7

Small Boy

Date: July 14, 1962
Location: Nevada Test Site
Bomb yield: "low"
Length of release: not specified
Farthest location radiation detected: "seven miles south of Parowan, Utah, on Highway 143"
Most radiation detected: 140,000 picocuries @ Elko, Nevada

8

Bandicoot

Date: October 19, 1962
Location: Nevada Test Site
Bomb yield: 12.5 kilotons
Length of release: five minutes
Farthest location radiation detected: 14.5 miles south of Shoshone, California
Most radiation detected: 52,000 picocuries @ Death Valley Junction, California

9

Double Tracks

This test was not technically a nuclear explosion. Rather, it was more along the lines of what we now call a "dirty bomb." The US and British militaries wanted to study dispersal of radioactive particles, so they did the logical thing: Out in the open, they used conventional explosives to scatter plutonium to the four winds.

Date: May 15, 1963
Location: Nellis Air Force Range (adjacent to Las Vegas)
Bomb yield: N/A
Length of release: N/A
Farthest location radiation detected: not specified
Most radiation detected: "Alpha activity detected on air samplers at Beatty, Nevada and Scotty's Junction, Nevada"

10

Baneberry

Date: December 18, 1970
Location: Nevada Test Site
Bomb yield: 10 kilotons
Length of release: 24 hours
Farthest location radiation detected: Austin, Nevada, although, in a seeming contradiction, the military reported: "parts of the [nuclear] cloud moved over Nevada, Utah, and Wyoming; another fraction moved towards California."
Most radiation detected: 3,400 picocuries @ Stone Cabin Ranch, Nevada

11

Misty Rain

Date: April 6, 1985
Location: Nevada Test Site
Bomb yield: under 20 kilotons

Length of release: "controlled ventilation" occurred from two and a half to four days later
Farthest location radiation detected: Reed Ranch Road, Nevada; Rachel, Nevada
Most radiation detected: "No radiation intensities above background levels were detected." (Then how was the radiation detected in Reed Ranch Road and Rachel?)

12

Glencoe

Date: March 22, 1986
Location: Nevada Test Site
Bomb yield: 29 kilotons
Length of release: unspecified length on March 27
Farthest location radiation detected: Lathrop Wells, Nevada.
Most radiation detected: not specified

13

Mighty Oak

Date: April 10, 1986 (last known test in which radiation leaked offsite)
Location: Nevada Test Site
Bomb yield: under 20 kilotons
Length of release: From April 22 to May 19, eight "controlled ventilations" were performed
Farthest location radiation detected: "No radiation intensities above background were detected."
Most radiation detected: 430±15 picocuries @ Medlins Ranch, Nevada ⌂

The nuclear priesthood has a tradition of giving interesting names to test detonations of atomic weapons. Often, they're named after animals, food, Southwestern cities, Native American tribes, and everyday objects. Most are pretty mundane, but out of the hundreds of tests, a few monikers are memorable. Some reveal gallows humor (Dead, Bye, and Calamity), while others seem darkly humorous only in retrospect (Rummy, Waco). Many will make your mouth water (Brie, Chocolate, Cinnamon, and Cognac), and still others make me wonder what else was happening at the Nevada Test Site (Sappho, Climax).

1950s

1. **Annie**
2. **Climax**
3. **Eddy**
4. **Fig**
5. **Flathead**
6. **Koon**
7. **Tesla**
8. **Zuccini**

1960s

9. **Absinthe**
10. **Anchovy**
11. **Barracuda**
12. **Bye**
13. **Calamity**

Department of Energy photo of the Climax test detonation.

LIST **37** | 46 Nuclear Tests by the US

14. **Chinchilla**

15. **Chipmunk**

16. **Chocolate**

17. **Cinnamon**

18. **Cognac**

19. **Daiquiri**

20. **Dead**

21. **Diluted Waters**

22. **Fizz**

23. **Gerbil**

24. **Gum Drop**

25. **Mad**

26. **Marshmallow**

27. **Nipper**

28. **Numbat**

29. **Persimmon**

30. **Platypus**

31. **Red Hot**

32. **Tiny Tot**

37. **Gazook**

38. **Haplopappus**

39. **Rummy**

40. **Sappho**

41. **Sheepshead**

1980s

42. **Brie**

43. **Darwin**

44. **Midas Myth**

45. **Waco**

1990s

46. **Hunters Trophy**

1970s

33. **Backgammon**

34. **Diamond Dust**

35. **Diana Mist**

36. **Dido Queen**

Number of Civilians Killed by Bombing During World War II

Britain: over 60,500
Germany: 570,000 to 800,000
Japan: 442,000 to 1,000,000 or more

Unlike almost all other government agencies and offices, the Inspector General of the Defense Department still uses imaginative names for its investigations.

1. **Operation Electric Avenue**
2. **Operation Brown Bag**
3. **Operation Cobra Nest**
4. **Operation Afterglow**
5. **Operation Bad Back**
6. **Operation Kaboom**
7. **Project Knotdock**
8. **Operation Bad Gas**
9. **Operation Goldbrick**
10. **Operation Shrinkwrap**
11. **Project Mongoose**
12. **Emergentology**
13. **Operation Busted Dreams**
14. **Operation Treasure Trolls**

33 Names of Defense Department Internal Investigations

15. **Operation Wingit**

16. **Project Excess**

17. **Operation Big Foot**

18. **Project Crank Call**

19. **Project Easy Pickings**

20. **Operation Aquaknot**

21. **Project Can't Be**

22. **Project Crypto Night**

23. **Operation Kill-Dare**

24. **Operation Kick the Can**

25. **Project Deadpool**

26. **Project Back Orifice 2000**

27. **Operation The Craft**

28. **Project Walk Along**

29. **Operation Chosen Path**

30. **Project Blue Lagoon**

31. **Project: X-Files**

32. **Operation Hack in the Box**

33. **Operation Gold Coat**

The investigations listed above have been closed in the past few years. If you'd like to find out more about any of them, write a letter mentioning the Freedom of Information Act and asking for the final report and/or closing memo on whichever investigations tickle your fancy. Mention how much you're willing to pay. Mail, fax, or email it to:

Inspector General, Department of Defense
Freedom of Information Act & Privacy
Act Office
400 Army Navy Drive, Room 223
Arlington, Virginia 22202-4704
fax: 703-602-0294
email: FOIA@dodig.osd.mil ﾑ

Thanks to Michael Ravnitzky

After 9/11, the Defense Advanced Research Projects Agency (DARPA)—the group that develops technology for the military and homeland defense—formed the Information Awareness Office. The IAO's most famous project was Total Information Awareness, a system to gather and interpret in real-time the activities of whomever the government wanted to watch. The man in charge was Iran-contra felon Admiral John Poindexter.

The IAO started backtracking as soon as the public, the press, and privacy watchdogs expressed alarm. First, the biographies of Poindexter and the other senior staff of the IAO disappeared from the website. Then the IAO's famously creepy logo—a Masonic pyramid with an eye shooting a beam that envelops the Earth—was pulled. Then TIA was changed to *Terrorism* Information Awareness. Next, Congress outlawed funding for the program (in name only—similar projects under a different moniker could be, and probably are, funded). Finally, in late 2003, DARPA scrapped the entire Information Awareness Office. A few of its programs were transferred to DARPA's Information Processing Technology Office. Below are all the projects that IAO was working on, with official descriptions from the website before it was deleted.

Babylon

"The goal of the Babylon program is to develop rapid, two-way, natural language speech translation interfaces and platforms for the warfighter for use in field environments for force protection, refugee processing, and medical triage. Babylon will focus on overcoming the many technical and engineering challenges limiting current multilingual translation technology to enable future full-domain, unconstrained dialog translation in multiple environments." The first four languages to be tackled were Pashto, Dari, Arabic, and Mandarin.

Bio-Surveillance

"The goal of the Bio-Surveillance program is to develop the necessary information technologies and resulting prototype capable of detecting the covert release of a biological pathogen automatically, and significantly earlier than traditional approaches.... The Bio-

13 Programs From DARPA's Defunct Information Awareness Office

Surveillance program will dramatically increase DoD's ability to detect a clandestine biological warfare attack in time to respond effectively and so avoid potentially thousands of casualties. The Bio-Surveillance program is seeking to achieve its objective by monitoring non-traditional data sources such as animal sentinels, behavioral indicators, and pre-diagnostic medical data."

3

Communicator

"The specific goal of the Communicator program is to develop and demonstrate 'dialogue interaction' technology that enables warfighters to talk with computers, such that information will be accessible on the battlefield or in command centers without ever having to touch a keyboard. The Communicator Platform will be wireless and mobile, and will function in a networked environment. Software enabling dialogue interaction will automatically focus on the context of a dialogue to improve performance, and the system will be capable of automatically adapting to new topics so conversation is natural and efficient."

"Hands-on exercises have been conducted involving small unit logistics operations with the Marines designed to stress test the technology in extreme environments."

4

Effective, Affordable, Reusable Speech-to-Text (EARS)

"The Effective Affordable Reusable Speech-To-Text (EARS) program is developing speech-to-text (automatic transcription) technology whose output is substantially richer and much more accurate than currently possible. This will make it possible for machines to do a much better job of detecting, extracting, summarizing, and translating important information. It will also enable humans to understand what was said by reading transcripts instead of listening to audio signals. EARS is focusing on natural, unconstrained human-human speech from broadcasts and telephone conversations in multiple languages."

5

Evidence Extraction and Link Discovery (EELD)

"The goal of the Evidence Extraction and Link Discovery (EELD) program is development of technologies and tools for automated discovery, extraction and linking of sparse evidence contained in large amounts of classified and unclassified data sources. EELD is developing detection capabilities to extract relevant data and relationships about people, organizations, and activities from message traffic and open source data. It will link items relating potential terrorist groups or scenarios, and learn patterns of different groups or scenarios to identify new organizations or emerging threats."

"EELD's initial activities demonstrated the feasibility of extracting relationships from text, and validated the detectability of patterns representing terrorist groups and scenarios."

6

Futures Markets Applied to Prediction (FutureMap)

"FutureMAP will concentrate on market-based techniques for avoiding surprise and predicting future events. Strategic decisions depend upon the accurate assessment of the likelihood of future events. This analysis often requires independent contributions by experts in a wide variety of fields, with the resulting difficulty of combining the various opinions into one assessment. Market-based techniques provide a tool for producing these assessments.

"There is potential for application of market-based methods to analyses of interest to the DoD [Department of Defense]. These may include analysis of political stability in regions of the world, prediction of the timing and impact on national security of emerging technologies, analysis of the outcomes of advanced technology programs, or other future events of interest to the DoD. In addition, the rapid reaction of markets to knowledge held by only a few participants may provide an early warning system to avoid surprise."

7

Genisys

"The Genisys program's goal is to produce technology enabling ultra-large, all-source information repositories. To predict, track, and preempt terrorist attacks, the US requires a full-coverage database containing all information relevant to identifying: potential foreign terrorists and their possible supporters; their activities; prospective targets; and, their operational plans. Current database technology is clearly insufficient to address this need."

8

Genoa

"Project Genoa is developing information technology for the intelligence community to rapidly and systematically accumulate evidence, facilitate collaboration (while protecting critical information), and test hypothesis that support decision-making at the national level. Bases on successful demonstrations, the Defense Intelligence Agency has agreed to be a transition partner for Project Genoa technology."

9

Genoa II

"It will focus on developing information technology needed by teams of intelligence analysts and operations and policy personnel in attempting to anticipate and preempt terrorist threats to US interests...."

"Genoa II will develop and deploy: 1) cognitive aids that allow humans and machines to 'think together' in real-time about complicated problems; 2) means to overcome the biases and limitations of the human cognitive system; 3) 'cognitive amplifiers' that help teams of people rapidly and fully comprehend complicated and uncertain situations; and, 4) the means to rapidly and seamlessly cut across—and complement— existing stove-piped hierarchical organizational structures by creating dynamic, adaptable, peer-to-peer collaborative networks."

10

Human ID at a Distance (HumanID)

"The goal of the Human Identification at a Distance (HumanID) program is to develop automated biometric identification technologies to detect, recognize and identify humans at great distances. These technologies will provide critical early warning support for force protection and homeland defense against terrorist, criminal, and other human-based threats, and will prevent or decrease the success rate of such attacks against DoD operational facilities and installations. Methods for fusing biometric technologies into advanced human identification systems will be developed to enable faster, more accurate and unconstrained identification of humans at significant standoff distances."

The three main modes of automatic identification planned were face recognition (including long-range and infrared), iris recognition, and gait recognition. This last would involve using radar to analyze the way a person walks and I.D. them based on that. This form of Big Brotherism was accurately predicted by George Orwell in *1984*.

11

Total Information Awareness System

"The goal of the Total Information Awareness (TIA) program is to revolutionize the ability of the United States to detect, classify and identify foreign terrorists—and decipher their plans—and thereby enable the US to take timely action to successfully preempt and defeat terrorist acts. To that end, the TIA program objective is to create a counter-terrorism information system that: (1) increases information coverage by an order of magnitude, and affords easy future scaling; (2) provides focused warnings within an hour after a triggering event occurs or an evidence threshold is passed; (3) can automatically queue analysts based on partial pattern matches and has patterns that cover 90% of all previously known foreign terrorist attacks; and, (4) supports collaboration, analytical reasoning and information sharing so that analysts can hypothesize, test and propose theories and mitigating strategies about possible futures, so decision-makers can effectively evaluate the impact of current or future policies and prospective courses of action."

12

Translingual Information Detection, Extraction and Summarization (TIDES)

"The Translingual Information Detection, Extraction and Summarization (TIDES) program is developing advanced language processing technology to enable English speakers to find and interpret critical information in multiple languages without requiring knowledge of those languages."

13

Wargaming the Asymmetric Environment (WAE)

"The goal of the Wargaming the Asymmetric Environment (WAE) program is the development and demonstration of predictive technology to better anticipate and act against terrorists. WAE is a revolutionary approach to identify predictive indicators of attacks by and the behavior of specific terrorists by examining their behavior in the broader context of their political, cultural and ideological environment.

"Test results have demonstrated the feasibility of developing automated and adaptive behavior prediction models tuned to specific terrorist groups and individuals. Specifically, WAE has developed, in conjunction with DoD and the intelligence community, indications and warning models for select terrorist individuals and organizations. These indication and warning models have been tested historically, and in some cases operationally, to predict an active terrorist group's next action (attack/no attack, target characteristics, location characteristics, tactical characteristics, timeframes, and motivating factors), and test results have been shown to be statistically significant. To date, several models have been transitioned to DoD and the Intelligence Community partners. WAE will extend its predictive technology research to model a larger set of terrorist groups and individuals, and will strive to increase the level of detail for each predictive model." ◘

The US didn't become a world power until after World War I, but was a hemispheric power for much of the nineteenth century. Indeed, US troops paid regular visits to Latin America throughout the 1800s in order to protect American private property and trade routes, to thwart postcolonial revolutionaries, and sometimes just to avenge "insults" of various sorts. The American resource-stretching imperialism we see today can be found in miniature here.

1

1823. While the US was not yet a world power, President James Monroe nonetheless declared the US the sole military protector of the Western Hemisphere against European powers.

2

1833. US troops to Buenos Aires to protect assets during insurrection.

3

1835–1836. Marines to Peru during attempted revolution.

4

1835–1836. Texas declared independence from Mexico; Sam Houston defeated Mexican Army in Battle of San Jacinto on April 21, 1836, leading to independent, white-ruled Republic of Texas.

LIST : 40

40 US Interventions in Latin America in the 1800s
Nick Mamatas

5

1845. Texas annexed to the US by mutual agreement, over Mexican and British objections.

6

1846–1848. After winning the presidential election partially based on promises to bring Oregon and California under American control, James Polk precipitated the Mexican-American War. The US occupied Mexico City and compelled Mexico to surrender roughly half of its territory. The Mexican Cession consisted of present-day California, Nevada, and Utah, plus parts of Arizona, Colorado, New Mexico, and Wyoming.

7

1850–1855. US and Britain signed the Clayton-Bulwer Treaty, which brought the two powers together in managing trade across the Nicaraguan isthmus. Nicaragua was not consulted in this treaty, which superceded an 1849 US-Nicaragua treaty giving US businessman Cornelius Vanderbilt exclusive rights to transit routes. US and British interests retained control over trade routes, leading to civil war among Nicaragua's elite.

8

1852–1853. Marines back in Buenos Aires to protect assets during another revolution.

9

1854. US sloop-of-war *Cyane* shells Nicaraguan town of San Juan del Norte after residents mock an American diplomat and refuse to pay restitution for damage to American-held assets.

10

1855–1857. American William Walker invaded Nicaragua with a mercenary army and conquered the nation. The US recognized the Walker-installed puppet government of Patricio Riva; later Walker installed himself as President, legalized slavery, and requested annexation to the US as a slave state. He was expelled by a Vanderbilt-backed coalition. In December, US Marines captured Walker and brought him back to the US. Commodore Hiram Paulding was forced into retirement for heading up that mission.

11

1855. US naval forces spent four days in Uruguay guarding American assets during attempted revolution in Montevideo.

12

1856. US troops dispatched to what is now Panama to protect Atlantic-Pacific railroad assets after American Jack Oliver steals a slice of watermelon from a vendor and starts a brawl that turns into the riot known as the Watermelon War.

13

1856. Facing soil depletion and agricultural disaster, the US passed the Guano Island Act, allowing for the annexation of any uninhabited island in the world, so long as it has large supplies of bird waste for export. Ninety-four islands, some around Latin America, were ultimately seized. Nine guano islands remain US territory at the present.

14

1858. Two US warships landed troops in Montevideo, Uruguay, during another attempted revolution.

15

1859. US warships performed a show of force on Paraguay's Parana River after an attack on a US naval vessel.

16

1859. US troops crossed Mexican border in pursuit of legendary bandit and former South Texas Democratic Party boss Juan Cortina. Cortina had raided Brownsville, Texas, freed some Mexican prisoners, and declared the "Republic of the Rio Grande" at a nearby ranch.

17

1860. US troops were dispatched to the Bay of Panama to protect US assets during a struggle for Panamanian independence.

18

1861 and **1862**. Colombia requested presence of US troops in Panama on two occasions, primarily to protect American-owned rail and trade assets.

19

1865. Back to Panama, protecting US assets during a very short-lived revolution (March 9 and 10).

20

1866. General Sedgwick and 100 soldiers occupied Matamoras, Mexico, for three days for no particular reason. US demanded Sedgwick's withdrawal.

21

1867. US Marines occupied Managua and Leon in Nicaragua.

22

1868. US troops protected American customhouse during another insurrection in Montevideo.

23

1868. US troops to Aspinwall, Colombia, to protect travelers during crisis after death of Colombia's President.

24

1870. US ships chased pirates flying a Salvadoran flag into Mexican waters on the Rio Tecapan. Two Americans were killed in the battle.

25

1873. US troops were sent to Panama again during conflict between Panamanian factions and the Colombian government, sans Colombian or Panamanian request or assent in May. In September, troops landed to protect railroad during local riot.

26

1873. US troops repeatedly crossed the Mexican border to hunt cattle thieves and bandits. Some crossings, including the Remolina Incursion in May, may not have been authorized by the US government.

27

1875. US troops crossed the Mexican border to hunt bandits, getting into a dust-up with the Mexican military at Las Cuevas.

28

1876. US troops to Matamoras, Mexico, after town government collapses.

29

1876. US and Mexican troops played footsie along border over the bandit issue.

30

1880. US ships to island of Ciare (Mexico) in Gulf of California to protect property of American citizens.

31

1885. US troops again were sent to Colon, Panama, for a single day in January to protect rails and goods in transit. In March, after an uprising in Colon, Marines landed and marched to Panama City. Colombia acceded to the intervention after it was a *fiat accompli*.

32

1890. US troops to Argentina to protect Buenos Aires consulate.

33

1891. US troops to Chile to defend consulate, August 28-30. On October 16, a confrontation between a crowd of angry locals and sailors assigned to the *USS Baltimore* lead President Harrison to consider war.

34

1894. US Navy flexed muscle in Rio de Janeiro after rebellious Brazilian naval units interfere with trade.

35

1894. Troops summered in the Bluefields region of Nicaragua during local unrest.

36

1895. After local authorities give permission, two days spent in Bocas del Toro, Colombia, guarding American assets during an assault on the town by well-organized bandits. Naval vessels stayed in the area for a month after the Marines were pulled back.

37

1896. Two days in Corinto, Nicaragua, during riots.

38

1898. Two days in San Juan del Sur, Nicaragua, protecting American assets during local unrest.

39

1898. The Spanish-American War. Under Ulysses S. Grant, the US avoided becoming embroiled in Cuba, even after revolutionary Carlos Manuel de Cespedes wrote a constitution annexing the island to the US in 1869. However, by the 1890s, the closing of the Western frontier, industrialization, and mass culture, along with an extensive history of smaller interventions, set the stage for a conflict with Spain. Yellow press reports from publisher William Randolph Hearst and others fueled the fire for war. After the probably accidental destruction of the *USS Maine*, which was blamed on a Spanish mine, war was declared, eventually leading US troops to intervene in Cuba, the Philippines, Puerto Rico, and Guam.

40

1899. A military landing, along with British troops, at Bluefields and San Juan del Norte in Nicaragua, at the request of the besieged Nicaraguan government, which was threatened by insurrectionist General Juan Reyes. ✷

+ Corporate Responsibility

Granted, in these cases—involving corporations and the federal government—it's hard to feel sorry for the aggrieved party, like when a crook steals from a thief. Grand curmudgeon H.L. Mencken once observed that "when the government is robbed, the worst that happens is that certain rogues and loafers have less money to play with than they had before." Still, that's taxpayer money being swindled. First, it was stolen from us citizens by the government; then it's swiped by greedy corporations, which will keep almost all of it since they don't pay nearly their fair share of taxes. Maybe every April 15, instead of making out a check to the IRS, we should send our income tax directly to Texaco, Halliburton, or Pfizer.

The following corporations were prosecuted under the False Claims Act, a Civil War-era law that specifically criminalizes overcharging, falsely charging, selling defective junk, or otherwise scamming the federal government or the military. Most settled, while some took it all the way to judgment and lost.

1. **HCA**

HCA holds the disgraceful distinction of paying the largest fines ever levied under the False Claims Act—not once—but *twice*. In 2000, HCA The Health Care Company settled for a staggering $731.4 million, the biggest amount in the Act's 140-year history. It pled guilty to charges involving bilking Medicare and other federal healthcare programs, paying kickbacks to doctors, and claiming advertising expenses as reimbursable public education expenses.

Three years later, HCA, Inc. (as it became known) forked over $631 million, the second largest amount ever. This was related to a new crop of charges regarding ripping off Medicare, bribing doctors, and other such behavior. On top of this, HCA had to pay Medicare and Medicaid an additional $250 million.

2. **Abbott Labs**

3. **AT&T**

4. **B.F. Goodrich**

LIST 41

36 Corporations That Ripped off the US Government

5. **BP Amoco**

6. **Bayer**

7. **Boeing Company**

8. **Chevron**

9. **Conoco**

10. **Frigidaire/Electrolux Home Products**

11. **General Dynamics**

12. **General Electric**

13. **GlaxoSmithKline**

14. **Goldman Sachs & Co.**

15. **Honeywell**

16. **Lehman Brothers**

17. **Lockheed Martin**

18. **Merrill Lynch Pierce Fenner & Smith**

19. **Morgan Stanley & Co.**

20. **Motorola**

21. **Northrop Grumman**

22. **PaineWebber**

23. **Pfizer**

24. **Philips Electronics North America Corporation**

25. **Prudential Securities**

26. **Salomon Smith Barney**

27. **Shell Oil Company**

28. **Smithkline Beecham Clinical Laboratories**

29. **Sprint Corp.**

30. **TAP Pharmacuetical Products**

31. **Teledyne**

32. **Texaco**

33. **Toshiba**

34. **United Airlines**

35. **Unocal**

36. **Westinghouse Electric**

Worker Safety Priorities, part 1

Maximum jail sentence for causing the death of a worker by willful safety violations: 6 months

Maximum jail sentence for "harassing a wild burro on federal lands": 12 months

1

May 1964: **Mark Maples**, a fifteen-year-old Long Beach, California, resident, was killed when he tried to stand up on the Matterhorn Bobsleds. Maples (or his companion) foolishly unbuckled his seatbelt and attempted to stand up as their bobsled neared the peak of the mountain. Maples lost his balance and was thrown from the sled to the track below, fracturing his skull and ribs and causing internal injuries. He died three days later.

2

June 1966: **Thomas Guy Cleveland**, a nineteen-year-old Northridge, California, resident, was killed when he attempted to sneak into Disneyland along the Monorail track. Cleveland scaled the park's sixteen-foot high outer fence on a Grad Nite and climbed onto the Monorail track, intending to jump or climb down once inside the park. Cleveland ignored a security guard's shouted warnings of an approaching Monorail train and failed to leap clear of the track. He finally climbed down onto a fiberglass canopy beneath the track, but the clearance wasn't enough—the oncoming train struck and killed him, dragging his body 30 to 40 feet down the track.

LIST 42

9 Visitors Who Died at Disneyland

Barbara and David P. Mikkelson, Urban Legends Reference Pages [snopes.com]

3

August 1967: **Ricky Lee Yama**, a seventeen-year-old Hawthorne, California, resident, was killed when he disregarded safety instructions and exited his People Mover car as the ride was passing through a tunnel. Yama slipped as he was jumping from car to car and was crushed to death beneath the wheels of oncoming cars.

4

June 1973: **Bogden Delaurot**, an eighteen-year-old Brooklyn resident, drowned trying to swim across the Rivers of America. Delaurot and his ten-year-old brother managed to stay on Tom Sawyer Island past its dusk closing time by climbing the fence separating the island from the burning settlers' cabin. When they decided to leave the island a few hours later, they chose to swim across the river rather than call attention to their rule-breaking by appealing to cast members for help. Because the younger brother did not know how to swim, Delaurot tried to carry him on his back as he swam to shore. Bogden Delaurot went down about halfway across the river. The younger boy remained afloat by dogpaddling until a ride operator hauled him aboard a boat, but Bogden was nowhere to be found. His body was not located by searchers until the next morning.

5

June 7, 1980: **Gerardo Gonzales**, a recent San Diego high school graduate, was killed on the People Mover in an accident much like the one that had befallen Ricky Lee Yama thirteen years earlier. Gonzales, in the early morning hours of a Grad Nite celebration, was climbing from car to car as the People Mover entered the SuperSpeed Tunnel adjacent to the former America Sings building. Gonzales stumbled and fell onto the track, where an oncoming train of cars crushed him beneath its wheels and dragged his body a few hundred feet before being stopped by a ride operator.

6

June 4, 1983: **Philip Straughan**, an eighteen-year-old Albuquerque, New Mexico, resident, also drowned in the Rivers of America in yet another Grad Nite incident. Straughan and a friend—celebrating both their graduations and Straughan's eighteenth birthday—had been drinking quite heavily that evening. They sneaked into a "Cast Members Only" area along the river and untied an inflatable rubber maintenance motorboat, deciding to take it for a joyride around the river. Unable to adequately control the boat, they struck a rock near Tom Sawyer Island, and Straughan was thrown into the water. His friend traveled back to shore to seek help, but Straughan drowned long before his body was finally located an hour later.

7

January 3, 1984: **Dolly Regene Young**, a 48-year-old Fremont, California, resident, was killed on the Matterhorn in an incident remarkably similar to the first Disneyland guest death nearly 20 years earlier. About two-thirds of the way down the mountain, Young was thrown from her seat into the path of an oncoming bobsled, her head and chest becoming pinned beneath its wheels. An examination of Young's sled revealed that her seatbelt was not fastened at the time of the accident, but because she was riding alone in the rear car of a sled no one could determine whether or not she had deliberately unfastened her belt.

8

December 24, 1998: In a tragic Christmas Eve accident, one Disneyland cast member and two guests were injured (one fatally) when a rope used to secure the sailing ship *Columbia* as it docked on the Rivers of America tore loose the metal cleat to which it was attached. The cleat sailed through air and struck the heads of two guests who were waiting to board the ship, **Luan Phi Dawson**, 33, of Duvall, Washington, and his wife, Lieu Thuy Vuong, 43. Dawson was declared brain-dead two days later and died when his life-support system was disconnected.

This accident resulted in the first guest death in Disneyland's history that was not attributable to any negligence on the part of the guest (it was the result of a combination of insufficiently rigorous ride maintenance and an insufficiently experienced supervisor assuming an attraction operator's role) and prompted a movement for greater government oversight of theme park operations and safety procedures.

9

September 5, 2003: A 22-year-old man, **Marcelo Torres** of Gardena, California, died, and several other guests were injured, when a locomotive separated from its train along a tunnel section of Big Thunder Mountain Railroad. Torres bled to death after suffering blunt force trauma to the chest. ◻

> **Corporate Quote #2**
> *"I don't know that smoking causes lung cancer. It may. It may not. Certainly I conceded the point that smokers are more likely to develop some diseases than non-smokers."*
> —*Gareth Davis, chief executive officer of Imperial Tobacco, February 4, 2004 (yes, he actually said this, not in 1954, but in 2004).*

The complete list of substances added to cigarettes, as compiled by the Indiana Prevention Resource Center at Indiana University, contains 599 entries. Below are some of the more interesting ones....

1. **ambergris tincture**
2. **ammonia**
3. **amyl butyrate**
4. **apple juice concentrate, extract, and skins**
5. **benzoic acid**
6. **1-butanol**
7. **caffeine**
8. **carbon dioxide**
9. **carrot oil**
10. **chocolate**
11. **civet absolute**
12. **coffee**
13. **cognac white and green oil**
14. **dimethyltetrahydrobenzofuranone**
15. **ethyl alcohol**
16. **fig juice concentrate**
17. **guaiac wood oil**
18. **hexyl phenylacetate**
19. **honey**
20. **hops oil**
21. **maple syrup and concentrate**
22. **2-methoxy-4-vinylphenol**
23. **2-methylheptanoic acid**
24. **beta-napthyl ethyl ether**
25. **nutmeg powder and oil**
26. **phosphoric acid**
27. **rum**
28. **skatole**
29. **1,5,5,9-tetramethyl-13-oxatricyclo(8.3.0.0(4,9))tridecane**
30. **urea**
31. **vinegar**
32. **yeast**

LIST 43 | 32 Cigarette Additives

According to government, media, and investor reports, the following companies do business with at least one of the countries deemed by the US to be an enemy state: Libya, Cuba, North Korea, Iran, Iraq, Syria, Sudan, Zimbabwe, Liberia, the Balkans, and Burma (Myanmar). It should be noted that in a lot of these cases, the transactions appear to be legal, either because a non-US subsidiary of the company is dealing with the rogue state or because the Treasury Department granted a special license. In other cases, though, the corporations have been fined for their activities.

1. **AAA Travel**

2. **Alcolac International**

3. **Amazon.com**

4. **American Express Bank**

5. **American Type Culture Collection**

6. **Axel Electronics**

7. **Baker Hughes**

8. **Bank of America**

9. **Bank of New York**

10. **Bank One**

11. **Barclays Bank**

12. **Bechtel**

13. **Canberra Industries**

14. **Carl Zeiss, Inc.**

15. **Caterpillar**

LIST 44

55 Companies Reportedly Doing Business With Enemy Nations

16. **Cerberus**

17. **Chevron Texaco**

18. **Citibank, N.A.**

19. **Conoco-Phillips**

20. **Consarc**

21. **Deutsche Bank**

22. **Dow Agrosciences**

23. **Dupont**

24. **Eastman Kodak**

25. **Electronic Associates**

26. **ESPN**
    (Entertainment & Sports Network)

27. **Exxon Mobile**

28. **EZ Logic Data Systems**

29. **Finnigan MAT (US)**

30. **Four Seasons Hotels**

31. **General Electric**

32. **Halliburton**

33. **Hewlett-Packard**

34. **Honeywell**

35. **Hyundai Group**

36. **International Computer Systems**

37. **JP Morgan Chase**

38. **Leybold Vacuum Systems**

39. **New York Yankees**

40. **Pepsi Cola Co.**

41. **PetroCanada**

42. **PetroChina**

43. **Playboy Enterprises**

44. **Rockwell**

45. **Samsung**

46. **Semetex**

47. **Siemens**

48. **Spectra Physics**

49. **Sperry Corp.**

50. **Standard Chartered Bank**

51. **Tektronix**

52. **TI Coating**

53. **Unisys**

54. **Wal-Mart**

55. **Wells Fargo Bank**

When the North American Free Trade Agreement was passed, we were assured that it would create at least 200,000 jobs in the US. Showing that politicians live in a Bizzaro world where everything is reversed, that's approximately the number of jobs the US *lost* due to NAFTA, either because companies move their facilities to Mexico or Canada, or because cheaper imports from those countries have forced the closing of US facilities.

Workers who lose their jobs because of NAFTA are eligible to receive special benefits. Toward the end of 2003, the famously non-partisan Congressional Research Service tallied the number of workers that US companies signed up for these benefits from the implementation of NAFTA (on the first day of 1994) to September 24, 2002.

The list below represents the 100 companies giving the boot to the most workers. The total comes to 201,414, and would be even higher if companies beyond the top 100 were included. In the ranked list below, the number of workers follows the name of each corporation.

Top 100 Corporations Laying off US Workers Due to NAFTA

1. **Vanity Fair or VF** 16,095

2. **Levi Strauss and Co.** 15,676

3. **Burlington House & Industries**
   total: 9,679

4. **Motorola, Inc.** 7,347

5. **Tyco** 5,751

6. **General Electric** total: 5,674

7. **Fruit of the Loom** Texas - 5,352

8. **Russell Corporation** 3,630

9. **Lucent Technologies** 3,416

10. **Honeywell, Inc.** 2,754

11. **Niagara Mohawk Power Corporation**
    2,600

12. **Lexington Fabrics** 2,461

13. **Anchor Glass Corporation** 2,419

14. **Brown Group** 2,400

15. **Louisiana Pacific** 2,397

16. **Dana Corporation** 2,306

17. **Emerson Electronic Connector Components** 2,246

18. **Stroh Brewery Company** 2,222

19. **Trinity Industries** 2,203

20. **Sarah Lee** 2,124

21. **Viasystems Technologies** 2,100

22. **Eaton Corporation** 2,052

23. **TRW/Auto Electronics Group of North America** 2,050

24. **Thomas and Betts Corporation** 1,987

25. **Nokia** 1,980

26. **Oxford Industries** 1,960

27. **Solectron Corporation** 1,932

28. **United Technologies Corporation**
    1,899

29. **Allied Signal, Inc.** 1,883

30. **Henry I. Siegel** 1,857

31. **Autoliv ASP** 1,720

32. **Haggar Clothing Co.** 1,717

33. **Hewlett Packard** 1,683

34. **Goodyear Tire and Rubber Company** 1,671

35. **AMP, Inc.** 1,654

36. **Thomaston Mills** 1,649

37. **Kemet Electronics** 1,631

38. **Freightliner, LLC** 1,595

39. **Lockheed Martin** 1,584

40. **Tultex Corporation** 1,547

41. **Hasbro Manufacturing Services** 1,531

42. **Exide Technologies** 1,470

43. **PL Industries and Subsidiary** 1,446

44. **FCI USA, Inc.** 1,436

45. **Kimberly Clark Corporation** 1,415

46. **Woodward Governor Company** 1,390

47. **Ithaca Industries** 1,359

48. **Regency Packing Company** 1,334

49. **AI Tech Specialty Steel Corporation** 1,330

50. **Master Lock** 1,324

51. **Square D Corporation** Group Schneider - 1,322

52. **Newell Manufacturing** 1,308

53. **Aalfs Manufacturing** 1,276

54. **Mattel Operations** 1,259

55. **Borg-Warner Automotive Diversified Trans** 1,259

56. **Sola Optical USA, Inc.** 1,252

57. **Federal Mogul Wiper Products** 1,201

58. **Household Products** 1,200

59. **Plaid Clothing Group** 1,180

60. **L.G. Philips Display** 1,163

61. **Magnetek** 1,160

62. **John Deere Consumer** 1,150

63. **Copper Range Co.** 1,133

64. **Sunbeam** 1,130

65. **Sony** 1,126

66. **Scientific Atlanta** 1,121

67. **Lear Corporation** 1,120

68. **Champion Products** 1,116

69. **KLH Industries** 1,100

70. **SMTC Manufacturing Corporation of Wisconsin** 1,085

71. **Zenith Electronics Corporation** 1,057

72. **Crown Pacific Limited Partnership** 1,050

73. **Flexel, Inc.** 1,050

74. **Hamilton Beach/Proctor Silex, Inc.** 1,046

75. **Johnson Controls, Inc.** 1,036

76. **Gulford Mills** 1,032

77. **United States Leather** 1,011

78. **Monon Corporation** 1,000

79. **Ametek** total: 1,000

80. **Singer Furniture** 1,000

81. **J.R. Simplot Company** 995

82. **Flextronics International** 991

83. **Greenwood Mills** 991

84. **Georgia Pacific West** 966

85. **Celestica Corporation** 965

86. **Seton Company** 960

87. **Kraft Foods North America** 955

88. **Bassett Furniture Industries** 954

89. **Grove US, LLC** 950

90. **C-Cor.Net** 930

91. **Jeanerette Mills** 926

92. **Boise Cascade Corporation** 918

93. **Strick Corporation** 912

94. **Xerox** 893

95. **A.O. Smith Electrical Products** 878

96. **Smith Corona Corporation** 874

97. **Siemens** 874

98. **Mitsubishi Consumer Electronics America** 870

99. **The Budd Company** 868

100. **Cross Creek Apparel** 863

Worker Safety Priorities, part 2

From 1982 to 2002, number of governmental investigations of workers' deaths: 1,798

Number of those cases referred to federal or state prosecutors: 196

Number of convictions: 81

Number of convictions resulting in jail time: 16

+ Sex

1

"Priapeum" by Virgil

Ancient Rome's greatest poet, the author of the epic *Aeneid*, also wrote the poem "Priapeum," in which he chastises his limp dick: "Goodbye, I am forsaken, wretched cock." He laments that no "tender boy" or "jolly girl" (it's a British translation) will have anything to do with him, although—for reasons not made clear—he can get it up for an ancient crone with icy skin and cobwebs around her pussy. Pretty racy for the first century BC.

2

Historia de duobus amantibus (*a/k/a* The Goodli History) by Pope Pius II

I covered this forgotten gem in my previous book, *50 Things You're Not Supposed to Know*, much to the delight of interviewers who loved telling their audiences about a fifteenth-century bodice-ripper written by a man who would soon be Pope. For a book written in 1444 (and published 44 years later), the action is pretty shocking, though not to us jaded members of the twenty-first century. "O fair neck and pleasant breasts, is it you that I touch? Is it you that I have? Are you in my hands? O round limbs, O sweet body, do I have you in my arms?... O pleasant kisses, O dear embraces, O sweet bites, no man alive is happier than I am, or more blessed."

3

Les Bijoux Indiscrets by Denis Diderot

Philosopher Diderot is known to history as a lynchpin of the Enlightenment. For a dozen years, he edited the monumental *Encyclopedie*, which sought to codify and expand all knowledge at the time. Voltaire and Rousseau were among the contributors. But before helping turbocharge scientific and literary progress in the West, Diderot spent

LIST 46 12 Erotic Works by Well-Known Writers

two weeks writing a sexy little book, *Les Bijoux Indiscrets* (1748). Being a French genius, he couldn't resist adding literary criticism and political satire to this tale of a Turkish sultan who magically discovers the sexual histories of the ladies in his court. An alleged version was published in English in 1968 (as *The Talking Pussy*), but it was much different than the original.

4

White Stains *and other works by Aleister Crowley*

Maybe it's not too surprising that occultist Aleister Crowley—"the wickedest man in the world"—wrote a book of unapologetically filthy poetry, but his main claim to fame is his numerous writings on magick. In 1898, he published *White Stains*, brimming with his raunchy, sacrilegious verse involving necrophilia, bestiality, golden showers, shit, STDs, Jesus, and menstruation ("How my dry throat, held hard between thy hips, / Shall drain the moon-wrought flow of womanhood!"). The poems even have their moments of strange beauty, as in "Abysmos," when the narrator laments that he will never again "bite her lips, as once my teeth / Met in her cheek, to cull a rosy wreath."

The year 1904 saw the publication of Crowley's *Snowdrops from a Curate's Garden*, about which he later wrote: "My object is not merely to disgust but to root out ruthlessly the sense of sin." It's self-consciously over-

the-top, a humorous attempt to massacre every taboo in sight. In describing his adventurous past, the Archbishop says:

> At the great Gold Medal competition of the Spunk Society in 1904, I was able to satisfy no less than twenty-seven ladies, besides an exhibition frig in which I extinguished fourteen candles in sixteen attempts, thus taking the eighth prize, and special mention as the sole representative of my cloth who was able to support a child weighing fifty-six pounds on my erect lance-of-love alone, and thus accomplishing the act of sex with my hands tied behind my back. Poor little devil!

In 1910, Crowley—using the pseudonym Major Luity—published *The Scented Garden of Abdullah the Satirist of Shiraz* (a/k/a *Bagh-i-Muattar*). It was presented as a volume of Arabic poetry translated by Luity, when actually Crowley wrote all the verse. It's unabashedly homoerotic, as in "The Love-Potion":

> If Suleiman with all his concubines
> From dusk to dawn consecutively lay,
>
> Yet at thy buttocks' velvet, O Habib,
> The man would rise erect from mudded clay.

Elsewhere, Crowley published "Leah Sublime," 26 verses in which he spits filthy commands at his degraded and degrading lover:

> Stab your demonical
> Smile to my brain!
> Soak me in cognac
> Cunt and cocaine;
> Sprawl on me! Sit
> On my mouth, Leah, shit!

As poetry, it's not the greatest, but it works as erotica mainly because Crowley just didn't give a rat's ass about any kind of propriety or correctness.

5

Various novels by Robert Silverberg

Here we have the first of many science fiction giants who took pen and penis in hand to write one-handed material. The prolific winner of five Nebula awards and five Hugos, while trying to make ends meet, cranked out almost *200* erotic pulp and stroke novels, almost all between 1960 and 1967. He most often used the name Don Elliot when speed-writing such nuggets as *The Bra Peddlers*, *A Change for the Bedder*, *Cousin Lover*, *Dial O-R-G-Y*, *Dyke Diary*, *Les Floozies*, *Kept Man*, *Love Bums*, *The Orgy Boys*, *Sexteen*, *Till Love Do Us Part*, and 26 titles beginning with the word *Sin*.

During this time, Silverberg also wrote sixteen nonfiction books about sex under various pseudonyms. Titles include *90% of What You Know About Sex Is Wrong*, *I Am a Nymphomaniac*, *Sex and the Armed Forces*, and *Virgin Wives*.

6 7

Image of the Beast *and* Blown *by Philip José Farmer*

Farmer is one of the big names of science fiction. His best-known works are two series: *Riverworld* and *World of Tiers*. Besides having won three Hugo awards and one Nebula (the Grand Master Award), Farmer is credited with introducing sex into science fiction in 1960-61 with *Flesh*, *A Woman a Day*, and *The Lovers*, all of which are extraordinarily tame by today's standards. What's not tame—and probably never will be viewed as such—are the erotic SF/horror books that he wrote in the late 1960s.

Image of the Beast was the first of these, opening with a scene that will live in infamy: Police are watching a homemade film that was anonymously mailed to them. In it, one of their detectives, tied down, has his cock bitten off by a woman with razor-sharp metal teeth. The penisless man's detective partner, Herald Childe, determines to find the people responsible for gruesomely killing his partner. It turns out that they're a bunch of vampires, werewolves, ghosts, and other strange beings. Really strange.

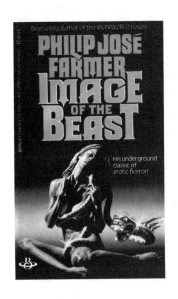

In one of the most memorable scenes, Childe is in a secret passageway of the mansion that serves as the headquarters for the weirdos. Looking through a one-way mirror, he spies the incredibly beautiful Vivienne masturbating. But then "a tiny thing, like a slender white tongue, spurted from the slit. It was not a tongue. It was more like a snake or an eel." This long, thin creature with smooth, white skin lives in the woman's womb and comes out during sexual activity. Its head, the size of a golfball, "was bald except for a fringe of oil-plastered black hair around the tiny ears. It had two thin but wet-black eyebrows and a wet black Mephistophelean moustache and beard." The vagina-snake with a man's face puts its head in the woman's open mouth, sliding in and out. The woman appears to have a long, violent orgasm, and the strange being withdraws, with a "thick whitish fluid" leaking from its mouth. It then retreats back into the woman's womb.

In the sequel, *Blown*, we find out that the various beings are two groups of aliens stranded on earth. One faction draws its power from sex, the other from blood. Childe, it just so happens, is the only person who can get the space creatures back to their home world by drawing on his sexual energy. He takes part in an orgy with the aliens, and while Vivienne is blowing him, another man yanks the pseudosnake out of her vagina:

Vivienne fell apart.

Childe stood with her head between his hands and his penis in her mouth. The eyes stared up at him with a violet fire, and the lips and tongue kept on sucking and thrusting. The other parts of her body, having gotten onto their legs, began to scuttle around the room. The big black who had been sucked off by Vivienne picked up the many-legged cunt and stuck it on the end of his cock and began sliding it back and forth. The cunt's legs kicked as if it were having an orgasm.

Farmer's two other ventures into weirdcore are *A Feast Unknown*, featuring Tarzan and Doc Savage, and the gothic horror *Love Song*.

8

The Gas *by Charles Platt*

Platt is a hard guy to pin down. He's written some well-received science fiction, such as *The Silicon Man*, plus a lot of articles on cyber-topics in *Omni*, *Wired*, and mainstream newspapers. Then there are his numerous interviews with legendary science fiction writers and his *Christina* erotic horror trilogy. Before *Christina*, though, there was *The Gas*. In this outrageous novel from 1970, an experimental biowarfare gas leaks in Southern England, causing people's inhibitions to vaporize and their most primal urges to surge to the forefront. A nonstop carnival of sex, violence, and combinations thereof ensues. Everyone is fair game for the unleashed lust and bloodlust—men, women, children, animals, priests and nuns, corpses, immediate family members, anything....

In one scene, a passing car sputters out, and its driver—a young punk—angrily hops out. Repeatedly screaming "fuck you!" at his ride, he gets an idea. After taking the cap off the gas tank:

> He pulled out his prick. "I'll make you fuck-ing go," he muttered. "Fuck you, fuck this!"
>
> He lunged forward, jamming his prick into the pipe, and started fucking it with crude angry movements. He groaned, spurting jism down into it, whipped his prick out, zipped his jeans up again.
>
> Vincent watched him trudge back to the front of the car, open the door and get in. He started the engine, revved it, drove off down the street and out of sight.

The novel could never be published in its original form today, which is why even bad-boy publisher Loompanics—when reissuing *The Gas* in 1995—cut out a lot of the forbidden sex scenes.

9

The Repentance of Lorraine *by Andrei Codrescu*

Those of us used to hearing the highly liter-ate, Romanian-accented thoughts of Andrei Codrescu on National Public Radio might be a little shocked to find out about his porn novel, *The Repentance of Lorraine* (originally pub-lished under the pseudonym Ames Claire).

We will, however, be less shocked when we read it and find that the highly accomplished author, poet, and essayist has applied his intel-lectual power to the task of writing an explicit but psychologically convincing novel about a triad of a male budding writer, a female busi-ness student, and a female professor. You don't see much porn peppered with words like "curvilinearly," "pedagogue," "petit-bour-geois," and "Huysmanesque non sequitur."

Not that it isn't enjoyable. Codrescu is witty and regularly uses memorable turns of phrase: "Colline is virginal, in that sexy French-nun way"; "She exuded sexuality and mystery like an oriental stage set"; while looking at two naked women holding each other: "The view of their two graceful backs, buttocks and legs is my coat of arms." There's humor throughout, and things get downright hilarious when, while the three-some is in Paris, Lorraine is kidnapped by a left-wing terrorist group, from whom she learns about "the people's orgasm."

When the writer and the prof have their first encounter: "I unbuttoned the top of her loose garment, and her beautiful breasts bounded into view, her nipples sublimely erect. It is unfortunate, but nature has decreed that one breast must be chosen first over the other. I chose the left. Begin-ning at the outermost edge, my tongue climbed toward the pink aureole in the mid-dle of which the nipple rose. A flicker of my tongue would set this sheikhdom on fire."

The narrator comments on the second time all three of them get together: "The frenzy of a bacchanalia seized us. We made love to each other in a timeless furor. This prolonged activity (it was midnight when we finally stopped to order a pizza) brought to the surface the amazing fact of our absolute compatibility. We fit into each other like a three-way lock. Our pleasures fitted together at their jagged edges as described by the Continental Drift Theory."

Reflecting on the 1973 novel 20 years later, Codrescu said that it was written purely "for money," yet he didn't want to write a stroke novel. "I felt that sex was transcendental, which is to say, untranslatable. What made the flesh rise was precisely what sank the page." With its sex scenes far between and too short, *Repentance* is meant more for the cerebrum than the genitalia.

10

The Beauty trilogy *by Anne Rice*

After making a name with her debut novel *The Vampire Chronicles*, and in the midst of writing *The Vampire Lestat*, Anne Rice published three erotic SM novels, one each year from 1983 to 1985. Under the pseudonym A.N. Roquelaure—so as not to alienate her fans—she works an erotic retelling of the Sleeping Beauty fairytale, with Beauty becoming the willing submissive of the Prince who awakens her. The three books— *The Claiming of Sleeping Beauty*, *Beauty's Punishment*, and *Beauty's Release*—are generally regarded as excellent erotic lit. All

three have now been issued under Rice's real name and are easily available.

Also easy to obtain are the two erotic novels Rice originally wrote under the pseudonym Ann Rampling. *Belinda* is really mislabeled as erotic, since there's almost no onstage sex, but Rice does venture into forbidden territory with this story of the love affair between a man and a slightly underage girl. *Exit to Eden* is literate SM that was all but ruined by Hollywood. The portions of the film that are faithful to the book are quite good, and seeing this love story between a dominant woman and her male slave is pretty radical. Too radical for the studio execs, who ham-fistedly inserted a hackneyed detective plot featuring Rosie O'Donnell and Dan Aykroyd, so as not to frighten the proles too much with all the whips and chains. The film would be much better if some rogue videographer would make an unauthorized edit—*a la The Phantom Menace*—in which all the detective scenes are left on the cutting room floor like the trash that they are.

11 12

Pornucopia *and* The Magical Fart *by Piers Anthony*

Certainly one of the most prolific writers of SF and fantasy, Anthony has written many series, including *Xanth*, which now includes almost 30 volumes. A lot of his novels are tinged with playful T&A, but he went balls-out in a couple of his books. *Pornucopia* was originally written for Playboy Press, but they rejected it as "too gross for words." They were probably expecting mainstream porn in sci-fi clothing and had to pick their jaws off the floor after reading this insanely imaginative, explicit novel, which somehow manages to retain the humor and lightheartedness of the *Xanth* works.

The plot revolves around Prior Gross, who has an uncircumcised dick that measures 3.97 inches when erect. As it turns out, the smegma that Prior's penis produces has curative properties, and this makes his organ the target of an abduction by the beautiful doctor Tantamount Emdee. The rest of the novel focuses on Prior's attempts to regain his pilfered gland. Anthony has commented that when writing this book, he tried to break every taboo he could think of, even those of the erotic publishing industry itself. Indeed, *Pornucopia* brazenly ventures into such *verboten* areas as smegma, VD, small penis size, bestiality, circumcision, tampon insertion, and a three-pronged prosthetic penis(?!):

> Oubliette got on her hands and knees again and presented her handsome posterior. "Stations, men," she said.
>
> Seeing her there, Prior finally realized what this weird divided member was for. The two small penises lifted as his hot blood filled them.
>
> He came at her as he had the prior night, but with a difference. He had three members to insert. The long one passed between her legs and curved by her falling breasts to reach her mouth. The two lesser ones prodded simultaneously at her vagina and anus.

> It was tricky getting them aligned, but with patience and steady nerves, he made it.

The *Magic Fart* catches up with Prior a year after recovering his cock. A succubus tells him that his dream woman—the one he's destined to marry—has been abducted to Fartingale, and he has one week to rescue her. As you may have surmised by now, this sequel adds a record amount of toilet humor to the mix, in the time-honored literary tradition of Chaucer, Rabelais, Swift, Twain, and Benjamin Franklin.

In the land of Fartingale, people break wind as a greeting, make their buildings out of dried shit, engage in literal pissing contests, and community life centers around a gigantic central public bathroom (the homes in Fartingale have no private loos). Eliminatory functions and sexual functions are entwined. As a female character tells Prior while seducing him: "Folks who poop together, whoop together. We have shared shit."

Honorable Mention 1: Two speeches by Mark Twain

Twain's love of tweaking convention shows up most strongly in some of his rarer writings on religion, farting, and sex. In the latter category we find his speech "Some Thoughts on the Science of Onanism," in which he devilishly propounds on masturbation:

> Of all the various kinds of sexual intercourse, this has the least to recommend it. As an amusement, it is too fleeting; as an occupation, it is too wearing; as a public

exhibition, there is no money in it. It is unsuited to the drawing room, and in the most cultured society it has long been banished from the social board. It has at last, in our day of progress and improvement, been degraded to brotherhood with flatulence.

Scarcer still is his speech "The Mammoth Cod Club," in which he gives several facetious reasons why he won't join. The fourth one being:

Largeness of organ is proof positive that it has been cultivated. The blacksmith gets an enormous arm by constantly exercising that limb, and I suppose a man by constantly using his private member will increase the size of it. Membership in your Society is a confession of immorality.

Honorable Mention 2: The love letters of James Joyce

Literary giant James Joyce destroyed and redefined every notion of what a novel could be with his stream-of-consciousness masterworks *Ulysses* and *Finnegans Wake*. Joyce wasn't just an experimentalist on paper, though. He was pretty kinky in the sack. Although his works stirred up trouble because of some racy passages, it's his letters to his common-law wife Nora Barnacle that are downright filthy. So filthy, in fact, that Joyce's literary estate has sworn that they will never again be published. But they *were* published around 40 ago in *The Selected Letters of James Joyce*. If you can get your hands on a copy, you'll read things like "my dirty little fuckbird!" "pull out my mickey and suck it like a teat," "I would love

to be whipped by you," "the heavy smell of your behind," and "a little brown stain on the seat of your white drawers." Yep, Joyce reveled in the sound and smell of Nora's farts and turds. "I think I would know Nora's fart anywhere," he wrote on December 8, 1909. "I think I could pick hers out in a roomful of farting women."

On December 2, 1909, he explained to Nora the twin feelings of love that he has for her— the spiritual side and the earthy, physical side:

It allows me to burst into tears of pity and love at some slight word, to tremble with love for you at the sounding of some chord or cadence of music or to lie heads and tales with you feeling your fingers fondling and tickling my ballocks or stuck up in my behind and your hot lips sucking off my cock while my head is wedged in between your fat thighs, my hands clutching the round cushions of your bum and my tongue licking ravenously up your rank red cunt.

These gloriously filthy, unashamed missives are truly some of the best erotic writing I've ever read. Joyce's literary genius, his raging horniness, and his devotion to Nora are a combination that can never be beat. It's a crying shame that his heirs now deprive the world of such high-caliber smut.

Honorable Mention 3: "Man of Steel, Woman of Kleenex" by Larry Niven

Like Philip José Farmer and Piers Anthony, Niven is another name familiar to SF fans. Winner of five Hugos and one Nebula, his crowning creation is the *Ringworld* series. In his 1971 essay "Man of Steel, Woman of Kleenex," he meditates on the problems that Superman and "a human woman designated LL" would have if they tried to make a kid. One of the problems is that Superman might kill LL while spasming during orgasm. Even if that didn't happen, "he'd blow off the top of her head. Ejaculation of semen is entirely involuntary in the human male, and in all other forms of terrestrial life. It would be unreasonable to assume otherwise for a kryptonian. But with kryptonian muscles behind it, Kal-El's semen would emerge with the muzzle velocity of a machine gun bullet."

Niven suggests artificial insemination, but this too presents challenges. Superman's supersperm would be unstoppable: "A thickened cell wall won't stop them. They will *all* enter the egg, obliterating it entirely in an orgy of microscopic gang rape." But they won't stop there; all several billion of them will travel outside of LL's body and fly around Metropolis, causing all kinds of microscopic damage and immaculate conceptions.

Honorable Mention 4: "Sisters" by Lynne Cheney

The novel *Sisters* has become legendary for two reasons. First, it was written by Lynne Cheney, the rigidly uptight fundamentalist wife of oil baron Vice President Dick Cheney. Second, almost no one has ever read it. It was published by New American Library's Canadian division in 1981, and almost

instantly went out of print. You simply cannot find a copy, even among rare book dealers.

Consequently, rumors about its contents swirl. For instance, legend has it that *Sisters* contains lesbian action. Having read it, I can tell you that this isn't correct. The misunderstanding stems from the fact that the main character's sister, dead by the time the novel starts, was a lesbian. Just like the Cheneys' daughter Mary.

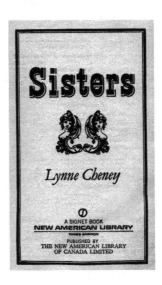

Sisters is thought of as a romance novel, but that's a misnomer. Although it was packaged as one, it's more correct to call it a Western mystery novel. In 1886, successful Sophie, the New York publisher of *Dymond's Ladies Magazine*, goes to Wyoming to find out why her sister died. Independent and intelligent, Sophie carries with her a little lacquer box filled with contraceptives. Goodness gracious!

There's only one sex scene—if you can even call it that—in the whole book. When Sophie can no longer resist the studly James Stevenson, she joins him in the library room after hours:

> He turned to her, leaned down, and put his hand gently on the side of her face. "You are extraordinarily beautiful," he said quietly. They kissed, and then she lay with him in the firelight, unmindful of the past, unmindful of anything except this moment, this man, and herself.

That's how the chapter ends. When the next one starts, it's the following morning. The scene of attempted rape, on the other hand, is much longer and more detailed (which gives us some psychological insight into Lynne). Sophie is attacked by a drunken homesteader in his shack:

> He let his thick, blunt fingers slide down to her throat, then over the front of her dress, over her breast and down until his hand rested on her thigh....
>
> He kissed her, forced her lips open with his mouth. She could taste the whiskey he had been drinking, feel his whiskers and the scab on his face. A wave of revulsion swept over her, and she pushed him away. As he fell back, the white bulldog moved toward her, his growl becoming louder.
>
> "Ah, feisty, ain't she, Luper?" Wilson stroked the dog. "Well, sometimes that kind's the most fun."

The scene goes on for another page, ending when Wilson passes out before he can complete the attack. His abused wife had spiked his whiskey.

Besides the sex, rape, lesbianism, and contraception, *Sisters* also contains disfiguring violence, animal cruelty, feminist thought, anticorporate messages, and several instances of taking the Lord's name in vain. What would Jesus say? What would *Dick* say? ⌂

Lest we forget that erotic books didn't start with the stroke novels of the 1960s, or in the 1930s with Henry Miller, or even with the underground novels of the Victorians, here are some explicit pre-1800 tomes, many of which are still in print in some form or another.

1

Sonnets Lussuriosi *by Pietro Aretino (1524)*

After checking out sexual drawings by Giuliano Romano, who studied under Raphael and was named as his artistic heir, Pietro Aretino—an Italian satirist whose wit was the scourge of princes and popes—was inspired to put pen to paper. He wrote nasty sonnets based on the sexual maneuvers, one of which included the lines:

> Forced to lean on my arms and legs,
> O curse you for this clumsy position.
> A mule would conk over after an hour of it.

This collection of sonnets is sometimes named as the first erotic book in the Western world, though this isn't true. (Pope Pius II's *Historia de duobus amantibus* appeared around 1488, and even that may not be the oldest.) Nevertheless, published way back in 1524, it's undoubtedly one of the earliest.

2

Ching P'Ing Mei *by Wang Shih-chêng (circa 1560)*

A Chinese classic, this novel has appeared in a large number of faithful and bastardized English translations, including *House of Joy*, *The Golden Lotus*, and *The Plum in the Golden Vase*.

3

Jou Pu Tuan [The Prayer Mat of Flesh] *by Li Yu (1634)*

4

Satyra Sotadica *by Nicholas Chorier (circa 1660)*

First appeared in Latin around 1660, with a French edition (*L'Academie des Dames*) 20 years later. An English translation—originally

LIST 47

12 Olde-Timey Porn Books

titled *The Duell*—showed up in 1688. *The Encyclopedia of Censorship* calls it "the earliest surviving piece of prose pornography in England." In it, Tullia initiates her 15-year-old cousin Ottavia into all manner of sexual deviancy.

5

Dialogues of Luisa Sigea *by Nicolas Chorier (circa 1660)*

6

La Galante hermaphrodite *by Francois Chavigny de la Bretonniere (1683)*

Adding to the book's frisson, the author was a defrocked monk.

7

Sodom, or The Quintessence of Debauchery *by John Wilmot, Earl of Rochester (1684)*

A proto-Sadean play featuring characters named Cuntigratia, Fuckadilla, and Buggeranthos.

8

A Lady of Quality *by Crebillon le Fils (Claude-Prosper Jolyot) (1700s)*

9

Memoirs of a Woman of Pleasure *by John Cleland (1748)*

Fanny Hill—as it is better known—"has the dubious distinction of being the most prosecuted literary work in history," says *The Encyclopedia of Censorship*. It was the subject of trials as late as the 1960s, well over two centuries after it appeared. The US Supreme Court overturned a ban in 1966, but it remains technically outlawed in the UK, although it's widely available.

10

Felicia *by Andre-Robert Andrea de Nerciat (1775)*

11

Justine *by the Marquis de Sade (1791)*

12

Juliette *by the Marquis de Sade (1798)*

♉

The rumor that the Vatican has an immense collection of erotic material may or may not be true, but for several decades, the Library of Congress definitely did. Called the Delta Collection, it was housed on the top floor of the Library, in Deck 38, to be exact. In what might be an exaggeration, a magazine article from the time said that the collection held "almost every erotic poem, essay and story ever written or translated into English."

Sometime in the 1880s, a wealthy businessman in California left his vast collection of rare books to the Library when he died. Almost all of it was erotic, much privately printed and irreplaceable. As a bonus, the librarians also received hundreds of the deceased's erotic artworks. Luckily, instead of pulping this scandalous material, the Library created a special, restricted area to house it. In any era this would be an admirably progressive stance, but in the latter 1800s it was downright revolutionary.

The Delta collection grew as other erotica collectors bequeathed their stashes to the Library. On top of that, US Customs started sending over some of the "obscene" material seized on its way into the country.

Moldering documents recently recovered from the Library by intrepid researcher Michael Ravnitzky reveal that, as of 1960, the Delta collection was contained in two rooms described as "cramped." In that year, plans were already being made to dissolve the collection, mainly by putting all but a few of the books into the open stacks. Only three books with "rather graphic illustrations" were pulled aside to be given to other libraries with erotic collections.

Some of the porn movies in the Delta Collection were destroyed in 1957, possibly earlier than that. A memo shows that in fall 1971, librarians incinerated thirteen large boxes of "other than printed matter," plus more boxes containing photos, transparencies, hundreds of magazines, dozens of monographs, and "miscellaneous advertising." At this point, the Delta collection seems to have gone the way of the dodo.

LIST 48

52 Items from the Delta Collection of the Library of Congress

1. **Attaining Manhood** by George Corner (Harper, 1938)

2. **Birth Control on Trial** by Lalla Secor Florence (London: Allen, 1930)

3. **The Bride of Ho Ling-Fu**

4. **The Decameron** by Boccaccio

5. **Encyclopedie de la Vie Sexuelle** by Ludwig Levy-Lenz

6. **Eugenics and Sex Harmony** by Herman H. Rubins (New York: Pioneer Publishing Company, 1933)

7. **Fanny Hill** by John Cleland

   This is a first edition bound in Morocco leather, allegedly from the collection of King George III.

8. **The Golden Ass** by Lucius Apuleius

9. **Kama Sutra** by Vatsyayana Mallanaga, translated by Richard Burton (New York, 1936)

10. **Lady Chatterly's Lover** by D.H. Lawrence

11. **Lolita** by Vladmir Nabokov

12. **A Love Starved World** by J.L. Pritcher (Los Angeles: Yale Publishing Company, 1932)

13. **My Lives and Loves** by Frank Harris

14. **Odoratus Sexualis** by Iwan Bloch (1933)

15. **The Perfumed Garden** by Sheikh Nefzaoui, translated by Sir Richard Burton

16. **The Sex Criminal** by Bertram Pollens (Macmillan, 1938)

17. **Sex Questions and Answers** by Fred Brown (Whittlesey, 1950)

18. **Sexual Misbehavior** by Arthur Hirsch (1955)

19. **Sonnets Luxurieux** by Pietro Aretino (Paris?, 1948)

20. **Tropic of Cancer** by Henry Miller

21. **Tropic of Capricorn** by Henry Miller

22-23. **The Kinsey reports** (Sexual Behavior in the Human Male and Sexual Behavior in the Human Female)

24-26. Works by **Catullus, Chaucer,** and **Rabelais**

27. **"Fuchs' multivolume set"**

28. **"A Gichner work"**

   This undoubtedly refers to Lawrence E. Gichner, who self-published three books: Erotic Aspects of Hindu Sculpture, Erotic Aspects of Japanese Culture, and Erotic Aspects of Chinese Culture.

29. One document notes that seized copies of **"certain Communist propaganda publications"** are to be sent to the Delta Collection.

30. Two documents mention that the Delta Collection houses **"three-dimensional materials,"** but no elaboration is given. Could this refer to dildos, diaphragms, and other types of sex toys and contraceptive devices? The mind reels.

31. The magazine article mentions **"drawings and etchings**, beautifully done by French, German and Italian masters—all portraying men and women engaged in the strangest types of sexual activities."

32. **"Girly" photos of nude and semi-nude women**

    Official descriptions include: "Nude girl lying prone on bearskin rug. Red background. Title: Grin and bare it." "Red-haired girl clutching frantically at torn halter of skimpy bathing suit. Title: Help!"

33. **Pornographic comic books**

    (certainly including the legendary Tijuana bibles) with titles such as "Maggie and Jiggs," "Toots and Casper," "Jimmy Durante and Mae West," and "Terry and the Dragon Lady."

34. **Stag films**

35. **Naughty postcards**

36. **"life-sized reproductions of the famous Marilyn Monroe nudes"**

37. "the original versions of cleaned-up **folk songs** sung by artists like Burl Ives, Josh White and Harry Belafonte." Specific songs include "Erie Canal" and "The Streets of Laredo."

38. **"torrid jazz songs"**

39. **"stag-party jingles"**

40. **English translations of non-erotic works in Greek and Latin**

    These books were considered "socially undesirable" because university students were expected to read them in their original languages, and having an English-language copy would've been cheating.

The following are movies seized by the Post Office or Customs 1950-1957, and sent to the Delta Collection:

41. ***Como Desnudarse Del Marido***

42. ***Crimines Sexuales***

43. ***Dos Entre Nudistas***

44. ***Kernesse Rouge***

45. ***Lectura Selecta***

46. ***Our Sinful Daughters***

47. ***El Profesor de Musica***

48. ***Story of Birth***

49. ***Vie Peccato***

50. ***Plastycy***

51. ***El Secreto de las Viciasos***

52. ***Test Tube Baby***

1

Autopederasty

The unlikely act in which a man inserts his partially hard penis into his own anus. Obviously, it's a trick that a very small percentage of men can achieve, but it is for real. The porn video appropriately titled *Go Fuck Yourself* is devoted to the act, and the Latino guy on the cover shows how it's done.

2

Axillism

Once you've exhausted the potential of your partner's mouth, vagina, and/or anus, it's time to look for new possibilities. In axillism, the virgin territory being invaded by the penis is the armpit. One famous axilliphile was Dada/Surrealist photographer Man Ray, who, when asked his favorite parts of a woman, replied: "The breasts and armpits."

3

Bestiality

Sure, we've heard about donkey shows in Tijuana and the rumor of gerbils in tailpipes, but things get a whole lot weirder than even that. In his 1894 book *Medical Jurisprudence*, German lawyer G. Herzog reports: "She would lie down on a sofa and separating her thighs would smear honey on and in the vulva. The flies thus attracted by the honey would tickle her until her sexual appetite was appeased." Elsewhere in his book, while commenting on guys committing bestiality, Herzog wrote: "In male animals the rectum is generally used, although in one reported case a man used the nostrils of a horse."

4

Cannibal fantasies

The sexually charged phrase "eat me" becomes almost literal with the kinksters into cannibal fantasies. They thrill to the thought of truly eating another person or, conversely,

---

LIST 49

12 Unorthodox Sex Practices

being eaten. On the Deviant Desires website —based on the book of the same title— Katharine Gates explains that some people bring these fantasies to life in consensual roleplaying. One of her friends "painted the woman's nude body with dotted lines to represent cuts of meat." She continues:

> One very tasteful (heh, heh) website, Muki's Kitchen [www.mukiskitchen.com], features photographs of lovely female models trussed up in pans filled with vegetables, and stuffed in their mouths, vaginas and assholes with flavorful treats like apples, bananas and carrots. Thus, erotic feeding, messy fun, bondage, gags and vaginal or anal penetration may be incorporated into the sexual scenario.

Docking

Involves two men, at least one of whom must be uncircumcised. With penises facing each other, the foreskin of the uncut guy is pulled over the cockhead—and part of the shaft, if it's really stretchy foreskin—of the other guy. One of the partners grabs the foreskin and uses it to stroke both dicks. On a Web message board, a "docker" shares his experiences: "I've been with a couple of guys with skin loose enough. Feels great. Cock head to cock head, inside his warm moist cover. One of the guys was loose, but not excessively. I could stroke and stretch his skin about 3" or so, or about 1/2 my cock. Felt all warm and 'comfy' inside there."

Erotic vomiting

Certainly it's hard to imagine two words that seem to belong together less than "erotic" and "vomiting." It might be the ultimate oxymoron. But vomiting and coming aren't as far apart as you may think. Both are reflex actions caused by a stimulus. Both trigger the release of hormones and neurotransmitters that make you feel warm and relaxed afterward. And in the case of male orgasm, at least, both result in fluid forced through a canal and out of a bodily opening. The main difference—and it's a big one—is that most people experience the act of vomiting as extremely unpleasant. Psychiatrist/sexologist Robert J. Stoller was the first to reveal the existence of erotic vomiting in medical literature. In a brief article, he describes the cases of three women.

One of the women doesn't herself barf. Instead: "I can reach a sure orgasm by imagining someone vomiting in a hard, humiliating fashion." The second woman actually experiences orgasm while she's throwing up. The final woman describes her feelings:

> Vomiting for me is like sex or an orgasm in that I'm tensed, I feel the rush or intense flood of good feelings almost continually throughout the vomiting and experience relief and quiet warmth in my body when I'm finished. It is not identical to an orgasm. I do not feel it intensely in my genitals alone, but I do feel it there as well as the rest of my body and feel pleasure in my mouth.

Additionally, a small number of people like to be puked upon, a practice known as Roman showers.

7

Felching

Involves licking, sucking or otherwise orally retrieving semen from a partner's pussy or asshole.

8

Meatotomy

To prepare for meatotomy, men enlarge the opening of their urethras by cutting or tearing. *The Encyclopedia of Unusual Sex Practices* informs us: "A few men have such a large opening that they were able to insert the glans penis of another man into the tip of their penis."

9

Mummification

A total-body form of bondage in which a person is completely wrapped from head to toe in bandages (sometimes overlaid with masking tape), strips of cloth, or—for those who want to feel less helpless—toilet paper.

10

Pediophilia

Not to be confused with pedophilia, pediophilia (note the extra "i") denotes sexual arousal from dolls. *The Encyclopedia of*

Unusual Sex Practices cites the case of one such man: "He shaved the hair from Barbie doll heads and then swallowed the heads to produce sexual arousal."

11

Ponyplay

A form of bondage and discipline, ponyplay involves a "pony" and a rider. The person in the pony part is typically outfitted with a leather saddle, straps, reins, and blinders, with a bit in the mouth. The other person, perhaps wielding a whip or riding crop, either rides the pony or gets pulled in a cart.

12

Pseudonecrophilia

If you like the idea of romancing the dead but you don't like the trouble and risk involved in actually doing it, pseudonecrophilia offers a more acceptable outlet. Just have your lover remain completely still and unresponsive during sex. For added realism, have him or her soak in cold water first. This form of sex reached a mass audience in an episode of *Law and Order: Special Victims Unit*, a show that has introduced middle America to a whole lot of sex practices it probably had been blissfully unaware of. ⌂

1

Adultery

In many states, not only is it a misdemeanor to nail someone else if you're married, it's also illegal to nail someone who's married even if you're single. For example, Arizona law states: "When the act is committed between parties only one of whom is married, both shall be punished." Michigan is biased on the issue, declaring that "both parties are guilty if the woman is married and the man is not; only the man is guilty if he is married and woman is not." Most of the states that outlaw adultery rank it as a misdemeanor, but in five states—including Idaho and Michigan—it's a felony.

2

Pretending to be a person's spouse or a medical professional

Like many other states, California defines sodomy as contact between the penis of one person and the anus of another. The act is not automatically illegal, but—being California—there are numerous conditions that make it against the law. One of these involves buttsex "where the victim submits under the belief that the person committing the act is the victim's spouse, and this belief is induced by any artifice, pretense, or concealment practiced by the accused, with intent to induce the belief…" Punishment is up to eight years in the state slammer, where no one ever breaks sodomy laws.

In a related vein, going up someone's rear in Cali is illegal when the recipient "[w]as not aware, knowing, perceiving, or cognizant of the essential characteristics of the act due to the perpetrator's fraudulent representation that the sexual penetration served a professional purpose when it served no professional purpose."

 **6 Sex Acts That Are Illegal**

Both of these statutes apply word for word to oral sex, as well. So when you're in the Sunshine State, don't fool someone into anal sex by pretending to be her husband, and don't tell someone that going down on him serves a professional purpose when it really doesn't, okay?

3

Incest

Sex with close family members is a felony in every state (and DC) with two exceptions: It's a misdemeanor in Delaware, and there's no law against it at all in Rhode Island. Maybe New England should be the butt of all those inbreeding jokes, instead of the South.

4

Necrophilia

Sexual contact with a corpse is specifically outlawed in several states, including Georgia, where it'll get you one to ten years in jail. Indiana considers it a felony if you merely open the lid of a coffin with the intent to molest the occupant, even if you never consummate.

5

Sexual intercourse

In a few states, it's illegal for an unmarried person to have sexual intercourse with *anyone*. Doesn't matter if your partner is of the opposite gender, of legal age, completely willing, etc. In Georgia, this is a misdemeanor punishable by a fine of up to $1,000 and up to a year behind bars. Idaho, Massachusetts, Utah, Virginia, and West Virginia have similar restrictions, and several other states consider it a misdemeanor for unmarried couples to live together if they're having sex on a regular basis.

6

Bestiality

Covering all its bases, Missouri specifies that its law against critter-humping also applies to *dead* animals.

Honorable Mention

In Washington, DC, having oral or anal sex with anyone is a felony, while adultery is a misdemeanor, and bestiality and peeping aren't specifically against the law. Besides being an upside down application of sex laws, it would appear that there are a whole lot of guilty politicians on the Potomac.

1. **almonds**

2. **calamus**

3. **chicken eggs** (raw)

4. **chocolate**

5. **dill**

6. **garlic**

   It's not necessarily an aphrodisiac for your partner, though.

7. **ginseng** (especially the Chinese variety)

8. **honey**

9. **licorice root**

10. **marijunana** (moderate amounts)

11. **musk** (taken internally)

12. **oats** (*Avena sativa*)

    From whence we get the phrase "to sow your wild oats."

13. **onion seeds**

14. **saffron**

15. **salep** (*Orchis morio*)

    The root of this orchid.

16. **saw palmetto**

17. **Spanish fly**

    An actual insect (*Cantharis vesicatoria*), this powdered beetle works by irritating the urinary system and is very dangerous.

18. **vanilla**

19. **wild carrot**

    Where do you think rabbits get all their sexual energy?

20. **wild celery**

21. **yohimbe**

    The bark from the African tree *Pansinystalia yohimbe* is widely regarded as one of the most unambiguous aphrodisiacs.

The Wonders of "Herbal" Medicine

In September 2003, companies were forced to recall 7 to 12 million tablets of supposedly natural supplements that boost sexual performance in men and women, a la Viagra. They contained ginseng, oats, saw palmetto, eucommia bark, hindo lotus seed, and...oh yeah, Viagra. Yep, these herbal concoctions were infused with sildenafil (the chemical name of Viagra), which the companies somehow forgot to mention on the labels.

LIST **51** # 21 Natural Aphrodisiacs

A triad is to three people what a couple is to two people. In other words, a relationship among three partners. It's sometimes called a threesome or *ménage à trois*, but these words have a primarily sexual connotation, usually being applied to a physical encounter that doesn't involve a long-term commitment.

This list is indebted almost completely to the amazing research of Barbara Foster, Michael Foster, and Letha Hadady. Themselves a triad, they went through history with a fine-tooth comb, digging up numerous examples of famous people involved in triads. The resulting book, *Three in Love*, is an unprecedented chronicle of this formerly unacknowledged type of relationship. (All quotes below are from this groundbreaking and highly readable book.)

1

Butch Cassady and the Sundance Kid

Wild West outlaws Butch Cassady and Harry Longabaugh (the Sundance Kid) committed crimes with Etta Place. All three of them lived together; details of the relationship are sketchy, but it appears that they thought of themselves as a family.

2

Catherine the Great

Imperial Russia's most famous Empress formed a triad with two of her closest staff members, chief deputy Gregory Poterakin and secretary Peter Zavadofsky.

3

Friedrich Engels

Benefactor of Karl Marx and coauthor of *The Communist Manifesto*, Engels lived and loved with two sisters, factory-workers Mary and Lizzie Burns.

32 Famous People Involved in Triads

4

Jacob Epstein

Called "one of the leading portrait sculptors of the 20th century" by the *Encyclopedia Britannica*, Epstein lived with his wife and mistress.

5

George Gordon, Lord Byron

The archetypal Romantic poet was involved for several years with Countess Teresa Guiccioli. He was her *cavaliere servente*, which is basically a combination of errand-boy and male mistress. Count Guiccioli was fine with sharing his wife, a not uncommon attitude among Italian aristocracy of the time.

6 7

Henry II and Catherine de' Medici

King Henry II was married to Catherine de' Medici and openly loved the aristocratic beauty Diane de Poitiers, who knew Henry since he was nine.

8

Victor Hugo

The French novelist who wrote *Les Miserables* was married to Adèle (née Foucher) and was involved for most of his life with a gorgeous but minimally talented actress, Juliette Drouet. (He routinely cheated on wife and mistress with other women.) For years, Adèle hated Juliette, whom Victor always set up in a nearby dwelling. However, the two grew to like and respect each other, with Juliette eventually running the household. Victor remained with both women until their deaths; his relationship with Ms. Drouet lasted exactly 50 years.

9

Lenin

Soviet leader Lenin was part of a fully cooperative triad involving his wife Nadezhda and mistress Inessa. The two women formed a friendship, and all three comrades worked together to further the revolution.

10

Lothar, King of Gaul

In the sixth century, Lothar was married to sisters Ingund and Aregund.

11

Harold Macmillan

As *Three in Love* sums up: "Harold Macmillan, the Conservative prime minister of England from 1957 to 1963, overlapping the Eisenhower and Kennedy administrations, lived in a thirty-year triad that included his wife Dorothy Cavendish and her lover, his closest political connection, Bob Boothby."

12

Marquis de Sade

The man whose name gave us *sadism* lived and loved for a while with his wife Renée and her sister, Anne. The sisters "performed together in the marquis's lost plays, playing his heroines who acquiesce in the acts perpetrated against them."

13

John Stuart Mill

One of the leading philosophers of freedom, Mill found his soulmate in the intelligent Harriet Taylor, who happened to be married to merchant John Taylor. After some initial friction, John came to accept the triad. After he succumbed to cancer, Harriet and John Stuart married and spent the rest of their lives together.

14

François Mitterand

President of France from 1981 to 1995, Mitterand equally loved his wife Danielle and his mistress Mazarine, fathering children with both of them. The families knew of each other but lived apart, though sometimes the triad would vacation together. Both women and all three offspring attended François' funeral.

15

Jawaharlal Nehru

The first Prime Minister of independent India formed a threesome with Louis, Lord Mountbatten (British Admiral of the Fleet) and Edwina, Lady Mountbatten.

16

Admiral Lord Nelson

One of history's most brilliant naval commanders, the man who saved England from France was famously involved with Emma, Lady Hamilton. Less known is the fact that her husband, Sir William Hamilton, approved of the relationship. In 1802, the triad sent cards bearing the greeting: "Sir William Hamilton, Lady Hamilton and Mr. Nelson desire to wish you a merry Christmas."

17 18

Henry Miller and Anaïs Nin

In perhaps the most well-known triad, pioneering erotic writers Henry Miller and Anaïs Nin formed a complex, rocky threesome with Miller's wife, June, in which all three were having sex with each other. Nin's husband stayed on the sidelines of this powderkeg relationship.

19 20 21 22

Pablo Picasso, Salvador Dalí, Paul Eluard, Max Ernst

Poet Paul Eluard, his wife Gala, and painter Max Ernst formed a triad that lasted several years. Gala's second husband, for 53 years, was Salvador Dalí. She had numerous affairs with artists he knew, which apparently didn't faze him.

Meanwhile, Paul Eluard became great friends with Picasso and married a Parisian prostitute, Nusch. She shows up in many of Picasso's paintings, and they formed a triad that lasted a decade, until Nusch's death in 1946.

23 24 25

Sigmund Freud, Friedrich Nietzsche, Rainer Maria Rilke

One of the great lyric poets, Rainer Maria Rilke was emotionally and sexually involved with Louise "Lou" Andreas-Salome, who later became a disciple of Sigmund Freud and a minor contributor to psychoanalytic theory. Lou at the time was in a sexless but loving marriage with an older scholar, F.C. Andreas. The three of them lived and traveled together, and Lou became Rainer's hands-on muse, helping him find his voice.

This was actually the middle of three triads that Lou would form. In the first, she was in an emotional but chaste threesome with philosophers Friedrich Nietzshe and Paul Ree. (Nietzsche had been in a previous sexless triad with Richard and Cosima Wagner.) In the last triad, Lou and Freud became very attached, though they never slept with each other; that honor was for the third party, psychoanalyst Victor Tausk.

26 27

Percy Byssche Shelley and Mary Shelley

Romantic poet Shelley had quite the complicated lovelife, with two aborted triads, one probable one, and an almost quadrad (i.e., involving four people). Early on, Shelley wanted to form a triad with his first wife Harriet and his best friend, Thomas Jefferson Hogg, but Harriet would have none of it. Later, he fell in love with Mary Godwin (daughter of pioneering feminist Mary Wollstonecraft), who would write Frankenstein. He proposed that he, Harriet, and Mary shack up, but again his wife said no.

Shelley and Mary went to Europe to frolic; accompanying them was Mary's half-sister, Claire Claremont. We don't know for sure, but it appears that Percy and Claire started hooking up, with Mary tolerating it.

Things got even more complex and ambiguous later—Percy, Mary, Clare, Lord Byron, his married lover, and her parents all lived under the same roof, along with Jane and Edward Williams, who had children and lived as a married couple though they weren't. (By this time, Harriet had committed suicide, and Percy had married Mary.) Percy fell in love with Jane, and it is likely, though arguable, that they got physical with each other. Percy and Edward became fast friends, sharing Jane's affections. Meanwhile, Mary also fell in love with Jane, who didn't return the feelings. Confused? Imagine how they felt!

28

Voltaire

The witty philosopher was deeply involved with the Marquis du Chatlet and his wife, Emilie. "The two men shared not only one woman but their money and influence at court."

29

Orson Welles' parents

The director of *Citizen Kane* essentially had three parents—his biological dad, Richard Welles; his mother, Beatrice Welles; and her lover, Dr. Maurice Bernstein, whom little Orson called "Dadda." The big, happy family lived together.

30 31

Victoria Woodhull and Henry Ward Beecher

Through the middle of the 1800s, Beecher was America's preacher, basically the Billy Graham of his time, except that he had progressive views. The most progressive he kept under wraps—he was an advocate and practitioner of free love. For many years he was involved with the wife of close friend Theodore Tilton, a situation that pleased all of them.

After a while, Tilton took a more active role in another triad when he began bonking pioneering feminist Victoria Woodhull. Her husband didn't mind; together he and Tilton wrote a biography of Victoria. Beecher enters the picture again, when Victoria started getting it on with him, plus Tilton, not to mention her husband. It also looks as though Victoria, her husband, and her sister Tennessee Claflin formed an emotional triad that may or may not have been sexual. Further complicating the issue is the fact that Victoria took on various lovers throughout the years. If you find these overlapping triads, quadrads, and even pentads confusing, you're not alone.

32

Emile Zola

French novelist Emile Zola split his time between two households—that of his wife and his mistress. The women tolerated each other, then became fast friends after Zola's death.

Others: **Marguerite Duras**; **Joseph Goebbels**; **Graham Greene**; **Ernest Hemingway**; **Jack Kerouac**, **Neal Cassady**, and **Carolyn Cassady**; **Frida Kahlo**; **D.H. Lawrence**; **Georgia O'Keeffe**; **Ezra Pound**; **Jean-Paul Sartre** and **Simone de Beauvoir**; and **Oskar Schindler**. ☐

1

Amputees

If this fetish gets your mast up, look out for *Stumpfuckers* starring Long Jeanne Silver.

2

Autofellatio

If your schlong is long enough and the rest of your body is flexible enough, you too can give yourself a blowjob. If you can't, you can still watch those who can. Ron Jeremy's early claim to fame was an act of autofellatio in 1981's *Inside Seka*. In the scene, the "Marilyn Monroe of porn" will blow everyone but Ron, who opts to service himself.

Videos like *Blow Your Own Horn*, *I Lick It Cuz I Like It*, and *Because They Can* feature guys going down (or is it up?) on themselves. And, yes, some of them swallow.

3

Bald women

Women with shaved pussies are a dime a dozen in porn, but only once in a while do you see women with bald heads. The *Q Balls* movies may be the only ones of their kind.

4

Cream pie videos

If you can't figure this out from the context, I'll spell it out for you: The latest trend to hit pornoland is the "internal cumshot" craze, as seen in such films as *Five Guy Cream Pie*, *Cream Filled Teens*, and *Internal Combustion*.

5

Enemas

Among the works in this genre are *XXXtreme Enemas*, *Ecstasy Waterworks*, and *The Enema Bandit Strikes Again*.

LIST 53

23 Strange Genres of Porn Movie

6

Face-sitting

Also called "queening," you can get an eyeful of this act in *Face-Sitting Fanatics* and *Clamsucker*.

7

Fingering

It may seem like one of the lesser sex acts, but it too is the subject of entire movies, including *Pussy Poppers* and *Finger Friggin'*.

8

Hairy women

In films like *Hairy Hippy Chicks*, *Hirsute Harlots*, and *Dirty Hairy*, the women have moustaches, and dense tangles of hair matting their crotches, legs, armpits, and other areas.

9

Little people

Seeing as how there are so few roles for dwarves in legit movies, I guess it's not too surprising that some have turned to the porn industry. A triumvirate of little men star in *Snow White and the Three Dwarves*, while short women get their moment in *Microslut* and *Bridget the Midget's Gangbang*.

10

Masturbation

Who needs more than one person to make a porn movie? Not the stars of *Stinkin' Fingers*, *Rub the Muff*, and *All Alone and No One to Bone*.

11

Menstruating women

Given our culture's aversion to the monthly cycle, *On the Rag*, *Period Pieces*, and *College Girls: 4th Period* rank as some of the most controversial porn films around.

12

Obese women and men

Starring horndogs who weigh hundreds and hundreds of pounds, *Chubby Chasers*, *Bulk Male*, and *Life in the Fat Lane* put lots of skin into skin flicks.

13

Pierced women

Women with more than the usual number of holes are featured in *Trendy Pierced Young Things*, *Pierced Be-atch!*, and *Pierced, Puntured and Perverted*.

14

Pissing

Waste not, want not with *Watch Me Tinkle*, *Piss Guzzlers*, and *Squirt 'Em Cowgirl!*.

15

Prego porn

Round bellies and milky breasts are the order of the day in porno featuring pregnant women—*Ready to Pop*, *Labor of Love*, *The Drop Zone*, etc.

16

Pubic areas getting shaved

Cream is for shaving in vids like *Shave Me Down!* and *Shaved and Depraved*.

17

Senior women

Some complain that our culture links sexual attractiveness exclusively to youth, but that's not always the case. Just ask the senior citizens who star in porn movies like the *Mature Women* series, *Granny Gets Her Cookies*, *Aged to Perfection*, *Grandma Does Dallas*, *Granny Does a Tranny*, *"Hey, My Grandma Is a Whore!"*, and many others. Women in their 60s are common, and porn

starlets in their 80s aren't unheard of. More rarely, you'll see some dirty old men, as in *Grandpa Gets a Woody*.

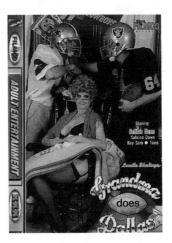

18

Tattooed women

Pierced girls shouldn't get all the attention. Watch *Rude, Screwed and Tattooed* and *Tattooed Love Girl* for women with serious ink on their skin.

19

Twins

Sisters are doing it for themselves and for *you*, the viewing public. Notable porno terrible twosomes are the Thai Sisters and the London Shaggers.

20

Women wearing only socks

Yes, every fetish has its corresponding movies. *The Joy of Socks* and *G-Strings and Bobby Socks* prove it.

21

Women who ejaculate

Those who deny the existence of female ejaculation obviously have never seen movies of women who shoot bigger loads than guys. Just look for anything with the word "Squirt" in the title.

22

Women who smoke

And not just with their mouths....

23

Women with strap-ons

Judging by the number of websites, photos, and movies available, there are a lot of people who love watching a woman strap on a dildo and nail everyone in sight with her plastic schlong. The two basic subcategories here depend on who's receiving the fem-penis— another woman or a guy (*Babes Ballin' Boys*). Some videos—like the *Sorority Strap-ons*

series—go both ways, showing guys and dolls getting humped by women who pack.

Honorable Mentions

Cat fights

Women clawing, scratching, and ripping can be seen in *Body Slamming Bitches*, *P.L.O.W (Punk Ladies of Wrestling)*, and *Mistress Kembra's Island of Hell*, all three directed by performance artist Kembra Pfahler of The Voluptuous Horror of Karen Black fame.

Nude workouts

Plenty of videos will let you watch buff people in the buff lifting weights, aerobicizing, or doing yoga and tai chi. ◘

The following animals have all been sited engaging in homosexual activities. Each one has been reported in the scientific literature, which was scoured by biologist Bruce Bagemihl for his mammoth survey, *Biological Exuberance: Animal Homosexuality and Natural Diversity*.

1. **Baboon**

2. **Barn owl**

3. **Bear** (including black, grizzly, koala, and polar)

4. **Bighorn sheep**

5. **Bonobo** (a primate)

6. **Brown rat**

7. **Caribou**

8. **Cat** (domestic)

9. **Cheetah**

10. **Chicken**

11. **Chimpanzee**

12. **Cockroach**

13. **Deer** (several types)

14. **Desert tortoise**

15. **Dog** (domestic)

16. **Dolphin** (several types)

17. **Dragonfly**

LIST 54

63 Gay Animals

18. **Duck** (several types)

19. **Elephant** (African and Asiatic)

20. **Emu**

21. **Flamingo**

22. **Gazelle**

23. **Giraffe**

24. **Goat**

25. **Gorilla**

26. **Gray squirrel**

27. **Guinea pig**

28. **Hamster**

29. **Herring gull**

30. **Horse**

31. **Housefly**

32. **Hummingbird** (several types)

33. **Indian rhinoceros**

34. **Lion**

35. **Lizard**

36. **Mallard duck**

37. **Monarch butterfly**

38. **Moose**

39. **Mountain zebra**

40. **Octopus**

41. **Orangutan**

42. **Ostrich**

43. **Penguin** (several types)

44. **Pig**

45. **Porcupine**

46. **Rabbit**

47. **Raccoon**

48. **Rattlesnake**

49. **Raven**

50. **Salmon**

51. **Sand shark**

52. **Sea otter**

53. **Seagull**

54. **Sheep**

55. **Swan** (several types)

56. **Tasmanian devil**

57. **Turkey**

58. **Vampire bat**

59. **Walrus**

60. **Warthog**

61. **Water buffalo**

62. **Whale** (several types, including bow head, fin, gray, killer, and—I'm trying not to make a wisecrack—sperm)

63. **Wolf**

1
"Cocksucker Blues" by the Rolling Stones

One of the most infamous unreleased songs in rock and roll history, "Cocksucker Blues" was the Stones' one-finger salute to their original record label. In 1970-1, the bad-boy Brits had started their own label (called, simply enough, Rolling Stones Records), but they still owed Decca a final single. Apparently, music contracts back then didn't stipulate that a single had to be *releasable*, because as fulfillment of their contractual obligation, Mick and the boys turned in a raunchy, bluesy song about a small-town boy who goes to London looking for hot gay sex. The chorus goes:

> When I get my cock sucked
> When I get my ass fucked
> I may not be good-lookin'
> But I know where to put it every time

At least two versions of the song exist—the demo done by Mick and Keith alone and a later, longer version with the whole band in the studio.

"Cocksucker Blues" is also the name of a gritty documentary that captured the Stones' 1972 tour, with all manner of groupie sex, drug use, various debauchery, and some of the band's most electrifying performances. Like the song, the film is officially unreleased, though both are available as bootlegs.

2
"Pussy Control" by Prince

The Purple One is certainly no stranger to sexual songs, and "Pussy Control" stands with the best of them, such as "Let's Pretend We're Married" and "Darling Nikki." In fact, it ranks among his best work, and it wouldn't be out of place on *Purple Rain* or *Sign o' the Times*, although it was recorded much later (probably 1994).

The music is ass-shakingly funky, decorated with lots of post-production sound effects. The lyrics tell the story of a woman with the unlikely name of Pussy Control. Then again, maybe this name isn't so unlikely when you realize that she's a pimp with an MBA. After being beaten by her peers when she was a girl, Pussy decided that living well would be the best revenge, so she studied hard, earned straight A's, and now runs an extremely successful ho operation. (The girls that beat her down are now turning tricks for her.) Her single-minded determination is spelled out in the second verse:

> Pussy got bank in her pockets
> Before she got dick in her drawers
> If brother didn't have good and plenty of his own
> In love Pussy never did fall

When some guy tries to impress Pussy by telling her she can sing backing vocals on a song of his, she replies:

LIST 55 | 4 Unreleased Raunchy Songs

"Niggah you're crazy if you don't know
Every girl in the world ain't a freak
You could go platinum four times
Still wouldn't make what I make in a week."

The song ends when the narrator macks on Ms. Control, and she gives him the brush-off. Prince has performed "Pussy Control" live, and he has been known to play the studio version to concert audiences before he takes the stage. So far, the song hasn't been released on a legitimate record.

3

"God's Gift to Women" by Jewel

Sure, dirty songs by the Stones and Prince aren't exactly out of character, but you might not expect such things from Jewel, who sweetly sings the mega-hits "Who Will Save Your Soul" and "You Were Meant for Me," not to mention "Ave Maria." During her pre-fame days, when she was writing and performing songs prolifically, she penned this ode to a guy who is well-hung and/or fucks really well. She starts off with a bit of boastfulness:

Would you like to ram your tongue down my throat
Would you like to grab my thighs
Yes, I have got nice tits
They are the perfect grab-me size

But she quickly does an about-face with some self-deprecating lines about being "so desperate" that "I'll do you on the front lawn" and "I'll do you and your mom." She certainly wasn't aiming for the feminist demographic when she wrote:

I was just thinking that it'd be really cool
If I got hit upside the head with a manly tool
That way he could have nothing left to say
And have his way with me all day

And who'd ever have thought that the young woman who once sang "I'm sensitive and I'd like to stay that way" would belt out the line:

"I've been saving myself my whole life for some motherfucker like you to come along"?

Besides being available as live bootleg, "God's Gift" was recorded in the studio for the demo CD, *Save the Linoleum*, that Jewel cut for record labels. Although some of the other tracks appeared on her debut album, *Pieces of You*, this one has yet to appear on a commercial release.

4

Unnamed song by Dean Martin

Perhaps even more shocking—or not, if you think about it—Dean Martin is alleged to have recorded a dirty ditty on a lark. In 1956, he and Jerry Lewis were in the studio to record a commercial for their new flick, *The Caddy*. They kept flubbing the lines, which started them cursing and cutting up. For several takes, they decided to be as nasty as they wanted to be.

This must've given Dino an idea, because he then laid down a musical number that the FBI—in Martin's file—later characterized as "extremely obscene." The song and the commercials were bootlegged, but the song still remains quite hard to find. A record collector on the Net says that the title is "All American Bum," but I've found no confirmation.

Honorable Mention

Craters of the Sac by Ween

College silly-rockers Ween quasi-officially released a set of songs only online, collectively know as *Craters of the Sac*. These MP3 tracks include "big fat fuck," "put the coke on my dick," "makin' love in the gravy," and "suckin' the blood from the devil's dick." ◨

Every one of the spam senders in this informal survey is trying—in the hope that you won't immediately delete them—to entice you into checking out their junk-email messages and purchasing their products. In that process, they will sometimes deliberately (but not always delliberately) misspell words in the subject lines of their spams in order to bypass any electronic filters you happen to set up.

As a friend writes to me:

> I just upgraded to AOL 9 which has a feature that takes out spam before it gets to you. Theoretically you submit and save a list of words you don't want in your subject line—in my case some are "Viagra," "Xanax," "cheerleaders" and "mortgages"—then *voila!* But, as always, the spammers are one step ahead. Now I'm getting spam for "Viagara," "Xannax," "cheer leaders" and "mort.gages." I don't know why they think I'd do business with anyone whose spelling skills were so faulty, but I guess their target audience may not care.

And from another friend:

> Has anyone had a problem with blocked email? I have had fully one-third of my mail blocked by my ISP that is running Norton's "Barracuda Spam Firewall." *Phooey!* It blocks email from friends and newsletters but lets the porn, Viagra and "grow your penis pills" through. I am ticked! Anyone else all of a sudden not hearing from friends?

Meanwhile, federal agents have arrested a man for repeatedly making death threats against employees of an Internet advertising firm. He faces a maximum penalty of five years in prison and a $250,000 fine if convicted. He had mistakenly believed that the company was the source of unsolicited email ads he received about penis enlargement. Well, everybody has their breaking point.

Carol Liefer observed on Comedy Central that apparently there are a lot of people who want *her* to have a bigger penis. And, on the all-female morning TV talk show *The View*, this rhetorical question was posed: "Which is worse, a tiny little penis or a lot of violence?" As if in response, a dwarf detective on a Comedy Central promo for their movie *Knee-High P.I.* observed, "Sometimes the best dick is a small dick," though you'll never see *that* in a subject line.

LIST 56

153 Bizarre and Revealing Spam Subject Lines Leading to Sexually Oriented Messages
Paul Krassner

Anyway, here's a quaint selection of penis-enlarger subject lines.

There's the impress-a-female approach:

1. "Women have always said: Size Matters!"
2. "No girl will give U a damn if U have little pe-nis"
3. "Hey My Girl Bought Me the Patch"
4. "She likes my new weenie"
5. "I am lookin for a big man like U! C*U*M* to me!"
6. "Wanna be big enough to shock people?"
7. "You will leave her speechless"
8. "Make her scream OHHH YEAAA!"

But men also like to impress other men:

9. "Feal proud when your in the locker room"
10. "Your friends will envy you" (guaranteed up to 4 rock hard inches)

Plus some more choices for the road:

11. "Keep praying eyes away!"
12. "Monster Cocks at Discount Price"
13. "impede her"
14. "dont worry about ur stupid little penis, ha ha"
15. "do u think u still can fuck like those who has macho dick?"
16. "Every man wishes he had a larger penis"
17. "Be a man and add a third leg"
18. "Enlarge your Manhood"
19. "Increase your penis size in one day"
20. "my hole was bored out by the reaper"
21. "Be happy when you make love!"
22. "With these pills you can shoot cum like a porn star!"
23. "Penus Enlarged in 2 Hours!"

The misleading subject line is a popular method of tricking you:

24. "Tickets arrived" led to this message: "there is no other way to enlarge your penis."
25-26. This vague subject line—"Hey, shit happens"—and this non sequitur subject line—"Do you like oranges"—both led to the same message: "Use this patch and it will grow i SWEAR...."

And then there was this charming misleader:

27. "Enlarge your Bank Account 2-3 inches in days"

All right, so now the good news is that every man has a larger penis. However, the bad news is that none of them can get it up.

"I remember a spam," writes a friend, "about free Viagra after a Penis Enlargement operation that would take place someplace in Kenya or Nigeria just before the search for my share of several hundred million dollars my new friend is cutting me in on. Seems his dad stashed bullion in foreign accounts to which they'd have no access until I brought several thousand dollars first. Could have gotten way rich while erect for days while I fucked myself."

Another friend quotes a spam—"Massive rock-solid erections, new natural product bmrgwhmsmnmb"—and adds, "I like how it turns into nonsense at the end. I kind of picture like it's a mild mannered guy at the beginning who takes the 'Natural' Viagra somewhere in the middle and then by the end he's like the incredible Hulk with a hard-on so powerful he can't even make coherent sounds. Also: 'From Keith Moon: Re: Generic Viagra'—At least they have a sense of humor. Maybe they'll start coming from 'Rush Limbaugh' next."

And now for your reading pleasure, here's an erection selection:

28. "Stick it on you then stick it to her" (Viagra-like patch)

29. "Bob Dole loves Viagra, so should you!"

30. "terrifying terpsichorean"

31. "The Assay Test"

32. "Men let the pillz do the talking"

33. "Is it time to upgrade your system?"

34. "You will be a sex machine"

35. "Are you hard at work?"

36. "You blocked my ICQ"

37. "Stay hard for 72 hours." Viagra ads in magazines state: "You should call a doctor immediately if you ever have an erection that lasts more than 4 hours. If not treated right away, permanent damage to your penis could occur."

38. This vague subject line—"Hi"—led to this message: "Sometimes people call it 'Magic Lubricant.' Sometimes 'Power Bottle.' Why? An amazing erection WITHIN SEVERAL SECONDS is guaranteed to you! Double-strengthed orgasm and full satisfaction."

39-40. Both "Can I Make It Up to You?" and "One Last Question" are spam subject lines for this message: "Did you know you could discreetly order Viagra over the Internet? You don't have to go through all the problems of getting it in a local pharmacy store or explaining your problems to the doctor."

Okay, so now all these horny men have gigantic penises and also the medical means to help them defy gravity and become oh so erect, but there's simply nobody around with whom to share these huge hard-ons. That's where Internet porn—a $10 billion industry—comes to the rescue. But please try not to ejaculate on the keyboard.

41. "Amateur Girls Never Before Seen"

42. "Fresh hot assets"

43. "Drunk party babes"

44. "Wow—Screwing Machines"

45. "Bondage at Mistress Shaved's Nasty Fetish Club"

46. "Pussies Getting Slammed"

47. "Pregnant Girls Getting Laid!"

48. "Look inside a pussy with our dildo-cam"

49. "watch this girl get her poousy lips get parted with a tongue"

50. "Big Clits—Monster Clits"

51. "enter this place and you willl see hard nipples and pink beavers"

52. "I have a multi-colored bush for you to see"

53. "The Executive's Dream" ("your secretary is a dirty little thing, and wants your Man Meat!")

Hey, psst, you wanna see some nice breasts? Try these for size:

54. "All we have are Breasts!"

55. "Do You Like Tits" ("100,000+ pics of big titty girls")

56. "Big Huge Breasts"

57. "Melon size boobies"

58. "Jumbo Juggy Jugs"

59. "Big juicy titties"

60. "Petite Little Boobs"

How about interracial?

61. "Choked white whores used as black cum recepticals"

62. "White Ladies and Dark Meat Look of Pain!"

Or what about international?

63. "Nasty Asian sex"

64. "Viet Yummy"

65. "Latin girls getting fucked"

66. "Re: travel plans" ("We've got girls from countries all over Asia spreading their pink pussies")

67. "I put the stalian back in Italian...."

Do you prefer four-legged friends?

68. "Watch me fuck a poodle"

69. "Oh my God, I had S-E-X With My Dog!"

70. "Meet Harvey the pussy eating wonder dog!"

71. "Teen takes a horse dong deep inside her flower"

72. "She takes the 20 inch horse pole"

73. "The real farm movie they tried to ban" ("guess Ramo's [the horse's] cock size and win a free ticket to the show")

74. "Dacy Does Donkeys"

75. "S*X WITH PETS" ("Taken to the Xtreme")

76. "This is sicker than Michael Jackson's daycare" (girls with farm animals)

77. "Hot women do everything in my car" ("You ever wanted to see a live donkey show?" Gosh, that must be a very large car.)

You dig first-timers?

78. "Angel's First Facial"

79. "Erika's First five finger Experience"

80. "First Time Lesbians!"

Know how to make (or take) a fist?

81. "Miss Fist-a-Lot!"

82. "Porn Queens Fistfucked for Real"

83. "Get Your Fisting Party Started!"

Got oral sex?

84. "Cum Squad Squat!"

85. "Free pics of teen Sluts Sucking Almight Cocks!"

86. "Young Pussy Lickers"

87. "Girls love to tasty cum"

88. "Shooting Incident" (Max Cumshot)

89. "See them spurt!" ("Cumshakes, Thousands of Hot Cum Covered Girls")

90. "I blew my load all over her" (Facial Fiasco)

91. "She swallowed it all, Cum splattered all over her face"

92. "Jizz drizzled all over my face help me!"

93. "Sarah sucking balls"

94. "Bite that cock!"

Or maybe anal?

95. "Doing Her Ass"

96. "My Girl Likes Anal Sex"

97. "Nasty Girls Doing Backdoor"

98. "I've applied to 4 Universities, but this one has the best programs" ("We're going to send you to Anal University")

Golden shower, anyone?

99. "She's a Pee Fanatic!"

100. "She peed on me!"

Age is no barrier:

101. "Virgin Schoolgirls"

102. "Cranky debutantes"

103. "Teen sluts gone wild"

104. "Tight Teen Cunts"

105. "watch me spread this teens Pucey lips"

106. "Ordinary Girls with Spread Legs— naughty girls fresh out of high school"

107. "Cute girls in college spreading their legs"

108. "Aged woman spreads legs"

109. "Loving for grannies"

110. "Hot Nude Granny" ("The Premier Mature Lady Site")

Neither is gender:

111. "Crazy Gay Action only the BIGGEST Gay Cocks Inside"

112. "New reality site with young boys"

113. "Gay closet movies"

114. "sex crazed lesbians"

Nor marriage vows:

115. "I'm ready to cheat on my husand"

116. "With the kids asleep, mom gets wild and kinky"

117. "Sit back, relax and get a blow job from a woman at EZ Cheatng tonight"

118. "watch these ladies get nailed while the kids are in bed"

119. "in here is over 5 hundred thousand pictures of hot moms naked"

120. "Look at a hot mom taking a shower and shaving her vagina"

121. "The State Survey" ("How many children do you claim? Real yummy mummys")

122-123. "Don't Be Shy" and "Please don't tell anyone" both lead to "a revolutionary new service connecting cheating wives with single men."

Celebrities, from Pamela Anderson to Paris Hilton, in home-made sex videos are of course a special treat on the World Wide Web:

124. "Hello! Paris Hilton just drinks love juice!"

125. "J. Lo's Nipples"

126. "J. Lo caught eating a booger" (whatever turns you on)

Here, have a subject-line montage:

127. "Bob said you'd want this"

128. "Naked Girls Next Door" ("Enter here to fuck these hot girls")

129. "(no subject)" ("Do you ever find yourself thinking about what it would be like to see naked girls all day?")

130. "lusty transvestites take picture for you"

131. "Upskirt panty peaks"

132. "Her cherrry gets popped!"

133. "Watch these young teens get exploited—severely!"

134. "100% hot bitches"

135. "As vulg@r as it getz"

136. "The sickest place on earth" (midgets, animals, trannies, fisting, pregnant, enemas)

137. "Unreal Penetrations"

138. "Security Guards F_ucking Hot Girls"

139. "Take care" ("Insane orgies")

140. "3 Girls gangbanged"

141. "These Guys Don't have a Chance!" ("Hot Young locals Seduce Unknowing Tourist!")

142. "Stop wasting money on women!"

Some spam subject lines have a certain sexual aura, but lead you to non-sexual messages:

143. "Do you know I love you" (money lender)

144. "See my newest movie" (wholesale prescription medicines)

145. "As good as it gets" (online poker)

146. "It is hard" ("Banned CD, Government don't want me to sell it. Your own FBI file, driving record, criminal databases")

147. "We Got the Spread" ("Nude, but click here to bet now! NFL odds")

148. "Beach Girls" ("Forget Aging and Dieting forever")

149-150. "First Time" (for both "Wholesale prescription medications at bargain prices" and "Term-life coverage at reduced rates is now available")

151-152. "I can come" and "Corrupted existentially" both lead to weight-loss messages.

153. And finally, here's my own personal favorite spam, which came from DarkProfits.com. The subject line reads: "Your credit card has been Charged for $234.65"—which leads to the following message, headlined "Important Notice:"

We have just charged your credit card for money laundry service in amount of $234.65 (because you are either child pornography webmaster or deal with dirty money, which require us to laundry them and then send to your checking account). If you feel this transaction was made by our mistake, please press "No." If you confirm this transaction, please press "Yes" and fill in the form below. Enter your credit card number here.

Enter your credit card expiration date.

In the immortal words of Bart Simpson, "I didn't think it was physically possible, but this both sucks and blows." ⌂

1 "If you're not going all the way, why go at all?"

–Joe Namath

2 "Those who restrain Desire, do so because theirs is weak enough to be restrained."

–William Blake

3 "Erotic impulses are a never-ending source of ingenious, even wondrous constructions. Almost any object or body function can be eroticized."

–Robert J. Stoller, M.D., sexologist and psychiatry professor at UCLA

4 "When a woman has tasted a dog, she will never want a man again."

–court transcript of "an unnamed 19th-century English serving girl"

5 "Chastity is the most unnatural of the sexual perversions."

–Remy de Gourmont

6 "Love ain't nothing but sex mis-spelled."

–Harlan Ellison

7 "The sex relation is not a personal relation. It can be irresistibly desired and rapturously consummated between persons who could not endure one another for a day in any other relation."

–George Bernard Shaw

8 "Playing to lose is like sleeping with your sister. Sure, she's a great piece of tail with a blouse full of goodies, but it's just illegal"

–"Topper Harley" (Charlie Sheen) in *Hot Shots!*

9 "Marriage finds its natural fulfillment in adultery."

–Simone de Beauvoir

10 "I also see sex in the joining win-dows, in the archways of doors, on the pattern a fence makes on the ground, in shadows. Who is to say those myriad of angles we see every day are not joined sexually?"

–Andrei Codrescu, *The Repentance of Lorraine*, 1973

11 "A sexual desire holds no interest for me unless it is accompanied by love, and for love I would leave every-thing."

–Benjamin Péret, Surrealist poet

11 Quotes About Sex

+ Religion

The Good Book is so pornographic and violent that several goodly Christians tried to make it fit for family reading, publishing five such versions in a 37-year period.

1

In 1796, the Bishop of London put out a Bible in which each chapter was rated with one of four designations. The fourth designation—which was actually no designation at all—was given to the nasty parts.

2

Swedenborg follower John Bellamy offered a G-rated version in 1818.

3

1824 saw the publication of The New Family Bible and Improved Version, which took a scalpel to the "offensive" parts.

4

Soon after, a Quaker released a Bible with the naughty bits toned down and printed in italics so they could easily be avoided (or easily read).

5

Legendary lexicographer Noah Webster, who created the first English-language dictionary, published a heavily reworded edition in 1833. ◘

LIST 58 5 Family-Safe Bibles

1

God burns whiners alive

And when the people complained, it displeased the LORD: and the LORD heard it; and his anger was kindled; and the fire of the LORD burnt among them, and consumed them that were in the uttermost parts of the camp. [Numbers 11:1, King James]

2

God poisons complainers

And the people spoke against God and against Moses, "Why have you brought us up out of Egypt to die in the wilderness? For there is no food and no water, and we loathe this worthless food." Then the LORD sent fiery serpents among the people, and they bit the people, so that many people of Israel died. [Numbers 21:5-6, New American Standard]

3

Smashing babies on rocks is a good thing

O Daughter of Babylon, doomed to destruction, happy is he who repays you for what you have done to us—he who seizes your infants and dashes them against the rocks. [Psalms 137:8-9, New International]

4

An angel commits mass murder

That night the angel of the LORD went out and put to death a hundred and eighty-five thousand men in the Assyrian camp. When the people got up the next morning—there were all the dead bodies! [2 Kings 19:35, New International]

 LIST **59** **18 Biblical Atrocities**

5

God commits genocide of babies

At midnight the LORD struck down all the first-born in Egypt, from the firstborn of Pharaoh, who sat on the throne, to the firstborn of the prisoner, who was in the dungeon, and the firstborn of all the livestock as well. [Exodus 12:29, King James]

6

God causes cannibalism

[God says:] I will make them eat the flesh of their sons and daughters, and they will eat one another's flesh during the stress of the siege imposed on them by the enemies who seek their lives. [Jeremiah 19:9, New International]

7

God demands heads

And the LORD said unto Moses, Take all the heads of the people, and hang them up before the LORD against the sun, that the fierce anger of the LORD may be turned away from Israel. [Numbers 25:4, King James]

8

God commands slaughter and rape

[Moses says:] Now kill all the boys. And kill every woman who has slept with a man, but save for yourselves every girl who has never slept with a man. [Numbers 31:17-18, New International]

9

God commands genocide and plunder

[Moses says:] And the LORD said unto me, Behold, I have begun to give Sihon and his land before thee: begin to possess, that thou mayest inherit his land. Then Sihon came out against us, he and all his people, to fight at Jahaz. And the LORD our God delivered him before us; and we smote him, and his sons, and all his people. And we took all his cities at that time, and utterly destroyed the men, and the women, and the little ones, of every city, we left none to remain: Only the cattle we took for a prey unto ourselves, and the spoil of the cities which we took. [Deuteronomy 2:31-35, King James]

10

God commands slaughter, rape, and plunder

When the LORD your God delivers it into your hand, put to the sword all the men in it. As for the women, the children, the livestock and everything else in the city, you may take these as plunder for yourselves. And you may use the plunder the LORD your God gives you from your enemies. [Deuteronomy 20:13-14, New International]

11

God assists slaughter and mutilation

When Judah attacked, the LORD gave the Canaanites and Perizzites into their hands and they struck down ten thousand men at Bezek. It was there that they found Adoni-Bezek and fought against him, putting to rout the Canaanites and Perizzites. Adoni-Bezek fled, but they chased him and caught him, and cut off his thumbs and big toes. [Judges 1:4-6, New International]

12

Gang rape, murder, and dismemberment

While they were enjoying themselves, some of the wicked men of the city surrounded the house. Pounding on the door, they shouted to the old man who owned the house, "Bring out the man who came to your house so we can have sex with him."

The owner of the house went outside and said to them, "No, my friends, don't be so vile. Since this man is my guest, don't do this disgraceful thing. Look, here is my virgin daughter, and his concubine. I will bring them out to you now, and you can use them and do to them whatever you wish. But to this man, don't do such a disgraceful thing."

But the men would not listen to him. So the man took his concubine and sent her outside to them, and they raped her and abused her throughout the night, and at dawn they let her go. At daybreak the woman went back to the house where her master was staying, fell down at the door and lay there until daylight. When her master got up in the morning and opened the door of the house and stepped out to continue on his way, there lay his concubine, fallen in the doorway of the house, with her hands on the threshold. He said to her, "Get up; let's go." But there was no answer. Then the man put her on his donkey and set out for home. When he reached home, he took a knife and cut up his concubine, limb by limb, into twelve parts and sent them into all the areas of Israel. [Judges 19:22-29, New International]

13

God gives men tumors and boils on their genitals

And they carried the ark of the God of Israel about thither. And it was so, that, after they had carried it about, the hand of the LORD was against the city with a very great destruction: and he smote the men of the city, both small and great, and they had emerods in their secret parts [i.e., tumors and boils on their genitals]. [1 Samuel 5:8-9, King James]

14

David collects foreskins

David and his men went out and killed two hundred Philistines. He brought their foreskins and presented the full number to the king so that he might become the king's son-in-law. Then Saul gave him his daughter Michal in marriage. [1 Samuel 18:27, New International]

15

Amnon rapes his sister, then kicks her out

Then Amnon said to Tamar, "Bring the food here into my bedroom so I may eat from your hand." And Tamar took the bread she had prepared and brought it to her brother Amnon in his bedroom. But when she took it to him to eat, he grabbed her and said, "Come to bed with me, my sister."

"Don't, my brother!" she said to him. "Don't force me. Such a thing should not be done in Israel! Don't do this wicked thing. What about me? Where could I get rid of my disgrace? And what about you? You would be like one of the wicked fools in Israel. Please speak to the king; he will not keep me from being married to you."

But he refused to listen to her, and since he was stronger than she, he raped her. Then Amnon hated her with intense hatred. In fact, he hated her more than he had loved her. Amnon said to her, "Get up and get out!" [2 Samuel 13:10-15, New International]

16

God mutilates jeering youngsters via two bears

From there Elisha went up to Bethel. As he was walking along the road, some youths came out of the town and jeered at him. "Go on up, you baldhead!" they said. "Go on up, you baldhead!" He turned around, looked at them and called down a curse on them in the name of the LORD. Then two bears came out of the woods and mauled forty-two of the youths. [2 Kings 2:23-24, New International]

17

Infanticide, rape, and looting for God

Whoever is captured [in Babylon] will be thrust through; all who are caught will fall by the sword. Their infants will be dashed to pieces before their eyes; their houses will be looted and their wives ravished. [Isaiah 13:15-16, New International]

18

Killing babies, slicing open preggies

The people of Samaria must bear their guilt, because they have rebelled against their God. They will fall by the sword; their little ones will be dashed to the ground, their pregnant women ripped open. [Hosea 13:16, New International] ⌂

1

A loving, merciful God?

The LORD is good to all: and his tender mercies are over all his works. [Psalms 145:9]

...God is love. [1 John 4:8]

But:

[God says:] I will not pity, nor spare, nor have mercy, but destroy them. [Jeremiah 13:14]

[God says:] If that nation, against whom I have pronounced, turn from their evil, I will repent of the evil that I thought to do unto them. [Jeremiah 18:8]

[Jesus says:] And fear not them which kill the body, but are not able to kill the soul: but rather fear him which is able to destroy both soul and body in hell. [Matthew 10:28]

Howl ye; for the day of the LORD is at hand; it shall come as a destruction from the Almighty.... Behold, the day of the LORD cometh, cruel both with wrath and fierce anger, to lay the land desolate: and he shall destroy the sinners thereof out of it.... Therefore I will shake the heavens, and the earth shall remove out of her place, in the wrath of the LORD of hosts, and in the day of his fierce anger. [Isaiah 13:6,9,13]

But God will smash the heads of his enemies, crushing the skulls of those who love their guilty ways. The LORD says, "I will bring my enemies down from Bashan; I will bring them up from the depths of the sea. You, my people, will wash your feet in their blood, and even your dogs will get their share!" [Psalms 68:21-23, New Living Translation]

2

A peaceful God?

Now the God of peace be with you all. Amen. [Romans 15:33]

But:

The LORD is a man of war: the LORD is his name. [Exodus 15:3]

21 Biblical Contradictions

3

Do children pay the price?

[God says:] The fathers shall not be put to death for the children, nor the children be put to death for the fathers; but every man shall be put to death for his own sin. [2 Kings 14:6]

[God says:] The son shall not bear the iniquity of the father, neither shall the father bear the iniquity of the son: the righteousness of the righteous shall be upon him, and the wickedness of the wicked shall be upon him. [Ezekiel 18:20]

But:

I the Lord thy God am a jealous God, visiting the iniquity of the fathers upon the children unto the third and fourth generation of them that hate me; [Exodus 20:5]

4

To swear oaths or not to swear oaths?

Above all, my brothers, do not swear—not by heaven or by earth or by anything else. [James 5:12, New International]

But:

When God made his promise to Abraham, since there was no one greater for him to swear by, he swore by himself, saying, "I will surely bless you and give you many descen-

dants." And so after waiting patiently, Abraham received what was promised. Men swear by someone greater than themselves, and the oath confirms what is said and puts an end to all argument. [Hebrews 6:13-16, New International]

5

Father and Son, or Father Is Son?

[Jesus said:] I and my Father are one. [John 10:30]

But:

[Jesus said:] If ye loved me, ye would rejoice, because I said, I go unto the Father: for my Father is greater than I. [John 14:28]

6

Sevens or twos?

Of every clean beast thou shalt take to thee by sevens, the male and his female: and of beasts that are not clean by two, the male and his female. [Genesis 7:2]

But:

Of clean beasts, and of beasts that are not clean, and of fowls, and of every thing that creepeth upon the earth, There went in two and two unto Noah into the ark, the male and the female, as God had commanded Noah. [Genesis 7:8-9]

7

The two deaths of Judas Iscariot

And he [Judas] cast down the pieces of silver in the temple, and departed, and went and hanged himself. [Matthew 27:5]

But:

Now this man [Judas] purchased a field with the reward of iniquity; and falling headlong, he burst asunder in the midst, and all his bowels gushed out. [Acts 1:18]

8

The last words (or not) of Jesus

And about the ninth hour Jesus cried with a loud voice, saying, Eli, eli, lama sabachthani? that is to say, My God, my God, why hast thou forsaken me? ...Jesus, when he cried again with a loud voice, yielded up the ghost. [Matthew 27:46,50]

But:

And when Jesus had cried with a loud voice, he said, Father, unto thy hands I commend my spirit: and having said thus, he gave up the ghost. [Luke 23:46]

But:

When Jesus therefore had received the vinegar, he said, It is finished: and he bowed his head, and gave up the ghost. [John 19:30]

9

Joseph had two dads?

And Jacob begat Joseph the husband of Mary, of whom was born Jesus, who is called Christ. [Matthew 1:16]

But:

And Jesus himself began to be about thirty years of age, being (as was supposed) the son of Joseph, which was the son of Heli, [Luke 3:23]

10

No kids or five?

Therefore Michal the daughter of Saul had no child unto the day of her death. [2 Samuel 6:23]

But:

But the king took the two sons of Rizpah the daughter of Aiah, whom she bare unto Saul, Armoni and Mephibosheth; and the five sons of Michal the daughter of Saul, whom she brought up for Adriel the son of Barzillai the Meholathite: [2 Samuel 21:8]

11

Hearing voices, maybe

And the men which journeyed with him [Saul] stood speechless, hearing a voice, but seeing no man. [Acts 9:7]

But:

[Saul says:] And they that were with me saw indeed the light, and were afraid; but they heard not the voice of him that spake to me. [Acts 22:9]

12

Omniscient or blind?

"Can anyone hide in secret places so that I cannot see him?" declares the Lord. "Do not I fill heaven and earth?" declares the Lord. [Jeremiah 23:24, New International]

Nothing in all creation is hidden from God's sight. Everything is uncovered and laid bare before the eyes of him to whom we must give account. [Hebrews 4:13, New International]

But:

Then the Lord said to Cain, "Where is your brother Abel?" [Genesis 4:9, New International]

Then the man and his wife heard the sound of the Lord God as he was walking in the garden in the cool of the day, and they hid from the Lord God among the trees of the garden. But the Lord God called to the man, "Where are you?" [Genesis 3:8-9, New International]

13

Should you honor or hate your parents?

Honour thy father and thy mother: [Exodus 20:12]

For God commanded, saying, Honour thy father and mother: and, He that curseth father or mother, let him die the death. [Matthew 15:4]

But:

[Jesus says:] If any man come to me, and hate not his father, and mother, and wife, and children, and brethren, and sisters, yea, and his own life also, he cannot be my disciple. [Luke 14:26]

14

Eye for eye, cheek for cheek

Breach for breach, eye for eye, tooth for tooth: as he hath caused a blemish in a man, so shall it be done to him again. [Leviticus 24:20]

But:

[Jesus said:] But I say unto you, That ye resist not evil: but whosoever shall smite thee on thy right cheek, turn to him the other also.... But I say unto you, Love your enemies, bless them that curse you, do good to them that hate you, and pray for them which despitefully use you, and persecute you; [Matthew 5:38,44]

15

The four deaths of Saul

Then said Saul unto his armourbearer, Draw thy sword, and thrust me through therewith; lest these uncircumcised come and thrust me through, and abuse me. But his armourbearer would not; for he was sore afraid. Therefore Saul took a sword, and fell upon it. [1 Samuel 31:4]

But:

And he [Saul] said unto me, Who art thou? And I answered him, I am an Amalekite. He said unto me again, Stand, I pray thee, upon me, and slay me: for anguish is come upon me, because my life is yet whole in me. So I stood upon him, and slew him, because I was sure that he could not live after that he was fallen: [2 Samuel 1:8-10]

But:

And David went and took the bones of Saul and the bones of Jonathan his son from the men of Jabeshgilead, which had stolen them from the street of Bethshan, where the Philistines had hanged them, when the Philistines had slain Saul in Gilboa: [2 Samuel 21:12]

But:

So Saul died for his transgression which he committed against the Lord, even against the word of the Lord, which he kept not, and

also for asking counsel of one that had a familiar spirit, to enquire of it; And enquired not of the Lord: therefore he slew him, and turned the kingdom unto David the son of Jesse. [1 Chronicles 10:13-14]

16

Forever isn't what it used to be

Generations come and generations go, but the earth remains forever. [Ecclesiastes 1:4]

But:

[Jesus says:] Heaven and earth will pass away, but my words will never pass away. [Matthew 24:35]

17

Thad or Jude?

Matthew [10:2] and Mark [3:16-19] list the Twelve Apostles as including Thaddaeus (Labbaeus), but Luke [6:13-16] doesn't include Thaddeus. Instead, the twelfth Apostle is Judas the son of James (different than Judas Iscariot).

18

Jesus judges?

[Jesus says:] You judge by human standards; I pass judgment on no one. [John 8:15, New International]

But:

Moreover, the Father judges no one, but has entrusted all judgment to the Son, [John 5:22, New International]

19

God judges?

Moreover, the Father judges no one, but has entrusted all judgment to the Son, [John 5:22, New International]

But:

Since you call on a Father who judges each man's work impartially, live your lives as strangers here in reverent fear. [1 Peter 1:17, New International]

Now we know that God's judgment against those who do such things is based on truth. [Romans 2:2, New International]

20

Jesus in Hell?

[Jesus says:] Whosoever shall say Thou fool, shall be in danger of hellfire. [Matthew 5:22]

But:

[Jesus says:] Ye fools and blind. [Matthew 23:17]

21

Omnipotent or impotent?

But Jesus beheld them, and said unto them, With men this is impossible; but with God all things are possible. [Matthew 19:26]

But:

And the LORD was with Judah; and he drave out the inhabitants of the mountain; but could not drive out the inhabitants of the valley, because they had chariots of iron. [Judges 1:19]

Note: All passages are from the King James version, unless otherwise noted. ⌂

Back in the days before groups of men decided what books would comprise the Bible, scads of Jewish and Christian writings were floating around. Here are some that the bishops and rulers didn't include in the Good Book.

1

The First Book of Adam and Eve

After being cast out of the Garden of Eden, Adam and Eve trudge up a mountain that looks down on their paradise lost:

> Then Adam threw himself down from the top of that mountain; his face was torn and his flesh was ripped; he lost a lot of blood and was close to death. Meanwhile Eve remained standing on the mountain crying over him, thus lying. And she said, "I don't wish to live after him; for all that he did to himself was through me." Then she threw herself after him; and was torn and ripped by stones; and remained lying as dead. But the merciful God, who looks over His creatures, looked at Adam and Eve as they lay dead, and He sent His Word to them, and raised them. [21:4-8]

2

The Book of the Secrets of Enoch

In this distinctly odd book, angels take Enoch to Heaven, where God shoots the breeze with him, explaining the Creation, Adam and Eve's fall, Satan, etc. Upon reaching the top level of Heaven, Enoch meets the Big G:

> On the tenth heaven, [which is called] Aravoth, I saw the appearance of the LORD's face, like iron made to glow in fire, and brought out, emitting sparks, and it burns. Thus I saw the LORD's face, but the LORD's face is ineffable, marvellous and very awful, and very, very terrible. And who am I to tell of the LORD's unspeakable being, and of his very wonderful face? And I cannot tell the quantity of his many instructions, and various voices, the LORD's throne very great and not made with hands, nor the quantity of those standing round him, troops of cherubim and seraphim, nor their incessant singing, nor his immutable beauty, and who shall tell of the ineffable greatness of his glory? [22:1-3]

The Almighty explains, more or less, what the scene was like before he pulled off the Creation:

LIST : 61 | 8 Books That Didn't Make it Into the Bible

For before all thing were visible, I alone used to go about in the invisible things, like the sun from east to west, and from west to east. But even the sun has peace in itself, while I found no peace, because I was creating all things, and I conceived the thought of placing foundations, and of creating visible creation. [24:4-5]

God gives the lowdown on making Adam:

"On the sixth day I commanded my wisdom to create man from seven consistencies: one, his flesh from the earth; two, his blood from the dew; three, his eyes from the sun; four, his bones from stone; five, his intelligence from the swiftness of the angels and from cloud; six, his veins and his hair from the grass of the earth; seven, his soul from my breath and from the wind. And I gave him seven natures: to the flesh hearing, the eyes for sight, to the soul smell, the veins for touch, the blood for taste, the bones for endurance, to the intelligence sweetness [enjoyment]." [30:10-11]

3

The First Book of Enoch

And it came to pass when the children of men had multiplied that in those days were born unto them beautiful and comely daughters. And the angels, the children of the heaven, saw and lusted after them, and said to one another: "Come, let us choose us wives from among the children of men and beget us children."...

And all the others together with them took unto themselves wives, and each chose for himself one, and they began to go in unto them and to defile themselves with them, and they taught them charms and enchant-

ments, and the cutting of roots, and made them acquainted with plants. And they became pregnant, and they bare great giants, whose height was three thousand ells: Who consumed all the acquisitions of men. And when men could no longer sustain them, the giants turned against them and devoured mankind. And they began to sin against birds, and beasts, and reptiles, and fish, and to devour one another's flesh, and drink the blood. [6:1-3, 7:1-6]

4

The Gospel of the Birth of Mary

This book fills the void about the life of the Virgin Mary. Angels appear to her parents, telling them they will conceive a miracle child who will eventually give birth to the Son of God. When little Mother Mary is three, her parents take her to a temple, where she performs what we are supposed to consider a miracle, even though crawling up some steps doesn't seem so hot compared to healing the sick and raising the dead:

And there were about the temple, according to the fifteen Psalms of degrees, fifteen stairs to ascend. For the temple being built in a mountain, the altar of burnt offering, which was without, could not be come near but by stairs; The parents of the blessed Virgin and infant Mary put her upon one of these stairs; But while they were putting off their clothes, in which they had travelled, and according to custom putting on some that were more neat and clean, In the mean time the Virgin of the LORD in such a manner went up all the stairs one after another, without the help of any to lead or lift her, that any one would have judged from hence that she was of perfect age. Thus the LORD did, in the infancy of his Virgin, work this extraordinary work, and evidence by this miracle how great she was like to be hereafter. [4:2-7]

In chapter 7, Mary asks the angel Gabriel how the hell she's going to conceive while remaining a virgin. He replies: "For the Holy Ghost shall come upon you, and the power of the Most High shall overshadow you, without any of the heats of lust." [7:19]

5

Gospel of Thomas

In this book, Thomas the Israelite writes about the early life of Jesus.

And after certain days, as Jesus passed through the midst of the city, a certain child cast a stone at him and smote his shoulder. And Jesus said unto him: Thou shalt not finish thy course. And straightway he also fell down and died. And they that were there were amazed, saying: From whence is this child, that every word which he speaketh becometh a perfect work? But they also departed and accused Joseph, saying: Thou wilt not be able to dwell with us in this city: but if thou wilt, teach thy child to bless and not to curse: for verily he slayeth our children: and every thing that he saith becometh a perfect work. [4:1-2, Greek text B]

6

The Gospel of Mary

Supposedly written by Mary Magdalene, this book exists only in fragments.

Peter said to him, "Since you have now explained all things to us, tell us this: what is the sin of the world?" The Savior said, "Sin as such does not exist, but you make sin when you do what is of the nature of fornication, which is called 'sin.' For this reason the Good came into your midst, to the essence of each nature, to restore it to its root."

7

The First Gospel of the Infancy of Jesus Christ

Early verses from this Gnostic Gospel remind me of *Look Who's Talking* or the many commercials featuring talking babies:

He relates, that Jesus spake even when he was in the cradle, and said to his mother: Mary, I am Jesus the Son of God, that word which thou didst bring forth according to the declaration of the angel Gabriel to thee, and my father hath sent me for the salvation of the world. [1:2-3]

Soon we learn the fate of Jesus' foreskin:

And when the time of his circumcision was come, namely, the eighth day, on which the law commanded the child to be circumcised, they circumcised him in the cave. And the old Hebrew woman took the foreskin (others say she took the navel-string), and preserved it in an alabaster-box of old oil of spikenard. And she had a son who was a druggist, to whom she said, Take heed thou sell not this alabaster box of spikenard-ointment, although thou shouldst be, offered three hundred pence for it. Now this is that alabaster box which Mary the sinner procured, and poured forth the ointment out of it upon the head and the feet of our LORD Jesus Christ, and wiped it off with the hairs of her head. [2:1-4]

Later, baby Jesus is put on the back of a man whom a witch had turned into a mule, and he is cured, changing back into human form. The tiny savior then casts Satan out of a little boy named Judas Iscariot, who definitely would *not* return the favor about 30 years later. This Gospel says that Joseph was a pretty lousy carpenter, so Jesus would miraculously adjust the size and shape of "gates, or milk-pails, or sieves, or boxes" that his stepdad made.

8

Questions of Saint Bartholomew

And Bartholomew said: LORD, when thou wentest to be hanged upon the cross, I followed thee afar off and saw thee hung upon the cross, and the angels coming down from heaven and worshipping thee. And when there came darkness, I beheld, and I saw thee that thou wast vanished away from the cross and I heard only a voice in the parts under the earth, and great wailing and gnashing of teeth on a sudden. Tell me, LORD, whither wentest thou from the cross?

And Jesus answered and said: Blessed art thou, Bartholomew, my beloved, because thou sawest this mystery, and now will I tell thee all things whatsoever thou askest me. For when I vanished away from the cross, then went I down into Hades that I might bring up Adam and all them that were with him, according to the supplication of Michael the archangel. [1:6-9] ⏁

1. **Kirstie Alley** actor

2. **Anne Archer** actor

3. **Sonny Bono** singer,
   US Congressman

4. **Nancy Cartwright** actor
   (voice of Bart Simpson)

5. **Erika Christensen** actor

6. **Chick Corea** musician

7. **Tom Cruise** actor

8. **Penelope Cruz** actor

9. **Jenna Elfman** actor

10. **Isaac Hayes** soul musician

11. **Juliette Lewis** actor

12. **James Packer** heir to the vast
    fortune of his father, media baron
    Kerry Packer, Australia's richest man

13. **Lisa Marie Presley** singer

14. **Priscilla Presley** actor

15. **Mimi Rogers** actor

16. **Greta van Susteren** cable news
    personality

17. **John Travolta** actor

18. **Edgar Winter** musician

Honorable Mentions

The following celebs were apparently never heavily or formally involved with Scientology but took a course or two before moving on.

William Burroughs writer

Nicole Kidman actor

Demi Moore actor

Brad Pitt actor

J.D. Salinger writer

Jerry Seinfeld actor

Oliver Stone director

Sharon Stone actor

LIST 62 18 Celebrities Involved with the Church of Scientology

1. **Kenneth Anger** director

2. **Sammy Davis, Jr.** singer, actor

3. **King Diamond** musician

4. **Jayne Mansfield** actor

5. **Marilyn Manson** musician

6. **Keenan Wynn** actor

LIST **63** **6 Celebrities Involved with the Church of Satan**

Perhaps the most controversial practice of Mormonism is baptism by proxy, in which dead souls are baptized. Live Mormons stand in for the dead during the dunking ceremony. In this way, a person who didn't accept the Church of Jesus Christ of Latter-Day Saints while he or she was alive has a chance to do it in the hereafter. According to the *Deseret News*—a daily newspaper owned by the Mormon Church—literally "millions" of dead people have been baptized by proxy.

At the end of 2002, the Mormon Church promised to stop baptizing dead Jews. They had promised the same thing several years earlier, but the practice was found to be continuing, so they promised again.

1. **Abigail Adams**
2. **Menachem Begin**
3. **David Ben-Gurion**
4. **Napoleon Bonaparte**
5. **Eva Braun**
6. **James Buchanan**
7. **Buddha**
8. **Christopher Columbus**
9. **Albert Einstein**
10. **Dwight Eisenhower**
11. **St. Francis of Assisi**
12. **Anne Frank**
15. **Frederick the Great**
14. **Sigmund Freud**
15. **George Gordon, Lord Byron**
16. **Patrick Henry**
17. **Adolph Hitler**
18. **Thomas "Stonewall" Jackson**
19. **Joan of Arc**
20. **Ghengis Khan**
21. **Abraham Lincoln**
22. **Golda Meir**
23. **Paul Revere**
24. **William Shakespeare**
25. **Josef Stalin**
26. **Leo Tolstoy**
27. **Martin van Buren**
28. **Daniel Webster**
29. **William Wordsworth**
30-86. **all signers of the Declaration of Independence**
87+. **numerous Jews who died in the Holocaust** (figures cited range from 20,000 to 380,000)

LIST 64

87+ People Mormons Have Baptized by Proxy

1

August 13, 1984: 38-year-old John Blue was being baptized in a river, when he and the preacher fell into deeper water. Though the man of the cloth survived, God saw fit to smite Blue, who drowned.

2

November 2001: In Bordeaux, France, a young couple was laying flowers on the grave of their baby. With them were their two children, a seven-year-old girl and an eleven-year-old boy. A heavy stone cross fell from a tomb, landing on the little girl, who soon died of her injuries.

3

December 20, 2001: A 71-year-old priest was trying to close an iron gate, weighing several hundred pounds, in front of St. Agnes Church in San Francisco, when it slipped off its tracks and crushed him to death.

LIST

65

815 People Killed by Religious Rituals and Objects

4

February 10, 2002: While officiating Mass at St. Agnes Church in Midtown, New York (is Agnes cursed?), a priest had a massive coronary, fell backwards, and met his Maker. A fellow priest was quoted: "He was giving the homily at Mass and keeled over immediately."

5 6

Many people, especially children, have died during exorcisms. In January 2004, Atlanta police found the body of an eight-year-old girl who had been strangled, stabbed, and had her back broken in what police believe was a ritual to drive out demons. They arrested Christopher and Valerie Carey, charging them with the murder. The previous August in Milwaukee, an eight year-old autistic boy was smothered to death allegedly by a storefront preacher as he kneeled on the child's chest and tried to chase out demons for two hours. Minister Ray Hemphill has been charged.

7-815

1997-2004: During the annual pilgrimage to Mecca known as the hajj, Muslims have been trampled to death in recent years. This happens during a ritual late in the proceedings, in which pilgrims throw pebbles at pillars, symbolically stoning to death various devils. The crowd goes wild, a stampede ensues, and anywhere from a dozen to hundreds of people are stomped into pulp. Death tolls from recent years include 180 in 1998, 35 in 2001, and fourteen in 2003.

The body count skyrocketed in 2004— around 244 people died, with hundreds more injured. Hajj Minister Iyad Madani said: "All precautions were taken to prevent such an incident, but this is God's will."

The worst hajj disaster of recent times occurred in 1997, when a tent city went up in flames, prematurely sending 340 worshippers to Allah.

Honorable mentions

September 25, 2001. After attending Mass, Australian Catholic schoolgirls in Merryland, New South Wales, were waiting for a bus to take them back to school. A storm suddenly hit, and before they could scramble to shelter, lightning struck the ground nearby, knocking down six of them. One of the teens was in critical condition with flash burns, another was in serious condition with unspecified injuries, and the other four were being held for observation. The *Sydney Morning Herald* reported: "Ambulance officers said the girls were lucky it was not a direct strike, which probably would have killed them."

February 25, 2004: During the gory crucifixion scene in Mel Gibson's *The Passion of the Christ*, 56-year-old Peggy Scott suffered a heart attack and immediately died in a Wichita, Kansas theater. And let's not forget that lightning struck twice during the filming of *The Passion*. An assistant director was hit both times, and during the second strike, the main bolt nailed Jim Caviezel, the actor playing Jesus. Smoke reportedly came out of one of his ears. If that's not a sign, I don't know what is. ◻

2

John Davis, on trial for torturing his two sons—who were found scarred, malnourished, and underdeveloped—told the court: "Proverbs tells you to discipline your children, or else they will grow up and kill their parents. All I did was discipline them."

3

Glynn Harding is a serial mail-bomber who wounded a little girl and disfigured a woman. A report in the London *Daily Telegraph* states: "The court heard how the bomber attributed the start of his campaign to the stillbirth of his baby in March 2000 and its burial inside a jam jar. In the weeks that followed, said Mr Bould, he heard 'the voice of Jesus' instructing him to send 100 bombs 'to ensure that the baby was allowed to go from Hell to Heaven'."

4

Dan Lafferty, who is serving two consecutive life terms for viciously killing a young woman and her fifteen-month-old daughter, said: "I had a calm peacefulness when I did it. I was being led by the Spirit."

1

Jennifer R. Cisowski killed her eight-month-old son by repeatedly throwing him to the ground and then down a staircase. A newspaper reports:

> Cisowski told police that killing her son, Gideon Fusscas, was a test of faith because she expected God to resurrect him, a prosecutor said Tuesday evening....
>
> "Apparently the mother of the child was telling her sister, Tabitha, that this was a test of her faith and that Christopher, the father, was possessed by some sort of demon and she needed to pray over him and drive some kind of demon from him," [chief prosecutor Robert E.] Belanger said....
>
> "[Tabitha] came in and she saw the baby laying dead in the house, and her sister said ... that God was testing her faith by having her do harm to her child and she was convinced her child would be brought back from the dead like Lazarus," Belanger said.

LIST **66** | **12 Godly People**

He also explained: "I'm not going to offend God by saying something inappropriate like, 'I wish I'd never done it.' I'll never say that. If you're a child of God, it'll make sense to you someday. I'll never say I'm sorry I did it."

The *Salt Lake Tribune* reported: "When one angry sheriff's deputy confronted the convicted murderer about his lack of remorse, Lafferty calmly replied, 'With all due respect, if God asked me to, I'd kill you right now.'"

5

Greg Martin, an American living in Ireland, was sentenced to three months in jail for killing and butchering his horse with an ax in an act that the judge called "absolute, wanton cruelty." Martin was upset because the mare had been eating a neighbor's grass. His defense: "The Bible says man has dominion over animals."

6

As reported by the BBC: "The police in Bangladesh say they have arrested a young Muslim cleric for allegedly killing his own son in a ritual sacrifice during Eid ul-Adha, the biggest Muslim festival. They say the cleric, **Golam Mustafa**, admitted to having killed the seven-month-old boy, Sulayman, after receiving what he called a revelation."

7

Lucille Poulin, a 78-year-old former nun and the spiritual leader of a commune on Prince Edward Island, Canada, was sentenced to eight years in jail for frequently beating five children, ages seven to twelve, who were in her care. The *Toronto Star* reported:

> Earlier in the day, a defiant Poulin told [Judge] Jenkins the blood of the children she assaulted is not on her hands. The self-described prophet of the commune near Summerside asked for the court's mercy but never said she was sorry for the pain and suffering she inflicted on the five youngsters. Poulin said God told her it was all right to punish children physically to drive out the devil.

8 9

Two Rastafarians attacked worshippers in a Catholic Church in the Caribbean island St. Lucia. One doused them with gas, while another set them aflame with a blowtorch. They also burned the priest, attacked people with machetes, and killed a nun. According to the Associated Press, the two men responsible "told police they were sent by God to combat corruption in the Roman Catholic Church. 'The way they're talking is that the world is going to end and that the time had come for what they had to do,' police Inspector Gregory Montoute, who interrogated the men, said Monday."

10

Angel Maturino Resendiz, the Mexican drifter who killed nine people in the US before turning himself in to authorities in July 1999, said: "I had to kill them. I could say I'm sorry, but I wouldn't mean it. They were promoting something that it clearly states in the Bible is wrong." (According to the British newswire Ananova, "Resendiz claimed he was on a mission from God to kill people who he said were 'evil' by stopping the spread of sins such as abortion, homo-sexuality and witchcraft.")

11

Andrea Yates, who famously drowned all five of her children in Texas, told a court-appoint-ed shrink: "It was the seventh deadly sin. My children weren't righteous. They stumbled because I was evil. The way I was raising them they could never be saved.... Better for someone else to tie a millstone around their neck and cast them in a river than stumble. They were going to perish."

12

And then there's this APBnews.com report from Florida: "Outraged that her 7-year-old son refused to go to Sunday school, a sin-gle mother allegedly tried to burn the boy to death in a bedroom, police said." A little later that day, she attempted to choke him with a belt. ☐

1 "Beware of the man whose god is in the skies."
–George Bernard Shaw

2 "In every country and in every age, the priest has been hostile to liberty. He is always in alliance with the despot, abetting his abuses in return for protection to his own."
–Thomas Jefferson

3 "A people who despise sex must also despise their god."
–Beth Brant

4 "Belief is messy, a violence that pushes life around into categories, choosing from infinite realities this truth or that."
–Robin Podolsky

5 "I believe that religion, generally speaking, has been a curse to mankind—that its modest and greatly overestimated services on the ethical side have been more than overcome by the damage it has done to clear and honest thinking."
–H.L. Mencken

6 "A few years ago we finally persuaded psychiatrists to remove homosexuality from the list of recognized mental disorders. Maybe it's time we started lobbying them to add belief in God to the list. Belief in an angry, intolerant one, anyway....

"I demand assurances that a given religion will not cause or potentiate mass homicidal psychosis or priestly pedophilia, before we let it indoctrinate helpless children and vulnerable adults. Bloodthirsty, authoritarian theology threatens Canada as much as tobacco, obesity and booze put together. It endangers our planet more than global warming, nuclear winter or rogue asteroids."
–Spider Robinson (Hugo- and Nebula-winning science fiction author)

7 "We must respect the other fellow's religion, but only in the sense and to the extent that we respect his theory that his wife is beautiful and his children smart."
–H.L. Mencken

8 "I not only maintain that all religions are versions of the same untruth, but I hold that the influence of churches, and the effect of religious belief, is positively harmful."
–Christopher Hitchens

9 "Hell is paved with priests' skulls."
–Saint John Chrysostom (347-407)

LIST 67 | 9 Religious Quotes

+ Movies, Music, and Pulp Fiction

1

Dolorita in the Passion Dance (1894)

Showing that film censorship is almost as old as film itself, this titillating little number was excommunicated from New Jersey after being shown in peepshows on the Atlantic City Boardwalk. The three-volume reference work *Censorship* says the film "was probably the first to be banned in the United States."

2

Reenactment of the Massacre at Wounded Knee (1906)

William Cody, better known as "Buffalo Bill," had been reenacting Wild West life—with a ten-gallon hatful of poetic license—in his traveling shows. When he decided to film a staging of the 1890 massacre of Native Americans at Wounded Knee, South Dakota, he enlisted the help of the US government. According to *Censorship*, the feds weren't too happy with the result, which displayed some sympathy for the slaughtered Indians, so they shelved the footage, permanently.

3

The Birth of a Nation (1915)

"The most banned film in American history," according to *The Encyclopedia of Censorship*. D.W. Griffith's racist, pro-KKK look at the Civil War and Reconstruction was outlawed in Ohio, Colorado, Boston, Pittsburgh, and dozens of other jurisdictions.

4

Birth Control (1917)

This lightly fictionalized film about eugenicist Margaret Sanger's quest to tell poor women about contraception in the face of suppression was banned by New York's film censor. It was written by and starred Sanger, who later founded the organizations that would become Planned Parenthood.

5

Scarface (1932)

The original, non-Pacino version of Al Capone's life—directed by Howard Hawks and produced by Howard Hughes—was

LIST 68 — 16 Movies Banned in the U.S.

banned in five states, including New York, and five cities, including Seattle and Chicago, owing to its violence and/or supposed glorification of crime.

6

Two-faced Woman (1941)

Greta Garbo's swan song was banned in New York City and elsewhere because of its theme of adultery.

7

Let There Be Light (1946)

Legendary director John Huston (*The African Queen*, *The Maltese Falcon*, etc.) made documentaries for the Army during the WWII era. The final one, *Let There Be Light*, focused on shell-shocked soldiers being treated at a Long Island Hospital. The Army confiscated the film and refused to release it, citing violation of the doughboys' privacy, although Huston was convinced it was pulled for PR reasons. It was finally screened in 1981.

8

The Vanishing Prairie (1956)

Censorship describes this idiotic incident succinctly: "Walt Disney's *The Vanishing Prairie*, an Academy Award-winning documentary, was banned in New York because it showed a buffalo giving birth; an American Civil Liberties Union complaint led to a reversal of the ban."

9

Titicut Follies (1967)

Director Frederick Wiseman was granted legal access to the State Prison for the Criminally Insane in Bridgewater, Massachusetts, for a month in 1966. He and his crew filmed scenes of mind-bruising degradation and sadness. Almost predictably, state officials went apeshit when they saw the final cut of *Titicut Follies*, and a Superior Court judge blocked the film's release.

The authorities charged that the documentary violated the inmates' privacy. Perhaps it did, but it's telling that they were suddenly so concerned about the privacy rights of the prisoners, while still uninterested in their human rights, which were obviously in a state of constant violation, as captured on film. The Massachusetts Supreme Court partially overturned the ruling, allowing the film to be screened only for doctors, sociologists, judges, and others who would have a professional interest in the subject. The Supreme Court refused to hear Wiseman's appeal of this unprecedented restriction, and there the matter stood until 1991, when a Massachusetts Superior Court judge dropped all restraints. Two years later, the documentary was aired a single time on public television. It has never been broadcast again, nor has it been released on video.

10

I Am Curious—Yellow (1967)

This Swedish hippie/art movie with explicit sex scenes was refused entry into the US by Customs. An appeals court slapped down the import ban, but then fifteen states barred it from their theaters.

11
Blue Movie (1969)

Also called *Fuck*, Andy Warhol's movie was banned as obscene by a New York criminal court, a ruling that was upheld on appeal.

12
Deep Throat (1972)

One of the first hardcore porno features, and still the most famous, *Deep Throat* was outlawed in 23 states, and the feds convicted a bunch of people, including starring penis Harry Reems, involved with its distribution. All convictions were later overturned.

13
Superstar: The Karen Carpenter Story (1987)

This unauthorized biopic is a double whammy. Todd Haynes used Barbie dolls as the "actors" with the Carpenters' recordings as the soundtrack. The only question was whether Richard Carpenter or Mattel would be the one to permanently block this film's release. It was Carpenter.

14
The Making of "Monsters" (1990)

John Greyson's short feature about gay-bashing includes an unauthorized, reworked version of "Mack the Knife," a gigantic hit for Bobby Darin and Louis Armstrong. The estate of the song's writer, Kurt Weill, had the movie pulled from circulation.

15
The Profit (2001)

Peter N. Alexander's movie follows the rise of a paranoid cult leader and his organization, obviously based on L. Ron Hubbard and the Church of Scientology. According to Alexander, Scientologists interfered with this movie at every step of the way. Lawyers and spokespeople for the Church professed that the movie bore absolutely no resemblance to Scientology, then turned around and sued the filmmakers after it had been showing for a few weeks. The Church claims that the only reason the movie was made was to taint the jury pool in a trial over the shadowy death of Lisa McPherson, a member of the Church. A Pinellas County Florida Judge apparently agreed and blocked the film from further release. The litigation continues.....

16
Ernest and Bertram (2002)

Described by *The Advocate* as "a retelling, in eight minutes, of Lillian Hellman's classic play of unrequited gay love, *The Children's Hour*, using the *Sesame Street* characters Bert and Ernie," Peter Spears' short film showed at several film festivals (including Sundance), but soon the Sesame Workshop made sure it would never flicker on a screen again. Another film by Spears, the 37-minute *Scream, Teen, Scream*, also met death by intellectual property law, this time over the song "Love Rollercoaster." ◘

1

Genetic music

The idea here is to take a sequence of DNA—whether a fragment, a gene, an amino acid, a protein—assign a musical characteristic (such as pitch, chord type, voice, or even a note) to various aspects of a mapped strand (bases, amino acids, molecular weight, light absorption frequencies, etc.), and then play the resulting composition.

David W. Deamer is a pioneer in the field, having created DNA music since the early 1980s. Using some simple rules, he started playing gene sequences on his piano. The first portion of human DNA he tried resembled a waltz; the insulin protein sounds like an Irish jig. Deamer currently has two albums available, with composer Riley McLaughlin.

More recently, Alexandra Pajak, a biology and music major at Agnes Scott College (Decatur, Georgia), created two works—a symphony based on the DNA of the school's founder and a CD of eight synthesized compositions, each one derived from a gene, including that of the Herpes B virus.

Other genetic musicians include Henry Alan Hargrove (*A Splash of Life*), Munakata Nobuo ("Duet of AIDS"), Susan Alexjander (*Sequencia*), John Dunn and K.W. Bridges ("Squid Eye Lens," "Scorpion Stinger," and "Slime Mold"), M.A. Clark and John Dunn (*Life Music*), Peter Gena and Charles Strom ("Collagen and Bass Clarinet"), Linda Long ("Calcium Chimes"), Aurora Sánchez Sousa (*Genoma Music*), and Larry Lang ("Oxy Fugue 9").

2

Other body music

DNA is the most popular basis for bodily music, but many others exist. In 2003, at a live event called "DECONcert: Music in the Key of EEG," 50 people were simultaneously hooked up to machines that made music out of their brain activity. Also, genetic musician John Dunn has created the fifteen-minute composition "Theta Music" from brainwaves (it's available on his self-published album *Algorithmic Music*). As you might imagine, full albums of gray matter music are few and far between; a couple include *Cerebral Disturbance* by Aube and the 1976 compilation *Brainwave Music*.

10 Unusual Forms and Genres of Music

In a small study at the University of Toronto, scientists measured the brainwaves of insomniacs, then had a computer translate the measurements into sound that was sometimes melodious, sometimes cacophonic. Listening to these CDs, the subjects fell asleep significantly faster and stayed asleep significantly longer than subjects who listened to *other* people's brainwaves.

A number of albums designed to put babies to sleep (they're said to work on adults, too) incorporate sounds based on heartbeats. At least one series—*Heartbeat Music Therapy* by Terry Woodford—uses an actual human heartbeat as gentle percussion for the lullabies.

Galvonic skin response (GSR) measures electrical activity of the skin, and is believed to reflect a person's internal state, particularly the actions of the parasympathetic nervous system. Several hardware-software devices, including Mental Games by Mind Modulations, will translate your GSR readings into music.

Beyond these forms, the trail goes pretty cold, with just fleeting references to music based on pulse, respiration, and other bodily activities or measurements of those activities. This is definitely a ripe area—practically *terra incognita*—for musicians to explore.

3

Plant music

"Sound ecologist" Michael Prime created the album *L-fields* by reading the bioelectric signals from plants, then feeding them into an oscillator. The All Music Guide says: "Prime later compresses, overlays, and integrates sounds from the surrounding environment to the signal and voilà: through a work aesthetically close to electroacoustics, the listener is invited to hear a plant live its life!" The three performers he chose are very telling: marijuana, peyote, and fly agaric mushrooms. Prime did similar things with fruit on David Toop's album *Museum of Fruit*.

Likewise, after measuring the electrical vibes given off by plants, Michael Theroux arranged the resulting sounds into musical compositions on the album *Plant Tones*.

Biochemist Linda Long creates compositions by transcribing 3-D models of proteins in parsley and other plants into music, making her work essentially a subgenre of genetic music (item #2, above).

Stretching the genre of plant music to its limit is the First Vienna Vegetable Orchestra, which jams on nothing but musical instruments made out of vegetables (with a few kitchen implements, such as a blender, thrown into the mix). Some of the instruments are simple, such as a tomato or turnip that gets thumped for percussion, but often they're more complex, like the wind instruments carved out of carrots, celery, and cucumbers, or the marimbas made out of radishes. The group's website says that their "musical spectrum ranges from traditional african pieces to classical european concert music through to experimental electronic music."

The eight musicians perform one or two concerts a month. After each performance, the group's chef chops and cooks the instruments, which the audience and band members then munch. If you can't make it to Europe, you can always buy their two CDs (meal not included).

4

Math music

Math was never my strong suit, so the ways that various numbers, constants, formulae, etc. are translated into music flies several thousand feet over my head. But it sure sounds purty. The largest subgenre is undoubtedly fractal music, though Daniel Cummerow has made compositions from trigonometric functions, prime numbers, and the Fibonacci sequence, among others.

In the Pi Project, over two-dozen musicians created compositions directly based on the ratio of a circle's circumference to its diameter. You know: π (3.141592....). Basically, any aspect of music that can be expressed as pi was employed—frequency, pitch, measure, etc. Others chose to take graphic representations of pi—either the Greek letter itself or the endless string of numbers that is pi—and convert them into sound

through various means. Each piece is exactly three minutes and fourteen seconds long.

On an even more complex level, classical composer Iannis Xenakis (1922-2001) applied calculus, probability, game theory, Boolean algebra, set theory, and other brain-crushing forms of mathematics to his work, which is regarded as some of the finest orchestral music of the twentieth century.

5

Underwater music

Michel Redolfi is the Neptune of underwater music. His album *Sonic Waters* contains original electronic music recorded in pools and the Pacific Ocean. The follow-up, *Sonic Waters #2: Underwater Music, 1983-1989*, showcases soundscapes derived from natural noises recorded by submerged microphones. In his concerts, Redolfi—while on land—plays his music, which is broadcast on nearby speakers that are completely underwater. Landlubbers hear nothing; you must put at least your head into the drink in order to hear the songs. Redolfi has even written an opera meant to be sung by performers encased in specially-designed bubbles at the bottom of the sea, and vibraphone virtuoso Alex Grillo has been known to team up with him for live sets *performed* underwater.

Jim Nollman—by virtue of the fact that he plays music with whales—is a *de facto* underwater musician. His live guitarwork is piped through speakers suspended under a boat. Through a hydrophone, he hears the cetaceans answer him. He then responds musically, and an underwater, interspecies jam session occurs. As part of the same series of experiments, chanting Tibetan monks and a reggae band have also had two-way musical encounters with the whales.

6

Palindromic music

"Palindrome" usually refers to a word or sentence that reads the same backwards as forwards: *mom*, *dad*, "Do geese see God?" But anything composed of discrete units, such as music, can be a palindrome. Classic composers including Mozart, Bach, and Haydn created pieces in which time, pitch, and/or melody was reversed at some point (a trick called a "crab canon").

According to the Wikipedia: "The Icelandic music-band Sigur Rós composed a song ["Staralfur"] on their album *Ágætis Byrjun*, which partly sounds the same, playing forwards or backwards. Not only symmetric from the notes, but also symmetric in the sound by mixing the reverse music over the original…. The interlude from Alban Berg's opera, *Lulu* is a palindrome."

College radio staple They Might Be Giants has a song called "I Palindrome I" in which one verse is a word-by-word (but not letter-by-letter) palindrome:

> "Son, I am able," she said, "though you scare me."
> "Watch," said I.
> "Beloved," I said, "watch me scare you, though."
> Said she, "Able am I, son."

7

Toy instruments

The shtick for Pianosaurus, a trio from New York State, was that they played pop-rock on kiddie instruments bought at toy stores. Their only studio album, *Groovy Neighborhood*, includes covers of Chuck Berry's "Memphis" and John Lee Hooker's "Dimples."

Although their complete devotion to plinky pianos and Smurf drums is unique, other bands before and after have occasionally taken the same approach. Indie-rockers Self released an all-toy album in 2000, *Gizmodgery* (with an explicit lyrics warning sticker) replete with Mattel Star Guitar, a See 'n Say, Little Tykes Xylophone, talking stuffed animals, beeping robots, baby rattles, etc. None other than the Rolling Stones pioneered the approach, when Charlie Watts played a 1930s toy drum kit on the band's rowdy "Street Fighting Man."

Outside of rock and roll, avant garde pianist Margaret Leng Tan is billed by one of her record labels as "the world's only professional toy pianist." She plays the full-size version of the instrument, as well the string piano, but it's her 1997 album *The Art of the Toy Piano*, plus assorted shorter works, that earns her a spot on the list. Tan has played compositions by Philip Glass, Beethoven, Lennon-McCartney, and John Cage (his 1948 "Suite for Toy Piano" is "the first 'serious' piece ever written for" the instrument, according to Tan).

8

Corporate anthems

Companies have always sought to motivate employees, and some of them go to lengths far beyond taping up signs that say, "TEAM = Together Everyone Achieves More." One such method is to infect workers' minds with a song that practically deifies the corporation. IBM was an early—if not the earliest—pioneer of these efforts. The 1931 edition of "Songs of the I.B.M." has been reproduced online, and it contains such mind-numbing propaganda as "Ever Onward":

> Ever onward! Ever onward!
> That's the spirit that has brought us fame.
> We're big but bigger we will be,
> We can't fail for all can see,
> That to serve humanity
> Has been our aim.
> Our products now are known
> In every zone.
> Our reputation sparkles
> Like a gem.

Despite such a long track record, the existence of corporate anthems only hit the mass mind in spring 2001, when Chris Raettig started a little website to collect these capitalist ditties. Soon the site was swamped with visitors, who were downloading the songs by the thousand, over a gigabyte of material every hour. The jingle that first caught Raettig's attention was written for a European conference of international accounting firm KPMG's consultants. For simpleminded cheesiness, most of the lyrics would embarrass Barney the Dinosaur. The chorus goes: "KPMG—a team of power and energy. We go for the gold. Together we hold

to a vision of global strategy." Another line actually declared: "We'll be number one, with effort and fun." The song was remixed by amused Netizens into jungle, hard rock, industrial, and Nokia ringtone versions.

Not to be outdone, accounting firm PricewaterhouseCoopers commissioned a tune with the lyrics: "We don't sell no dogma. All we've got is skill. Doing each and every client's will." "Global Technology" by Deutsche Bank contains this bit of doggerel: "Global technology is no easy game to play. A new challenge for all of us, every day."

In perhaps the most ill-advised move in corporate music history, "Internet solutions provider" Asera wanted to kick it old-school style, so they chose to make "Asera Everywhere" into a rap song:

> Yo! Homeboys, homegirls, gather 'round.
> We're poppin' it, kickin' it, gettin' down.
> We're hot, we're bad, we're lean and mean.
> We're takin' control of the e-biz scene.

Other corporations who took the dive into sonic drivel include Ericsson, Novell, GE, Honeywell, and Ernst & Young. The fad of collecting and listening to corporate songs died rapidly, but companies are surely still making such numbers under the radar.

9

One-man bands

Being able to play two or more instruments at once is a musical tradition that has been much overlooked. Sure, guys like Prince,

Paul McCartney, Trent Reznor, and Dave Grohl have played all the instruments on some of their albums, but did they play them all *at the same time*? I think not.

The earliest known references to simultaneously playing two instruments come from Iceland in the eleventh century. In the journal *Musical Traditions*, Hal Rammel writes:

> [I]t was in vaudeville and the music hall, a setting that encouraged the unique and unforgettable performer, that the one-man band flowered in its wildest varieties. Ragtime composer Wilbur Sweatman in the early 1900s did a vaudeville act playing three clarinets at once and Vick Hyde, a vaudevillian of the 1940s did his finale playing three trumpets at the same time and twirling a baton as he exited the stage. Virtuoso Violinsky concluded his act with a piano-cello duet by fastening a bow to his right knee while his right hand fingered the strings, leaving his left hand to accompany himself on the piano. The piano, generally thought to be a two-handed instrument was played with only the right hand by Paul Seminole in the 1920s while he played guitar with his left, and for jazz musician and comedian Slim Gaillard playing the piano and guitar at the same time was possible by turning up the volume on his electric guitar "...it'll play itself—you just make the chords and hit the strings, feedback!"

This almost unrecognized musical genre is alive and well. In Boston, Eric Royer comprises the totality of Royer's One Man Band. He plays traditional bluegrass with a banjo in his hands, a dobro (related to the slide guitar) across his lap, an acoustic guitar at his feet (he built the contraption that allows him to play it footsie-style), and a harmonica held to his mouth by a brace. Royer has released five albums, including *Barefoot Breakdown* and *Bluegrass Contraption*. Alternative music mag *The Noise* believes that his music sounds "more blended than most five piece bluegrass bands."

If you think playing a guitar with your feet is impressive, you ain't heard nothing yet. Choctaw one-man band Joe Barrick built a device that allows him to use his tootsies to play guitar, bass guitar, banjo, and snare drum at the same time. With his hands he works a double-necked instrument (also his own creation) that is half mandolin, half guitar, sometimes switching to a fiddle. Around his neck is that staple of one-man bands, the harmonica. That's a total of six or seven instruments, plus vocals, simultaneously.

Hasil Adkins, according to his official website, has been playing "true lonesome country, hopped up blues, and boogie woogie rockabilly nonstop since 1949." As of early 2004, he's *still* touring. Considered the progenitor of the psychobilly genre, Adkins wails on an untold number of instruments at once. He claims to play piano and organ with his elbows, and on some tracks he can be heard somehow playing spoons.

Some purists feel that a *true* one-man band not only plays at least three instruments at once, but must be able to remain mobile while cranking out the jams. Among this extremely rare breed is Australian industrial designer and jazz musician Tom Nicolson, who walks around playing banjo, bass drum, cymbals, kazoo, and whistles, while singing.

Animal music

Humans aren't the only animals that make music. Birds and whales are known for their beautiful songs, and they've supplied the content for many "sounds of nature" albums. Recordings of other life forms in the act of singing are harder to come by, but they're around. The bland title *Animal Music* masks the fact that this album of a team of sled dogs howling together is quite a stunner. A German reviewer marvels: "The chorus of dogs definitely seems to have its lead vocalists and harmonizers and after a while one can hear the motifs of the leading parts being expressed in stretto as though in a fugue, but then also inverted and even, dare I say, in retrograde form."

At times, humans have attempted to incorporate animal sounds into their music. Mozart swiped some melodies from his pet bird. The Paul Winter Consort played with animal sounds, and on the hopelessly obscure Euro-album *Bugs & Beats & Beasts: Natural Techno*, Ammer & Console go heavy on the insect sounds and light on the artificial music.

Graeme Revell—cofounder of the experimental German performance group/band SPK—created *The Insect Musicians*, an album built on the sounds made by crickets, grasshoppers, cicadae, beetles, flies, gnats, wasps, bees, and moths. In many cases, the creepy-crawlies make noises that are inaudible to humans, but through the magic of technology, Revell has brought these hidden sounds to our limited ears. The liner notes of the album explain:

> I thus chose to make Volume I of The Insect Musicians a series of vignettes of a multicultural nature.
>
> Each traces a development from the raw sound to its digital transformation and its position in the musical structure. At most 8 different sounds are used in one piece, the better for the ear to trace the modification and its development as syntactic and semantic component in musical organisation. Some sounds (the scrapes & clicks) lend themselves more to rhythm, whilst those more tonal (chirps & buzzes) to melody. I have tried to remain faithful to the essential "nature" of each sound, and where possible to use an insect native to a particular continent in the context of a musical theme based on the ethnic music of that continent.

On the album *Natural Rhythms* by Ancient Futures, musicians including Michael Morfort play with frogs in Bali and Cali. The album *Experimental Musical Instruments: Early Years* has a similar track on it in which the aforementioned Jim Nollman (see item #5) plays guitar with a group of whales.

Similarly, the avant-garde/jazz pianist-composer Kirk Nurock has used vocalizations, didgeridoo, and piano to coax dogs, cats, guinea pigs, wolves, sea lions, an owl, and other animals into making yips, howls, squeals, and other noises. He only chooses to work with the individuals who have the most melodic and interesting vocalizations. His live compositions include "Sonata for Piano and Dog," "The Bronx Zoo Events," and the three-dog, 20-human chorus of

"Howl," performed at Carnegie Hall. He's currently working on a CD in which jazz musicians and various furry or feathered creatures improvise with each other.

Another form of animal music—probably the rarest—occurs when the critters play instruments, either manmade or improvised. At one point, circuses—including Barnum and Bailey—featured "elephant bands," but no recordings appear to be extant. At least one entire album of pachyderm music is available—*Thai Elephant Orchestra*. In it, six young elephants at a conservation center in Thailand play *renats* (similar to a xylophone), a bow bass, slit drums, and a gong, while sometimes trumpeting with their trunks. Beforehand, David Soldier—founder of Mulatta Records, the label that released the tusked ones' album—thought he'd have to sample the sounds the elephants made, then mix them into a human composition. Turns out the elephants were so musically inclined that the tracks are exactly as they were performed live. Soldier played the songs blind for many people, who all thought they were performed by *homo sapiens*. A critic at the *New York Times* even named chamber music groups who play near Lincoln Center as the likely performers!

A *New York Times* critic—who knew the true source of the music—wrote: "The players improvise distinct meters and melodic lines, and vary and repeat them. The results, at once meditative and deliberate, delicate and insistently thrumming, strike some Western listeners as haunting, others as monotonous." *The Economist* remarked: "They clearly have a strong sense of rhythm. They flap their ears to the beat, swish their tails and generally rock back and forth."

One of the few other such recordings is "Monkey Business"—the first cut on the epic percussion box-set *The Big Bang*—in which leading nature-recorder Bernie Krause caught chimps making excited guttural sounds and beating on trees in the rain forest. It sure sounds like they're trying to make music. ◻

Unusual Band #1

Burqa Band

This trio of Muslim women is known to have performed only once. Sometime during the summer of 2003, a German music producer and his colleagues were running a workshop in Kabul to reintroduce Afghans to their musical heritage. They asked the only female in attendance, their translator, if she'd like to play drums. On the spur of the moment, she and two friends donned their blue burqas and banged out a rock song, with the translator on skins, another woman on bass, and a third singing in English: "You give me all your love, you give me all your kisses, and then you touch my burqa, and don't know who it is." Agence France-Presse reports: "All that remains of the ephemeral alliance of the Burqa and rock is an amateur video clip and a song remixed by Berlin DJ Barbara Morgenstern which has become a modest summer-time favourite [in Germany]."

1

An Oakland band formed in 1993, **Fuck** has a name that may make you think of death metal or industrial noise, though they're actually an alt pop/rock band along the lines of The Church and Belly. (Incidentally, when KISS was getting started, they considered naming the band Fuck.)

2

With two women and two men, **Nashville Pussy** sounds like its name—loud, harsh, and rude. Two years after forming (in Georgia, not Tennessee), they released their debut album: *Let Them Eat Pussy*.

3

Not surprisingly, the grindcore band **Anal Cunt** trafficks in extremely dark, obscene humor. Their songs rarely last more than a minute, meaning you get 50 to 60 cuts per album. With titles like "Jack Kevorkian Is Cool," "I Became a Counselor So I Could Tell Rape Victims They Asked for It," "Recycling Is Gay," "I Sent Concentration Camp Footage to America's Funniest Home Videos," "I Fucked Your Wife," and "You're Pregnant, So I Kicked You in the Stomach," maybe brevity is a good thing.

LIST 70 — 19 Profanely-Named Bands

4

Songs by the experimental industrial band **Tit Wrench** include "Corporate Sponsored Sex Change Operation," "Everybodily Orifice Needs School Prayer," "Stomach Lining of God," "Pit Bull With AIDS," and "Cops Hate Firemen."

5

The punk band **Schlong** ground out such ditties as "I Wanna Scratch My Butt," but they're best known for their cover album *Punk Side Story*, which gives the entire classic musical *West Side Story* a loud, debauched makeover.

6

Just as Nine Inch Nails is really Trent Reznor, the "band" **Prick** is simply Kevin McMahon. Its only full-length album—produced and released by Reznor—failed to make a dent, just a prick.

7

Heavy metal band **3 Way Cum** released only one album, 1997's *Killing the Life*.

8-19

The most oft-used profanity in band names is "bitch," hands down. Two bands use the word as their full name, and are joined by **Bitch Magnet**, **Bitch Alert**, **Bitchcraft**, **Bitch & Animal**, **Anvil Bitch**, **Son of a Bitch**, **Psycho Bitch**, **Southern Bitch**, **Little Bo Bitch**, **7 Year Bitch**, and others.

Several bands have names that are raunchy only if you're in on the joke. **Steely Dan** is named after an industrial-strength dildo in William Burroughs' *Naked Lunch*. At least three band names are references to cum—the **Lovin' Spoonful** and **10cc** (both reflect the amount in a typical ejaculation), and **Thin White Rope** (another Burroughsism). Although I've never heard anything to support the idea, I wonder if **Pearl Jam** doesn't also fall into this category.

Richard Metzger, the creative director of The Disinformation Company (the publisher of this book), relates that he was once a part of a punk band called **Jizz Janitors**. ◻

Unusual Band # 2

The Transplant Band
This musical outfit is/was comprised of organ transplant surgeons. The cover of their album, Gift of Life, *shows four guitar cases covered in stickers bearing slogans such as, "Recycle Yourself." (They're not to be confused with a band of the same name that plays at fundraisers for organ transplants. That band's founder, heart recipient Robert Seeback, is apparently the only member with direct transplant experience.)*

1. **Ababeal** (death metal)

2. **Alookal**

3. **Amertad**

4. **Arteebun**

5. **Black Blooms**

6. **Fanoos**

7. **Fara**

8. **Fat Rats** (punk)

9. **Hack**

10. **Khak**

11. **Kharazmi** (Gothic trance)

12. **Kooch**

13. **Kuarash** (acid jazz)

14. **Lunatics on the Grass**

15. **Mud**

16. **Namjoo**

17. **Nefrin** (reggae-pop)

18. **Oolan Batoor**

19. **Saar**

20. **Soma**

21. **Stainless Steel**

22. **StoNail**

23. **The Angels of Hell**

24. **Uzima**

25. **Xakestar**

Unusual Band # 3

Rondellus
The Estonian band Rondellus plays music of the Middle Ages and the Renaissance on period instruments, such as the lute, harp, and hurdy-gurdy. That's not terribly unusual, but what earns them a spot in the book is their fourth album—Sabbatum, an entire disc of Black Sabbath songs recorded on medieval instruments and sung in Latin. I can only imagine a perplexed Ozzy Osbourne listening to "Verres Militares" ("War Pigs") and "Oculi Filioli" ("Junior's Eyes").

LIST 71

25 Iranian Rock Bands

Pulp novels, printed on dirt-cheap paper (hence, the name) and selling for a trifle, are an extinct genre of American writing/publishing. The golden age of the pulps was pretty much 1945 to 1955, but they were around for over a decade before and after this period. A tiny portion of this throwaway lit is still remembered and read today; Louis Lamour, Dashiell Hammet, H.P. Lovecraft, and Ian Fleming are among the few pulpsters who rose above the genre. But they wrote pulp that is still acceptable "genre fiction"—science fiction, horror, Westerns, spy novels, mystery fiction, etc.

What have been almost completely forgotten (except by collectors, bibliophiles, and pulp cultists) are the exploitation pulps that dealt with sex (orgies, adulterous spouses, homosexuality, promiscuous women, etc.), drugs, and violence, sometimes in combination, almost always with as much sensationalism as possible. Sure, 98 percent of the writing was hackneyed and the content didn't live up to its titillating promise, but those lurid titles, taglines, and covers are worthy of immortality.

1. ***AC-DC Stud***
   author: J.X. Williams
   tagline: "A lover and his lady…and his laddie!"

2. ***Acid Orgy***
   author: Tony Calvano
   tagline: "Psychedelic sin-trippers…way out and wanton!"

3. ***All on Sunday***
   author: Don Elliott (pseudonym of Robert Silverberg)
   tagline: "The family shame was their only fame!"

4. ***Basement Game***
   tagline: "Your children know—but they won't tell you!"

5. ***Beatnik Wanton***
   author: Don Elliott
   tagline: "She lusted in sin orgies and reefer brawls!"

6. ***Blondes Are Skin Deep***
   author: Louis Trimble

7. ***Boss Lady***
   author: Ursula Grant
   tagline: "How could she expect a teenage stock-boy to sense her shameless need and shocking desires?"

LIST **72**

56 Pulp Novels

8. ***By Love Depraved***
   author: Arthur Adlon
   tagline: "Portraying the frightening
   spread of lesbianism among the
   white women of modern-day Africa."

9. ***Call South 3300: Ask for Molly!***
   author: Orrie Hitt
   tagline: "A candid novel that takes
   you behind the scenes at those
   sales conventions!"

10. ***Campus Kittens***
    author: Joan Ellis

11. ***Chain Gang***
    author: Don Holliday
    tagline: "Their sins were the shame
    of a changing society!"

12. ***The Cheaters***
    author: Orrie Hitt
    tagline: "Can an unhappy wife be a
    happy mistress?"

13. ***Farm Girl***
    author: Anneke de Lange
    tagline: "She lived like a wicked,
    little animal."

14. ***Freakout on Sunset Strip***
    author: Nick Rogers
    tagline: "Fags, freaks and the famous
    turn the street into a hippie hell."

15. ***Go Down, Aaron***
    author: Chris Davidson
    tagline: "Third-sex slave to the Third
    Reich's brutal lust!"

16. ***H is for Heroin***
    author: David Hulburd
    tagline: "A teenage narcotic tells
    her story."

17. ***High School Jungle***
    author: Alex Carter
    tagline: "Debbie's date in the park
    turned into gang rape… And her
    friends wouldn't let her forget…"

18. ***Hill Billy in High Heels***
    author: Jeff Boga
    tagline: "She was sixteen…and true
    to the code of the hills…ripe for love!"

19. ***Home to Harlem***
    author: Claude McKay
    tagline: "Love was cheap and life
    was high in the torrid zone of 'little
    old' New York."

20. ***Hypno-Sin***
    author: J.X. Williams
    tagline: "You feel very, very…sexy!"

21. ***If the Coffin Fits***
    author: Day Keene

22. ***Into Plutonian Depths***
    author: Stanton A. Coblentz
    tagline: "An exciting science-fiction
    novel of a world with three sexes
    on a faraway planet!"

23. ***It's My Funeral***
    author: Peter Rabe
    tagline: "Never give a killer an even
    break—shoot first and the blonde's
    all yours."

24. ***Jailbait***
    author: Jason Hytes
    tagline: "She wouldn't stay out of
    his bed…no matter what he said
    or did to her!"

25. ***King of New Lesbos***
    author: Curt Aldrich
    tagline: "Every man's day dream
    came true for him!"

26. ***Kiss My Fist!***
    author: James Hadley Chase

27. ***The Leather Girls***
    author: Una Mujer
    tagline: "She had the face of an angel,
    the body of a devil—and the passions
    of a lesbian!"

28. **Lez on Wheels**
    author: Dan Rader
    tagline: "They were she-studs in a free-wheeling trailer of depravity."

29. **Lovemaster**
    author: Lambert Lacy
    tagline: "LSD plunged them into an orgy of violence..."

30. **Lust Is No Lady**
    author: Stephanie Davis

31. **Luther: Amber Satyr**
    author: Roy Flannagon
    tagline: "A swamp Negro... A White trash woman... A tragic hunger."

32. **Marihuana**
    author: William Irish
    tagline: "A cheap and evil girl sets a hopped-up killer against a city."

33. **Marijuana Girl**
    author: N.R. DeMexico
    tagline: "She traded her body for drugs—and kicks!"

34. **Mulatto**
    author: Joan Ellis
    tagline: "She played upon men's lusts to get anything she wanted...then she tried to cross the color line"

35. **Murder Is Dangerous**
    author: Saul Levinson

36. **Musk, Hashish and Blood**
    author: Hector France
    tagline: "The adventures of a modern man among the cruel men and passionate women of Algiers."

37. **Naked She Died**
    author: Don Elliott

38. **Nautipuss**
    author: Clyde Allison
    tagline: "Agent 0008 battles the temptress of the deep!"
    note: This was part of a James Bond spoof series featuring the voluptuous but deadly Agent 0008.

39. **The Needle**
    author: Sloane M. Britain
    tagline: "Man or woman, sister or brother: her lust knew no bounds."

40. **Older Woman**
    author: Sheldon Lord
    tagline: "Where could this woman-boy love affair lead?"

41. **Perfume and Pain**
    author: Kimberly Kemp

42. **The Petting Generation**
    author: Lucius B. Steiner
    tagline: "The fine art of petting, completely described with authentic case histories."

43. **The Price of Salt**
    author: Claire Morgan (pseudonym of Patricia Highsmith)
    note: Generally considered the first lesbian pulp novel with a happy ending.

44. **Queer Patterns**
    author: Lilyan Brock
    tagline: "A delicate theme, treated honestly and candidly."

45. **Rally Round the Fag**
    author: Don Holliday
    note: This was part of a series spoofing *The Man from U.N.C.L.E.*, called *The Man from C.A.M.P.*

46. **Satan Was a Lesbian**
    author: Fred Haley

47. **Shayne**
author: John Burton Thompson
tagline: "A nymphomaniac who turned men into sex candles and burned them at both ends. Then she fell in love..."

48. **The Sins of Seena**
author: Don Elliott

49. **Slum Doctor**
author: Matthew Clay

50. **Tender Torment**
author: Randy Salem
tagline: "Her marriage was born in hell—her husband was a woman!"

51. **Those Sexy Saucer People**
author: Jan Hudson

52. **The Trailer Park Girls**
author: Glenn Canary
tagline: "Their love was as mobile as their home and just as carefree."

53. **TV Tramps**
author: Walter Dyer
tagline: "On camera they violate the Code of Decency. Off camera they violated each other."

54. **Widow's Delight**
author: J.X. Williams
tagline: "She wore black...but not much of it!"

55. **Women's Barracks**
author: Tereska Torres
tagline: "The frank autobiography of a French soldier girl."
note: This book was condemned by name by the House Un-American Activities Committee.

56. **69 Barrow Street**
author: Sheldon Lord
tagline: "Their love was right! But their sex was wrong."

+ Odd & Ends

The causes of such problems as depression, bipolar illness (manic-depression), extreme anxiety, and schizophrenia are the subject of much debate, but we do know that a lot substances, deficiencies, and physical maladies can cause symptoms that are often considered a mental illness. A lot of people who are diagnosed as crazy are really suffering from one or more of the problems listed below, which are drawn primarily from the series *Healthy Mind Guides* by Stephanie Marohn.

1

Diseases and disorders

It's universally recognized that stroke, lupus, mono, and Parkinson's are among the medical problems that can make you feel bipolar, while brain tumors, epilepsy, migraines, low blood oxygen, and liver disease can cause psychotic symptoms.

2

Medications

Practically any given drug can cause depression, other mood disorders, and schizophrenia in some people. Pain relievers, tranquilizers, birth-control pills, antihistamines, muscle relaxants, and several other categories of pharmaceutical are the most likely to mess with your head.

3

Heavy metal poisoning

Even the medical establishment accepts that heavy metals are highly toxic to the nervous system, yet for some reason they rarely link them to the symptoms of mental illness. Mercury was what made hat-makers "mad as hatters" in the olden days, and many of us now have this poisonous substance right in our mouths. Silver amalgam tooth fillings are at least half mercury, so this neurotoxin is constantly leaking into our bodies. (Ninety percent of depressed people who have their silver fillings removed feel their depression lift.) Many types of fish consumed by humans

LIST 73   15 Things That Cause or Mimic "Mental Illnesses"

are loaded to the gills with mercury. Predatory fish (like sharks), shellfish, tuna, and cod are said to be the worst.

Like mercury, the metals copper, aluminum, and lead—all present in our environments—trigger hallucinations, depression, anxiety, irritability, and mental fog.

4

Omega-3 deficiency

Most people don't get enough omega-3. This type of essential fatty acid is absolutely crucial to keeping your brain humming along smoothly, and the lack of it has been clinically tied to depression, bipolar disorder, and schizophrenia. Fish oil is rich in omega-3, but then you have to worry about the mercury! Instead, try the seed oil of flax, pumpkin, or hemp. Some supplements mix these vegetable oils together for maximum effect.

5

Amino acid deficiency

Derived from ingested proteins, amino acids are the building blocks of neurotransmitters. In a two-step process, tryptophan is turned into serotonin, which plays a crucial (though not understood) role in mood. *Natural Mind* author Stephanie Marohn notes: "Research has found that tryptophan may be beneficial in the treatment of mania, depression, anxiety, panic disorders, sleep disorders, and psychosis." Other amino acids have been shown to help alleviate depression, and if a

person doesn't have enough GABA, he often becomes manic.

6

Vitamin B deficiency

All of the vitamins in the B family are vital to keeping you sane. Being low on any of them can touch off depression. Not having enough folic acid, B_1, B_3, B_6, or B_{12} makes you unstable and psychotic. Lack of B_3 actually causes a recognized disease, pellagra, which is virtually indistinguishable from schizophrenia.

7

Vitamin C deficiency

Hey, vitamin C fights more than colds—it also staves off depression, mental fog, and even psychosis.

8

Out-of-whack hormones

If your thyroid is overactive or sluggish, you can feel bipolar or even have delusions. In women, not enough estrogen means depression; too much means anxiety. Whacked-out adrenal glands can cause problems often mistaken for schizophrenia.

9

Hypoglycemia

Chronically low blood sugar often causes depression and related mood swings, which can be quite severe. I can testify to this, since I'm hypoglycemic. The minute my blood sugar dips, I get extremely irritable (just ask my girlfriend!) and I hate the world. Cutting out sugar and caffeine, minimizing carbs, and eating five or six small, protein-rich meals a day keeps blood sugar at a constant, optimal level and eliminates hypoglycemia.

10

Candida albicans

In order to function properly, your body needs a certain amount of the fungus *Candida albicans* in your intestines. Candida is kept in check by good bacteria, such as acidophilus, but sometimes the balance is disrupted. When acidophilus is killed by mercury, antibiotics, or the Pill, the yeast-like Candida takes over, producing a laundry list of "mental" problems: "depression, fatigue, anxiety, irritability, memory and concentration problems, dizziness, insomnia, headaches, feelings of unreality, and even delusions, mania, psychosis, and suicidal or violent tendencies," according to Marohn.

My ladylove Anne suffered a Candida overload brought on by antibiotics, and I can tell you, it ain't pretty. She had never felt physically or mentally worse in her entire life, and, of course, doctors had no idea what was wrong. When a kinesiologist-chiropractor-nutritionist corrected the imbalance, she felt better in less than two weeks and was back to her old self in six weeks.

11

Food intolerance

If you pay attention, you might notice that symptoms start soon after you ingest certain foods or drinks. This is because your body is intolerant to a given substance, triggering your immune system to attack this invader, and this process can directly impact the brain. In *Natural Prescriptions*, Dr. Robert Giller writes that a "study found that 85 percent of a group of depressed children and adults was allergic" to something they were eating. Wheat, especially the gluten it contains, is the most common edible culprit when it comes to depression, bipolar disorder, and schizophrenia.

12

Food additives

Aspartame (NutraSweet), MSG, and sulfites are three big causes of depression and anxiety. Lots of other preservatives, taste enhancers, and artificial colorings and flavorings are to blame, as well.

13

Skull squeeze

If your skull is misshapen due to traumatic birth or later incidents, it may be putting pressure on your brain. This can lead to malfunctions, which can be at least partially alleviated by craniosacral therapy.

14

Sleep deprivation

Take a perfectly sane person, deprive her of sleep for 72 hours, and she'll start displaying classic psychotic symptoms—hallucinations, paranoia, delusions. Actually, it's not sleep in general that's so necessary; it's the REM stage (in which we dream). In experiments, scientists have let people fall asleep but wake them up the second they enter REM. The result is virtually identical to being deprived of all sleep. Not sleeping on a regular schedule can cause similar problems.

15

Light deprivation

Not getting enough sunlight (or, alternatively, light from full-spectrum bulbs) is known to cause depression and numerous other physical/mental problems. With its creation of Seasonal Affective Disorder, the mental health establishment has officially recognized this effect. ⌁

Here are tips to alleviate 11 common medical problems. In spite of proven track records and convincing research, they're not going to be offered to you at your traditional doctor's office. Ignorance keeps them from you in some cases; in others it's a malignant territorial protection racket. Here they are, by ailment with explanations from experts in the related fields.

1

Carpal tunnel syndrome – avoid surgery

Expert opinion: Dr. James C. Edmondson, Brooklyn, New York, board-certified adult and child neurologist.

A pinched nerve in your wrist from repetitive motion or physical stress, Edmondson says, seriously weakens the most essential muscle in your thumb. When you flex and extend the weakened thumb, it may ache, so you tend to avoid using it. Instead you may claw or scoop at items using the four fingers.

In order to increase your range of motion while using just the fingers, you have to twist your forearms, arms, shoulders and neck into awkward positions. The chronic overuse of these muscles, Edmondson explains, creates nagging spasms throughout the upper half of your body, which can trigger back pain, chest pain, all types of headaches, blurry vision, ringing in the ears, numbness of face and tongue, floating sensations, loss of balance, and dizzy spells.

For these reasons, Edmondson says, thumb problems must be addressed by protecting the nerves from further injury and reducing stresses. Many undergo surgery unnecessarily. (Edmondson sees hundreds of patients a week for this condition and refers only about 1 percent of those for surgery— ten out of 1,000.)

Here's his full treatment protocol:

- Wear wrist splints while sleeping. While awake, too, if you like.
- Keep arms and hands warm at all times.
- Do stretching exercises every day for at least 20 minutes.
- Take hourly stretching breaks while working.

11 Super Cures Your Doctor Won't Tell You About
Diane Petryk-Bloom

- Relax tense muscles in a hot shower or bath (watch out if you have diabetes because it can impair sensitivity to heat).
- Use yoga exercises to help you relax muscles and mind.

At the same time, do not squeeze anything, like a ball or clay or sponge; do not repeatedly flex and extend fingers, lift weights or exercise with free weights, pull or stretch an elastic strap, or dangle heavy, filled plastic grocery bags from handles across fingers. Also, don't apply ice because it will knot muscles.

Edmondson is responsible for the neurological care of about 80,000 patients a year at Central Brooklyn Medical Group, P.C. He is a New York University Medical School developmental neurologist who identified the molecule neurons use to bind to and communicate with glial cells.

2

Childhood middle ear infections – avoid dangerous misuse of antibiotics

Expert opinion: Dr. Gerard Clum, President of Life Chiropractic College, Hayward, California.

Middle ear infection in children can cause severe pain and complications. Physicians usually treat it by giving an antibiotic. Studies have shown this to be of no use in curing the disease and dangerous because it sets up the potential for repeated infections by stronger and more antibiotic-resistant organisms, according to Dr. Clum.

Canada, he said, is the most aggressive in treating middle ear infections in children with antibiotics. The Netherlands does not use antibiotics at all in such cases. Studies show the rates of recovery and complications in the two countries are the same. While Canadians and Americans are wasting their money on antibiotics and contributing to their dangerous overuse, chiropractic practice offers a great track record in effecting cures through spinal manipulation.

Clum says blockage of the Eustachian tube causes such infections. Upper cervical spinal adjustment, he said, can aid muscular mechanisms in normalizing the Eustachian tube. But pediatricians continue to write prescriptions.

"I wouldn't take my dog to a chiropractor," he remembers the ophthalmologist telling his dad. That was the moment Dr. Clum decided to become a chiropractor. What the ophthalmologist called a miracle—his restored good vision—he knew, even at age twelve, had been brought about by chiropractic manipulation. In the intervening 30-plus years, the prejudice of medical doctors against chiropractors has been slow to decline. Few M.D.s write referrals to chiropractors. A national survey showed that among 36 percent of physicians who said they believed spinal manipulation would be helpful for lower back pain, only 2 percent would make a referral in such a case.

Cardiovascular disease – preventative/restorative known and slighted by doctors for three decades

Expert opinion: Dr. David Sands, associate dean for academic and clinical affairs, Institute for Natural Medicine and Prevention, Fairfield, Iowa.

Doctors are reluctant to acknowledge the connection between mind and body, but, Sands says, it's a fact that reduction of stress like that facilitated through Transcendental Meditation reduces coronary disease. There are fewer strokes and heart attacks among those who meditate. The effects begin immediately for every age group. Plaques and hardening of the arteries can be reversed just by practicing meditation, Sands says, but there's more. Calmness and sense of well-being while meditating carry over while the meditator is engaged in other activities. Anxiety is diminished at all times.

The key reason, according to Sands: Meditation enlivens the body's inner intelligence and restores fundamental vitality. "There are real physical effects—changes and repairs," he said. These were shown in collaborative studies between his institute and the University of Iowa, but not for the first time.

Back in 1975, Harvard cardiologist Dr. Herbert Benson had already gotten the same results in studies at Harvard and Boston's Beth Israel Hospital. His book, *The Relaxation Response*, first published 28 years ago, has become a classic in the field.

Other studies have had similar results. So it remains mind-boggling, according to Sands, that most doctors only pay lip service to the findings and still reach for the prescription pad first.

Infertility – documented dietary solutions

Expert opinion: Fern Reiss, author of *The Infertility Diet: Get Pregnant and Prevent Miscarriage*.

Reiss bases her diet on more than 500 documented medical studies, including such simple things as avoiding dairy products and ginger. And although her book is endorsed by several infertility specialists and the American Society for Reproductive Medicine, diet continues to take a back seat to medical treatment for infertility, "which," Reiss says, "is much more invasive, much more expensive, and no more likely to succeed."

"After more than three years of infertility and miscarriage, I now have three children because of this diet!" Reiss says.

Osteoporosis – hold the Fosamax

Expert opinion: Barbara Morris, registered pharmacist, author of *Put Old on Hold: The Only Guide You'll Ever Need to Go From Baby Boomer to Whatababe!*.

It's simply Vitamin D—2,000 units per day— says this 74-year-old pharmacist who works full-time for a national grocery chain and maintains a vivacity that belies her age. A doctor will prescribe products related to the material used to remove lime deposits from faucets, she says. "That's why patients are cautioned not to lie down for an hour after taking Fosamax—because if it gets caught in the esophagus it may erode it."

A check of the online National Library of Medicine turns up a recent Japanese study finding that "Vitamin D(3) may contribute to the local production of estrogen, thus leading to protective effect against osteoporosis especially after menopause."

Early in her life, Morris, a graduate of Rutgers University College of Pharmacy, became convinced that signs of "old age" associated with the normal aging process resulted not just from heredity but also from lifestyle choices and, as such, could be manipulated and controlled. She's dedicated to helping Boomers and others retain the vital characteristics of youth.

Other tips from Barbara:

6

Irritable bowel syndrome/overactive bladder – end "the runs"

Using five or more grams daily of l-glutamine is a "real wonder worker" for bringing bowel movements back to normal, assuming there is no underlying disease, she said. For women with a bladder retention problem, the answer is vaginal testosterone and Kegel exercises. "Most traditional docs don't know anything beyond Detrol L.A. As a plus, the proper testosterone regimen will restore libido."

7

High cholesterol – protect your muscles

To lower cholesterol, doctors will prescribe statin drugs, which are "diabolical," Morris warns. That's because they inhibit an enzyme called CoQ10, necessary for the strength of any muscle in the body. So if you take a drug to lower cholesterol, you need to take additional CoQ10. Or, she says, try policosanol. It's a plant derivative available in health food stores. "It works wonders, but most traditional M.D.s don't know it exists," she says.

8

Chronic fatigue syndrome/ fibromyalgia – yes, something can be done

Expert opinion: Dr. Jacob Teitelbaum, author of *From Fatigued to Fantastic*.

"Five different doctors told me there was nothing they could do" is the type of comment that floods the Amazon.com reviews of Teitelbaum's book. By their own testimonials, many chronic fatigue and fibromyalgia patients have finally been helped by Teitelbaum.

He rejects both the view that the ailments are nonexistent and that nothing can be done.

CFS comes because the body has "blown a fuse," he says. There may be a variety of causes, but the key fuse is in the hypothalamus, which controls production and release of hormones as well as temperature regulation, blood pressure, and other functions of the autonomic nervous system. Teitelbaum treats all symptoms involving these functions at once with four key steps:

- Eight to nine hours of sleep a night.
- Nutritional support.
- Normalizing thyroid function (blood tests don't tell the story here, he warns).
- Treating any infections—usually yeast.

Although some of the protocol for tests and supplements can tend to be expensive, Teitelbaum gives economical ways to accomplish them via his website, endfatigue.com.

Teitelbaum may be particularly compassionate with CFS sufferers because he battled the disease himself. In 1975, while in medical school at Ohio State, he had a bout of "drop-dead flu." After a month, he still couldn't get out of bed before noon. The debilitating fatigue forced him to drop out of school even though pursuing a medical career was his life-long dream. After a year of studying his own illness he recovered enough to continue—and devote his career to helping others similarly afflicted.

9

Hormone replacement – the hottest topic going

Expert opinion: Dr. Charles E. Anderson, Burlington, Vermont, author of *Rage Against Age* and *Secrets to Healthy Aging*.

For years, menopausal women had no options. There was Premarin and there was Premarin—a substance made from the urine of female horses.

"Not exactly analogous to the human body," says Dr. Anderson. Today, Anderson offers three options.

- A compound utilizing three components of estrogen—estrone, estradiol, and estriol. It's called Triest and is derived from plants. Alternative and complimentary physicians use it.
- A low-progesterone cream.
- Or an herbal blend of black cohosh, Don-Quai, and Vitex.

Years ago Anderson became convinced that the increase in breast and cervical cancers was due to the western diet and Premarin. Most doctors were slow to see the danger, now supported by research, in Premarin.

Although Anderson may seem out on a limb, compared to the huddled masses of physicians, he is supported by a growing cadre of divergent thinkers. These doctors make up the memberships of the American College for Advancement in Medicine, formed in the 1980s, today with about 1,300 members, and the more recent A4M—American Association of Anti-Aging Medicine.

Talking to most doctors outside these groups, Anderson said, is a dead end. They are not interested in learning.

What Anderson and his colleagues have learned so far is that most ailments, aging along with them, are related to diet.

"What is killing us?" Anderson asks. "Destruction of our cells through toxicity or deficiency of nutrients.

"We have free radicals, which cause irritation, impacting every cell."

What do we do to protect ourselves? Anderson advises eliminating sugar as much as possible (yeast feeds on it), get the heavy metals and toxins out if present in our systems (arsenic, lead, and mercury are among the top dangers), alleviate our allergies, supplement hormones, support the immune system, and weed out infections.

Dr. Anderson, who has been in practice more than 30 years, veered from the traditional medical path in the 1980s when his wife developed a cancerous lump on her leg. After the tumor was surgically removed, they decided on heavy dosages of anti-oxidants. Anderson, a favorite referral physician of the late Dr. Robert Atkins, said he doesn't mind criticism from colleagues. "Sooner or later they usually end up bringing a family member to me." His wife, by the way, is doing fine.

Also from Dr. Anderson, advice on:

10

Hyperactivity and Attention Deficit Disorder – food is the prime suspect

Anderson says a vast proportion of children with these problems are allergic to foods they're eating. When he is consulted in a suspected ADD or hyperactivity case, he suggests blood tests for food allergies, being careful to use a reliable lab.

As Teitelbaum, too, noted, different labs can come up with remarkably different results with the same blood sample. The same lab, with a sample submitted under different names, can come up with different results.

So what's a person to do? Test with a reputable lab and retest until results are consistent.

11

Asthma – the magnesium method

Asthma sufferers can often reduce the frequency and dosage of inhalers with 800 to 1,000 milligrams of magnesium a day, Anderson says. Sometimes they no longer need them at all.

Anderson treats the whole spectrum of medical problems, but says that with almost anything, "You're going to walk away with a diet." So why wait for disease? Start eating right, now. ◘

1

Major General
Smedley D. Butler

Imagine one of the most highly-decorated military men in US history. Imagine a Marine who was awarded two Congressional Medals of Honor, the Army Distinguished Service Medal, the Navy Distinguished Service Medal, and the French Order of the Black Star. Imagine a Marine still spoken of with awe within the Corps, whose name is now the name of the base in Okinawa. Now imagine that, upon retiring, this "hero" and "legend" (two words the military uses to describe him) realized that America's foreign interventions are done "to protect some lousy investment of the bankers." Then imagine that he spoke out about this.

You can stop imagining now, because this really happened. Major General Smedley D. Butler was a brilliant, brave military man who realized that he had been used as the enforcer in a global shakedown. In 1935 he published a long essay titled "War Is a Racket," which has become an anti-war classic. Two years prior to that, he gave a speech along the same lines. The most widely quoted section contains the following confession:

> I spent thirty-three years and four months in active military service as a member of this country's most agile military force, the Marine Corps. I served in all commissioned ranks from Second Lieutenant to Major-General. And during that period, I spent most of my time being a high class muscle-man for Big Business, for Wall Street and for the Bankers. In short, I was a racketeer, a gangster for capitalism.

> I suspected I was just part of a racket at the time. Now I am sure of it. Like all the members of the military profession, I never had a thought of my own until I left the service. My mental faculties remained in suspended animation while I obeyed the orders of higher-ups. This is typical with everyone in the military service.

> I helped make Mexico, especially Tampico, safe for American oil interests in 1914. I helped make Haiti and Cuba a decent place for the National City Bank boys to collect revenues in. I helped in the raping of half a dozen Central American republics for the benefits of Wall Street. The record of racketeering is long. I helped purify Nicaragua for the international banking house of Brown Brothers in 1909-1912 (where have I heard that name before?). I brought light to the Dominican Republic for American sugar interests in 1916. In China I helped to see to it that Standard Oil went its way unmolested.

LIST 75 **11 Whistle-blowers**

2

Karen Silkwood

On November 13, 1974, Karen Silkwood was ready to blow the whistle on the unsafe conditions, faulty products, and missing radioactive material at a Kerr McGee plutonium plant, where she was a lab analyst and union organizer. She had already spilled the beans to union officials, and she was on her way to present a *New York Times* reporter with smuggled documents proving her claims when she died in that bane of troublemakers everywhere—the one-car accident on a lonely road. The documents were not found with her and have never been recovered. High amounts of plutonium in Silkwood's body and apartment indicated that she had been exposed to radiation within 30 days of her death.

3

Daniel Ellsberg

Ellsberg's name is now synonymous with leaking official secrets revealing government lies. But given his early life as a Marine, Harvard Ph.D. in economics, RAND consultant, and assistant in the Departments of Defense and State, he was an unlikely person to turn the establishment on its head. "From my first day in the Pentagon—August 4, 1964—I witnessed lies about US provocations and imaginary torpedos in the Tonkin Gulf," he wrote in 2000. "I became a participant in secret plans to escalate the war as soon as President Johnson won in a landslide by promising voters just the opposite."

While working on a highly classified study of the Vietnam War, Ellsberg got to the point where he could no longer stomach the lies. He clandestinely, and illegally, photocopied the 7,000-page study and gave it to the Senate Foreign Relations Committee. When it became apparent that they weren't doing anything meaningful with it, in 1971 he sent it to newspapers, including the *New York Times*, which published portions of it after winning an epochal Supreme Court ruling over prior restraint.

The government prosecuted Ellsberg on a dozen felony counts, but he beat the rap when it became known that the Nixon Administration had used dirty tricks against him. Since those heady days, he's been arrested around 60 times for civil disobedience against nuclear war and foreign interventionism. He now urges other government insiders to release bombshell documents about the 2003 Iraq invasion.

4

Mordechai Vanunu

Starting in 1976, Mordechai Vanunu worked as a technician in Israel's secret nuclear weapons program. Before leaving the country in 1985, he took photos of the inner workings of the Dimona installation. In October of the next year, the London *Sunday Times* ran an extensive interview with Vanunu—accompanied by his photos—in which he definitively revealed the existence of Israel's nukes. In September 1986, even before the *Times* had printed the story, Israeli agents kidnapped

Vanunu, drugged him, and shipped him back to his home country, where he was found guilty of espionage and treason. Sentenced to eighteen years in prison, he spent the first eleven and a half in solitary. He's due to be released before the *Disinformation Book of Lists* hits the streets, but the Israeli government is planning ways to extend his sentence or at least gag him and prevent him from leaving the country.

Control room of plutonium separation plant at Israel's Dimona nuclear facility.
Photo by Mordechai Vanunu.

5

Martin Jay Levitt

Martin Jay Levitt went from busting unions to busting the union-busters. For almost 20 years, he was a consultant for corporations that wanted to prevent their workers from organizing, becoming known as a ruthless, dirty-playing enemy of labor. But in 1988, during an alcoholic midlife crisis, he realized that—like all others in the field—he was the scum of the earth. He immediately created the Justice for Labor Foundation, wrote a book exposing the underhanded tactics of union-busters, and is now heavily in demand

as a pro-labor speaker, consultant, expert witness, etc. As someone who was once a master of this nasty game, he is in a prime position to reveal the way it's played.

He talks about the time he and his colleagues arranged for cocaine to be planted in the locker of a union organizer. "The employee went to open his locker," Levitt told National Public Radio, "and, conveniently, not one, but two supervisors were standing within six feet of the locker, saw a bag of white substance fall to the floor, confronted the employee, took the employee to personnel." The personnel director said that the cops should be called over this, but: "I'm gonna give you a break. You resign now and we'll forget the whole incident."

Levitt maintains that this is not an isolated incident. Every company that tries to prevent unions from forming "routinely" uses immoral and illegal methods, including lying, spying, threatening, harassing, and framing, as well as more subtle tactics like making superficial improvements for workers and turning organizers against each other.

6

Jeffrey Wigand

Disney made a movie about him; Russell Crowe portrayed him; and *The Insider* was nominated for seven Academy Awards, including best picture. But before this, Jeffrey Wigand had to endure hell when he became the highest level tobacco executive to expose the industry's dirt and ashes. In

1988, he had been made Vice President of Scientific Research at Brown & Williamson Tobacco Corp., and his mission—or so he believed—was to develop a less addictive cigarette. What he found is that Big Tobacco *wants* their products to be as addictive as possible.

In 1993, he started quietly, then overtly, revealing inside secrets to the government and the press. He appeared in a legendary *60 Minutes* interview that was temporarily spiked for fear that Brown & Williamson might sue. For his actions, Levitt was followed, physically threatened, and found a bullet in his mailbox. His former bosses launched a classic smear campaign against him, then sued him for violating trade secrets (they later dropped the suit).

Wigand's information sparked the successful multibillion-dollar lawsuits against Big Tobacco. He started the Smoke-Free Kids Foundation, and now he lectures, consults, and advocates against the nicotine pushers.

7

M. Wesley Swearingen

M. Wesley Swearingen was an FBI agent from 1955 to 1977. During those particularly volatile 22 years of American history, he was involved in the FBI's dirtiest deeds against US political dissidents, including burglaries, disinformation campaigns, and other unethical activities. On top of that, he has insider knowledge of even more extreme tactics, including assassination. After quitting the agency in disgust and spending a year in mental anguish, Swearingen became a whistle-blower.

When he arrived as a rookie agent in Chicago, he had visions of doing battle with mobsters. Instead, he was assigned to surveil the wives of two leaders of the Communist Party of the United States. Soon, he was participating in black bag jobs, in which he illegally and unconstitutionally broke into people's homes looking for incriminating documents. He estimates that the FBI performed 23,800 such break-ins over 35 years, and he personally participated in hundreds of them.

His accusations get even stronger: "...I learned how the FBI had arranged to assassinate members of the Black Panther Party by using hit men in the United Slaves organization, a black nationalist organization based in Southern California, who were FBI informers. I learned how the FBI had neutralized the charismatic leader of the Los Angeles Black Panther Party, Elmer 'Geronimo' Pratt, by framing him for murder." A colleague of Swearingen's disclosed to him that the FBI had orchestrated the murders of Chicago Panthers Fred Hampton and Mark Clark.

In his almost unprecedented exposé, he claims that the Bureau lied to the General Accounting Office during its audit of FBI files and that top FBI brass committed perjury before Congress. He also reveals internal problems within the FBI during his tenure— authorized cheating on training examinations, attitudes of extreme racism and sexism, anally retentive neatness rules, thievery and laziness, and the apparently random dismissals of agents.

8

Dr. Bernard Nathanson

Bernard Nathanson, M.D., was a founder of the National Abortion Rights Action League. "I worked hard to make abortion legal, affordable, and available on demand," he wrote in his autobiography. After *Roe v. Wade*, he performed thousands of the procedures himself, and he headed the Center for Reproductive and Sexual Health, which performed more abortions than any other clinic in the world. Nathanson eventually renounced abortion, converted to Catholicism in 1996, and now spills the beans about the movement to legalize abortion. He claims that he and his colleagues made up polls out of thin air, telling the media that 60 percent of people wanted no restrictions on abortion. In his essay "Confessions of an Ex-Abortionist," he writes:

> We aroused enough sympathy to sell our program of permissive abortion by fabricating the number of illegal abortions done annually in the US. The actual figure was approaching 100,000 but the figure we gave to the media repeatedly was 1,000,000. Repeating the big lie often enough convinces the public. The number of women dying from illegal abortions was around 200-250 annually. The figure we constantly fed to the media was 10,000. These false figures took root in the consciousness of Americans convincing many that we needed to crack the abortion law. Another myth we fed to the public through the media was that legalizing abortion would only mean that the abortions taking place illegally would then be done legally. In fact, of course, abortion is now being used as a primary method of birth control in the US and the annual number of abortions has increased by 1500% since legalization.

9

Anthony V. Bouza

After a 36-year career in law enforcement—including stints as police chief of Minneapolis and commander of the Bronx police—Anthony V. Bouza wrote a book, *Police Unbound*, that both honored cops for their good points and excoriated them for the rotten things they do. He confirms the existence of the "blue wall of silence," which most cops will swear is mythical, and he relays the term "testilying," police slang for giving false testimony under oath in order to convict someone. He tells of instances of police brutality, and admits: "Unquestionably, racism is endemic in the ranks." He also dishes up anger at the system that uses cops as a means of social control, deliberately underreports crime so the mayor looks good, and continues the mindless the war on drugs.

10

Joseph E. Stiglitz

At one time, Joseph Stiglitz was a leading force in economic globalization. As a senior vice president and the chief economist of the World Bank, this Nobel laureate thought he was helping undeveloped and underdeveloped countries to grow and prosper. Then he realized he wasn't. "And you know what the problem with globalization and the program of privatizations, deregulation, liberalization of capital markets is?" he asked in an interview. "They don't work"

The World Bank and International Monetary Fund loan scads of money to Second and Third World nations with an average of 111 conditions—often suicidal conditions—attached. The countries are forced to change their political and economic systems in ways that allow First World "vulture capitalists" to massively profit from the situation while the masses get screwed. Stiglitz calls it "briber-ization," not privatization.

Beyond that, he admits that every single nation that has gotten onboard the World Bank/IMF's globalization scheme has gotten trashed. China and Botswana have achieved growth, he says, because they told the glob-alizers to shove their money and conditions.

In his call to arms, *Globalization and Its Dis-contents*, Stiglitz confesses that "the policies of the international economic institutions are all too often closely aligned with the commer-cial and financial interests of those in the advanced industrial countries." He writes:

> Modern high-tech warfare is designed to remove physical contact; dropping bombs from 50,000 feet ensures that one does not "feel" what one does. Modern economic man-agement is similar: from one's luxury hotel, one can callously impose policies about which one would think twice if one knew the people whose lives one was destroying.

11

Katharine Gun

In spring 2002, the US and UK were trying to convince the United Nations Security Council of the need to invade Iraq over weapons of mass destruction that no longer existed. Six countries were seen as sitting on the fence, so, in order to figure out how to manipulate them, the National Security Agency was told to spy on their delegates. Phone calls and email of the representatives from Mexico, Chile, Angola, Cameroon, Guinea, and Pak-istan were intercepted.

We know about this shameful episode because Katharine Gun—who worked as a translator in Britain's eavesdropping facili-ty, GCHQ—bravely leaked a classified NSA memo to the London *Observer*. Right-wingers insinuated that the document was fake, but when the British government arrested and prosecuted Gun for leaking state secrets, it became obvious that this was for real and that America was spying on UN delegates. She says that she leaked the memos "because they exposed serious illegality and wrongdoing on the part of the US Government who attempted to subvert our own security services," as well as "to prevent wide-scale death and casualties among ordinary Iraqi people and UK forces in the course of an illegal war." In late Februrary 2004, Gun's trial for violations of the noxious Official Secrets Act was abrupt-ly called off, the British government saying that it would have to reveal sensitive infor-mation in order to prosecute her. ◻

The NSA Memo Leaked by Katherine Gun

To: [Recipients withheld]
From: FRANK KOZA, Def Chief of Staff (Regional Targets)
CIV/NSA
Sent on Jan 31 2003 0:16
Subject: Reflections of Iraq Debate/Votes at UN-RT Actions + Potential for Related Contributions
Importance: HIGH
Top Secret//COMINT//X1

All,

As you've likely heard by now, the Agency is mounting a surge particularly directed at the UN Security Council (UNSC) members (minus US and GBR of course) for insights as to how to membership is reacting to the on-going debate RE: Iraq, plans to vote on any related resolutions, what related policies/ negotiating positions they may be considering, alliances/ dependencies, etc - the whole gamut of information that could give US policymakers an edge in obtaining results favorable to US goals or to head off surprises. In RT, that means a QRC surge effort to revive/ create efforts against UNSC members Angola, Cameroon, Chile, Bulgaria and Guinea, as well as extra focus on Pakistan UN matters.

We've also asked ALL RT topi's to emphasize and make sure they pay attention to existing non-UNSC member UN-related and domestic comms for anything useful related to the UNSC deliberations/ debates/ votes. We have a lot of special UN-related diplomatic coverage (various UN delegations) from countries not sitting on the UNSC right now that could contribute related perspectives/ insights/ whatever. We recognize that we can't afford to ignore this possible source.

We'd appreciate your support in getting the word to your analysts who might have similar, more in-direct access to valuable information from accesses in your product lines. I suspect that you'll be hearing more along these lines in formal channels - especially as this effort will probably peak (at least for this specific focus) in the middle of next week, following the SecState's presentation to the UNSC.

Thanks for your help

Most people who don't have their heads in the sand realize that the US government, military, and intelligence agencies have been medically experimenting on citizens since World War II. And it's no secret that the Nazis and Imperial Japanese performed hideous human experimentation during the 1930s and 1940s. Except for the notable case of the Tuskegee syphilis experiment (1932-1972)—in which poor black men in Alabama went untreated for the venereal disease so doctors could observe the effects—human experimentation before the WWII era is still shrouded in obscurity. Digging through mountains of primary documents, professor Susan E. Lederer uncovered this hidden history and presented it in the Johns Hopkins University book *Subjected to Science*, which focuses mainly, but not exclusively, on the United States.

1

Lederer writes: "Before the civil war some southern physicians had actually used slaves as experimental subjects, advertising from time to time their wish to purchase Negroes with particular complaints in order to test new remedies."

2

In the latter part of the 1800s, Lederer found over 40 instances in which unknowing people—including toddlers and teenagers—were *deliberately* injected with gonorrhea or syphilis in order to see if they would develop the diseases.

3

A medical journal from 1874 reveals that some doctors injected children with smallpox to test whether a previously applied vaccination was effective.

4

In 1874, Dr. Roberts Bartholow stuck electrodes into the brain of a cancer patient (who happened to be an Irish domestic servant). His report documents her blue lips, frothing at the mouth, spasms, and convulsions. When she died days later, the autopsy showed that her brain had been trashed.

LIST 76
23 Early Cases of Involuntary Human Experimentation

5

The doctor who codiscovered the cause of leprosy was drummed out of the profession in 1880 for putting the mycobacterium in a patient's eye.

6

In 1883, the resident physician at a Hawaiian leper colony injected around 20 men, women, and girls with syphilis.

7

In the 1890s, Italian doctor Giuseppe Sanarelli jabbed at least five patients with yellow fever.

8

In 1891, a physician—apparently in Germany—removed cancerous tumors from the breasts of two women. Each time, he inserted some of the tumor into the patient's healthy breast to see if the cancer would take root.

9

Two doctors in 1895 vaccinated, then infected with smallpox, numerous boys at orphanages in Brooklyn.

10

In order to see if spinal taps were dangerous to kids, a Harvard researcher performed the agonizing procedure dozens of times on toddlers and babies fresh out of the womb in the early to mid-1890s.

11

In 1897, a Johns Hopkins researcher studied the toxicity of thyroid extract on eight mental patients.

12

In 1901, a doctor studying hookworm infection saw a patient who wanted a circumcision. Deciding to kill two birds with one stone, the doc put dirt containing hookworm larvae on the man's foreskin, implying that this was part of the procedure. The patient's penis was soon infested with the worms.

13

In the first decade of the 1900s, several physicians performed hundreds of experimental tests for tuberculosis on babies and children. One method of administration was in the eye, which caused severe pain for the youngsters.

14

A Rockefeller Institute physician gave an experimental test for syphilis—which contained the dead germs of the disease—to 400 hospital patients, including children, in 1911.

15

From 1913 till at least 1915, two doctors exposed infants—aged two days to 20 months—to repeated X rays to see how their digestive systems handled food.

16

To test his theory that syphilis bacteria were to be found in living brain tissue, a doctor used a dental drill to bore through the skulls and into the gray matter of six patients at Pontiac State Hospital in 1915. Needless to say, they had not been informed of the procedure.

17

Doctor L.L. Stanley was into the quackery of testicular transplantation. In 1920, he published an article about taking the balls from executed prisoners and putting them into still-breathing convicts, not to mention sewing ram testes into 23 other prisoners.

18

In 1921, three pediatricians deliberately induced scurvy and rickets in babies at an NYC orphanage.

19

While researching spinal taps, a physician performed lumbar punctures on 423 African American babies in Atlanta in the mid-1920s. None of them needed the excruciating procedure.

20

Germany, 1930: 76 children died from a contaminated experimental vaccine for tuberculosis.

21

In 1932, Dr. Pedro Albizu Campos published a manuscript about an experiment in which Puerto Ricans had been injected with cancer cells to study the disease's progression. At least thirteen eventually died from cancer. In his book *In the Name of Science*, professor Andrew Goliszek quotes lifelong human experimenter Dr. Cornelius Rhoades, who ran the experiment for the Rockefeller Institute: "The Puerto Ricans are the dirtiest, laziest, most degenerate and thievish race of men ever to inhabit this sphere."

22

In 1934 and 1935, over 20,000 children across the country received one of two experimental polio vaccines, one of which contained the live virus.

23

A 1942 issue of the *Journal of Pediatrics* features an article by a doctor who deliberately infected a 12-month-old baby with herpes. ☊

Stupid Government Trick

A scientist funded by the government has developed super-lethal strains of mousepox, cowpox, and rabbitpox. When tested, the mousepox killed all mice, even those that had been vaccinated against the disease. Rest easy, though. We've been assured that these 100-percent lethal bugs can't harm humans. No way. Not a chance.

1

"I am the commander, see? I do not need to explain why I say things. That's the interesting thing about being the President. Maybe somebody needs to explain to me why they say something, but I don't feel like I owe anybody an explanation."
–President George W. Bush

2

"See, free nations are peaceful nations. Free nations don't attack each other. Free nations don't develop weapons of mass destruction."
–President George W. Bush

3

"No President has ever done more for human rights than I have."
–President George W. Bush

8 Stupid Politician Quotes

4

"We know there are known knowns: there are things we know we know. We also know there are known unknowns: that is to say we know there are things we know we don't know. But there are also unknown unknowns—the ones we don't know we don't know."
–Secretary of Defense Donald Rumsfeld

5

"Death has a tendency to encourage a depressing view of war."
–Secretary of Defense Donald Rumsfeld

6

Senator Rick Santorum (Republican – Pennsylvania): "In every society, the definition of marriage has not ever, to my knowledge, included homosexuality. That's not to pick on homosexuality. It's not, you know, man on child, man on dog or whatever the case may be. It is one thing. And when you destroy that you have a dramatic impact on the quality—"

Associated Press reporter: "I'm sorry, I didn't think I was going to talk about 'man on dog' with a United States Senator. It's sort of freaking me out."

7

Regarding an invasion of Israel: "If Iraq came across the Jordan River...I would grab a rifle and get in the trench and fight and die."
–former President Bill Clinton at a Jewish fundraiser, July 30, 2002

8

"I know a little bit about how White Houses work. I know somebody picked up a phone, somebody got on a computer, somebody sent an email, somebody called for a meeting, somebody in that White House probably under instructions from somebody further up the chain told the EPA: 'Don't tell the people of New York the truth.'"
–Sen. Hillary Clinton, ostensibly talking about the Bush Administration covering up the health effects of the WTC collapse, but actually explaining how the executive branch *really* works ⊐

Federal Investigative Priorities

Amount of time for the US government to announce an investigation into 9/11: five months

Amount of time for the US government to announce an investigation into two senior Bush Administration officials leaking the name of an undercover CIA operative: two and a half months

Amount of time for the US government to announce an investigation into the exposure of Janet Jackson's right breast for four seconds during the 2004 Super Bowl halftime show: one day

When Senate Majority Leader Bill Frist (Republican – Tennessee) offered his self-published genealogy on Amazon, he might not have realized what he was doing. Sporting a price tag of $50 and the pro-eugenics title *Good People Beget Good People*, the vanity project inspired dozens of hilarious customer "reviews" slamming Frist on everything from his family's corrupt healthcare company (HCA) to his admission that he used to vivisect and kill cats he "adopted" at shelters. As I suspected they would, Amazon soon deleted the thrashings, so for the sake of preservation—and to add some levity to this book—here are some of the best. (All errors of grammar, punctuation, etc. remain uncorrected.)

This epic tale of a family that climbed from the pits of incest, congenital mental impairment, and sexual debauchery to be crowned first bootlick to the Monkey faced boy king is truly staggering.

From the opening where little Pansy, the slavering one eyed love child of siamese twin cousins, creates a family legacy by maiming her first feline to the closing chapter where the First bootlick himself parades through congress in his homemade dress of cat skins, we are taken on a non stop thrill ride.

Truly this is a tale of america as seen through the jaundiced eye of a slobbering third cousin who mated with his own mother to beget what we have today, Cat Killer First Bootlick Frist.

1

[one-star rating] **Frist in cat skins**, February 2, 2004
Reviewer: **Terry Duke Laslough** from Trinity South carolina

Not since the glory days of slavery have we seen such a heroic figure as Cat Killer Frist.

2

[one-star rating] **A triumph of antidisnonmiscegenation**, February 12, 2004
Reviewer: **A reader** from Jacksonville, FL USA

The genius of the Frist line is that, like the Jefferson and Thurmond lines, they kept the caucasian line entirely separated from the

 LIST 78 | **12 Amazon Reviews of Senator Bill Frist's Family History**

Negro/mulatto/quadrron/octaroon/hexade-caroon/high yellow/could-almost-pass-for-white-but-I-know-better line of the family.

This book of course represents the caucasian line which lived in houses like the one pictured on the cover. The miscegented line lived and died in shanties, hovels, lean-tos, slave quarters, ghettoes and other dwellings befitting the creatures produced when good people get a little reckless and beget with dark people. A second volume of the book is planned, to explore this side of the family history, to be entitled, "Good People Sometimes Make Youthful Errors with the Colored Help and Either Arrange for an Abortion, or Ship the Help Off to Another State Where They Beget Half-Good People Who Shall Never Know They Carry Frist Genes, So Help Us God."

3

[one-star rating] *ssholes beget *ssholes, too, February 4, 2004
Reviewer: solt from Way out west

Bill Frist disemboweled five of my littermates for the greater good of his offshore bank account, so I'd say this book is purr-fect.

4

[five-star rating] I begot what I was going to say..., February 3, 2004
Reviewer: A reader from Philadelphia, PA USA

Oh yeah...

If good people beget good people, do bad people beget bad people?

How can we tell bad people from good people?

These are some of the topics covered in this brilliant book by U.S. Senate Majority Leader, Bill Frist, M.D..

The answer, Dr. Frist informs us, is that good people make lots and lots of money, while bad people work just as hard but make very little. We must stop these bad people from begetting before they beget more bad people.

That's where forced sterilization comes in. Pioneering experimentation done on adopted kittens led Dr. Frist to his conclusion that the cheapest, most cost-effective means of forced sterilization is execution. Frist executed dozens of cats, both good and bad, and these cats did not beget any more.

Now if we just execute bad people (we can identify them by their low incomes) they will not beget either!

Dr. Frist opens a door to a bright new American future!

5

[one-star rating] Such an ambitious family!!, February 2, 2004
Reviewer: A reader from San Pedro, CA USA

I most enjoyed the tale of the plucky Frist family business stealing billions from me and my fellow tax payers, billions intended to provide health care for the poor, elderly and children. 14 felony convictions. That's gotta be some kind of record!

Oh. That's not mentioned in the book? Huh. Odd.

Well, Google around for "HCA Columbia frist fraud" and you can learn about it.

Excerpts

6

"I rate this book five tortured and slaughtered kitties out of a possible five. It's sure to win the Mengele Eugenics Award at The New Republic's Gala Celebration of the 25th Anniversary of the Publication of 'The Bell Curve'!"

7

"Frist explains the intricacies of human reproduction in a way sure to confound, bedevil, and infuriate his natural constituency of Tennessee creationists."

8

"Why strive to be good if your parents aren't WASPS?"

9

"it's like tennessee williams huffin' spray varnish!"

10

"Perhaps the Senator could take a look at my geneology and let me know whether I, too, spawn from 'good people.' If not, I guess I might as well just give up. This book makes me long for the literary company of a family with a bit more humility, like the Bushes."

11

"This book was so good, I changed my name to Frist so I could say it was about me. I read the whole thing while waiting [in] the reception area for subpar medical service."

12

"Move away from the kitten, Dr. Frist!"

Federal Investigative Priorities #2

Amount of time given to the federal commission investigating 9/11: 18 months

Amount of time given to the federal commission studying legalized gambling: 24 months

Amount of money given to the federal commission investigating 9/11: $3 million

Amount of money given to the federal commission studying legalized gambling: $5 million

1

"Every government is run by liars, and nothing they say should be believed."
–investigative journalist I.F. Stone

2

"You are more secure buying a book from Amazon than you are uploading your results to a Diebold server."
–Michael A. Wertheimer, former National Security Agency analyst, referring to electronic voting machines

3

"There is no act of treachery or meanness of which a political party is not capable; for in politics there is no honor."
–former British Prime Minister Benjamin Disraeli

4

"All political parties die at last of swallowing their own lies"
–John Arbuthnot

5

"A professional politician is a professionally dishonorable man. In order to get anywhere near high office he has to make so many compromises and submit to so many humil-
iations that he becomes indistinguishable from a streetwalker."
–H.L. Mencken

6

"[It is a] basic delusion that men may be governed and yet be free."
–H.L. Mencken

7

"I heartily accept the motto, 'That government is best which governs least'; and I should like to see it acted up to more rapidly and systematically. Carried out, it finally amounts to this, which also I believe—'That government is best which governs not at all'; and when men are prepared for it, that will be the kind of government which they will have."
–Henry David Thoreau

8

"[A]nyone who has spent any amount of time in Washington, DC can attest to this—the grant grazing conservative herd is rife with closeted gay men who sing the praises of Republican 'family values' by day and cruise for boy prostitutes at night."
–Bill Kauffman, *America First!*

LIST 79

11 Quotes About Politics and Government

9

"Politicians love the death penalty because it makes a bunch of candy-asses look like tough guys."
–Tony Fitzpatrick, "Idiot Whistle" (song)

10

"If one were to describe the American Revolution as a seditious conspiracy fomented by a band of extremists, misfits, malcontents, and troublemakers dedicated to the overthrow of recognized authority, one well might be right on the mark."
–John George and Laird Wilcox

11

"If you want a picture of the future, imagine a boot stomping on a human face—forever…"
–George Orwell

Bush Family Values

When President Bush's baby brother Neil—of Silverado Savings and Loan infamy—got a divorce, he was grilled by his wife's attorney, Marshall Davis Brown, in early 2003. Copies of the deposition were leaked. Here are some excerpts:

Bush: "I had sexual intercourse with perhaps three or four, I don't remember the exact number, women, at different times. In Thailand once, I have a pretty clear recollection that there was one time in Thailand and in Hong Kong."

Brown: "And you were married to Mrs. Bush?"

Bush: "Yes."

Brown: "Is that where you caught the venereal diseases?"

Bush: "No."

Brown: "Where did you catch those?"

Bush: "Diseases plural? I didn't catch…"

Brown: "Well, I'm sorry. How — how many venereal diseases do you suffer from?"

Bush: "I've had one venereal disease."

Brown: "Which was?"

Bush: "Herpes."

….

Brown: "Did you pay them for that sex?"

Bush: "No, I did not."

Brown: "Pick them up in a sushi house?"

Bush: "No…. My recollection is, where I can recall, they came to my room."

Brown: "Do you know the name of that hotel? I may go to Thailand sometime."

….

Brown: "Mr. Bush, you have to admit that it's a pretty remarkable thing for a man just to go to a hotel room door and open it and have a woman standing there and have sex with her."

Bush: "It was very unusual."

Brown: "Were they prostitutes?"

Bush: "I don't — I don't know."

1

Bumper-to-bumper

From 1950 to 1970, the US automobile population grew four times faster than the human population. Today, there are around 200 million cars in America. As a result, we Americans spend 8 billion hours per year stuck in traffic.

2

Cars kill people

During the twentieth century, 250 million Americans were maimed or injured in automobile accidents. Every single day in the US, an average of 121 people are killed in car accidents. The leading cause of death for children aged five to fourteen in New York City is pedestrian automobile accidents.

3

Cars kill animals

Automobiles, SUVs, trucks, and other fossil-burning vehicles kill a million wild animals per week in the US—not counting tens of thousands of family pets.

4

Cars exploit dead animals

Substances like anti-freeze, bio-diesel fuel, hydraulic brake fluid, and asphalt binder are all made with ingredients culled from the carcasses of departed animals.

5

Sprawling for dollars

During the last century, an area equal to all the arable land in Ohio, Indiana, and Pennsyl-

---

LIST :80

10 Reasons Why Cars Suck
Mickey Z.

vania was paved in the US. This area requires maintenance costing over $200 million a day. (The surreptitious cost of the car culture totals nearly $464 billion a year in the US alone, much of that going to the sustentation of a military presence in the Persian Gulf.)

6

Getting warmer?

Automobiles emit one-quarter of US greenhouse gases.

7

Oil in our veins

The US spends $60 billion per year on foreign oil. Eight million barrels of oil per day are combusted in US cars. That's 450 gallons per person per year.

8

They're all wasted

Cars create 7 billion pounds of unrecycled scrap and waste annually.

9

Leaving rubber

With approximately one billion discarded tires littering our increasingly paved landscape, meditate upon this: Every tire loses one pound of rubber per year, spewing minute grains of rubber into the stratosphere and then back down to find a new home in our water and/or our lungs.

10

Cars are hell

During the 40 days of the (first) Gulf War, 146 Americans died keeping the world safe for petroleum, while at home 4,900 Americans died in motor vehicle accidents.

Mickey Z. is the author of five books and hundreds of articles. His most recent books are: A Gigantic Mistake: Articles and Essays for Your Intellectual Self-Defense *(Prime Books) and* Seven Deadly Spins: Exposing the Lies Behind War Propaganda *(Common Courage Press). Contact him at mzx2@earthlink.net.*

1
Manure

Everyday, out of the hind ends of billions of living creatures, plops enough material to light up the world. Just heat shit in an extremely hot oven (a gasifier), and it gives off methane, which can be ignited to create steam for power. A slower method involves dumping the crap into an oxygenless tank, where anaerobic bacteria make the methane. The only byproduct is an environmentally-friendly ash that can be used as fertilizer.

Earth Resources, Inc. has set up a prototype chickenshit plant in Georgia that can power 25 homes with 6,000 pounds of dung a day. Several state governments—and those of Britain and Greece—have expressed interest in the operation. John C. McKissick of the University of Georgia says: "If we do it right, we're already the Saudi Arabia of the US with the potential chicken litter as an energy source."

A fully functional cow-flop facility was opened in Wisconsin in June 2001. The state's power companies buy the electricity generated, which is enough to juice up 250 homes. Similar efforts are underway across the globe, from Alberta to the Ukraine.

2
Sugar

In the "sugar platform" process, biomass—which includes anything from dung to trees, peanut shells to fats and grease—is broken down via enzymes. The resulting glucose is converted to fuels and chemicals, while the residue is used for heat and power. The US Department of Energy expects to see this process in use between 2006 and 2010.

3
Volcanoes

Geothermal energy is created by capturing and converting the natural heat of the earth. Presently, this type of energy almost always comes from reservoirs of hot water, but some successful attempts have harnessed the energy of volcanoes. In 1985 the US Geological Survey wrote: "The internal heat associated with young volcanic systems has been harnessed to produce geothermal energy. For example, the electrical energy generated from The Geysers geothermal field in northern California can meet the present power consumption of the city of San Francisco." Hawai'i has also been using volcano power.

LIST 81

3 Uncommon Sources of Power

1

Around the world

Vera Anderson always wanted to travel, but her emphysema and heart problems meant that she never made it out of the Midwest. When she died at 78 in early 2001, her son Ross arranged her final wish—a worldwide trip. Using half of her ashes, he sent a small packet to the postmasters at the capitol of each US state and each of the world's 191 countries, asking that they make sure the ashes were put in a proper place, perhaps with a ritual. The BBC reports:

> Vera's ashes have entered the stream in front of the Royal Castle in Stockholm, Sweden. They have toured Thailand, been to Malta, and dusted the snows of both the Earth's poles.... The Aymara Indians held a burial ceremony for them at Lake Titicaca in the Andes. And a nun at a South American orphanage now considers Vera Anderson her guardian angel. The ashes were sprinkled along the Choo Praya River in Thailand, on the Alabama state capitol grounds in Montgomery and within sight of Kiev, the capital of Ukraine.

2

Reef

If you'd like your body to become an octopus' garden, have Eternal Reefs handle the cremains. They'll mix the ashes in with a super-strong, environmentally-friendly concrete, casting it as an artificial reef. The reef—with or without a plaque—is put into the ocean, where it quickly gets covered in sea life and, if it's large enough, may become home to various fish or turtles. The cheapest option is $995, with prices up to $4,995.

3

Space

If your postmortem travel plans go beyond earth, you can get part of your ashes launched into space. Celestis will send one gram or seven grams of cremains into orbit around the Earth. (Approximately 100 people—including Gene Roddenberry and Timothy Leary—have put a pinch of their ashes on the space express.) Of course, the satellites containing the ashes will eventually re-enter Earth's atmosphere, burning to noth-

LIST 82 : 12 Things to do With Your Body After You're Dead

ingness, but it'll be fun while it lasts. For serious bucks, you can have one gram of ashes sent to the Moon's surface or launched into deep space.

4

Diamonds

One way to shine after your death is to become a diamond. LifeGem takes the carbon from cremated remains and turns them into an actual, certified, virtually flawless diamond with a yellow hue. Most people can be transformed into more than 50 one-carat stones. Not too many people will be turned into that much ice, though, since a 0.99-carat human-diamond costs $13,999 (for more than one, the cost is knocked down to $13,199 each).

5

Painting

The artists at Eternally Yours Everlasting Memorial Art will paint a canvas, sprinkle two to six tablespoons of cremains on it, then apply sealant. For abstract paintings, the colors will match the deceased's personality, or you can supply a photo to be turned into a painting.

6

Frisbee

Frisbee pioneer Ed Headrick asked that his ashes be molded into flying discs given to family and friends at his funeral.

7

Wild urns

All right, you want to be cremated, but you don't want your ashes shot into space, scattered all over the world, or tossed around in a park. Just because you're going to have them placed in an urn doesn't mean you have to be boring. Kelco Supply makes some wild receptacles that attain the level of sculpture: a twin set of urns that looks like stylized swans nuzzling each other, an eagle soaring across mountain cliffs, a man and woman cuddling on a bench, a book, a mantle clock, a pyramid, a golf bag, a duck decoy, cowboy boots, a teddy bear, a black lacquer egg with a Japanese landscape painted in gold leaf, a gray pseudo-granite box with a pink triangle... the choices are many. Materials used for these groovy containers include zebrawood, ebony, alabaster, onyx, ceramics, handblown glass, and polished pewter.

8

Ecopods

Let's say you don't feel like getting cremated. What is there in the way of alternative, ecofriendly coffins? AKRA's Ecopod is a streamlined casket based on the shape of a seed pod and constructed entirely of recycled paper that's been hardened using natural processes. These beauties come in green, red, blue, ivory, and goldleaf, and all but the latter can be silkscreened with doves, a Celtic cross, or an Aztec Sun. If you like the idea but still want to be cremated, the company's Acorn Urn—which looks just the way it sounds—is a snazzy holder for ashes also made out of hardened, recycled paper.

9

Other unorthodox bone boxes

People have been laid to rest in coffins made out of cardboard, willow, and wicker (demand for the latter tripled in the UK after 1960s pop idol Adam Faith was buried in one in 2003).

10

Natural burials

Why use a coffin at all? Britain is home to a growing movement in which the corpse is simply wrapped in a shroud and buried in a wooded area, in order to decay naturally. The UK is home to around 180 areas designated as woodland or green burial grounds, where people can also be buried *au naturel* or in coffins made of biodegradable materials.

11

Mummification

Started by a Mormon who has since been excommunicated, the religious organization Summum will mummify your body and encase it in a custom-made sarcophagus of bronze or stainless steel. The process—

which takes at least three months—supposedly combines the best of the old and new to create a modern form of mummification that preserves the entire body—skin, organs, DNA, and all. Summum's founder, Corky Ra, guarantees that your body will never decompose, that you eternally will look like you did on your dying day.

As of July 2003, 1,400 people had reportedly signed up for the pharaoh treatment, although none has yet died, which means that the process hasn't been tried on a human. It has been done to animals, specifically "more than 200 dogs, cats, parrots, cockatiels, a pet rat and a finch," according to the *LA Times*. The going rate for a human mummification is $67,000, plus tens of thousands to over a hundred grand for the burial casket. Animal rates start at $4,000 for a small pet, plus $2,000 to $100,000+ for the Mummiform sarcophagus.

12

Sweet rides

No matter what you decide to do with your earthly remains, if you're going to be the guest of honor at a funeral, you want to arrive in style. Instead of a humdrum hearse, try something different: a motorcycle with a hearse sidecar or a horse-drawn carriage. If you're lucky enough to croak in Australia, have the Classic and Vintage Funeral Coaches company fix you up with hearses made from a 1927 Buick, 1935 Dodge, 1946 Mercury, 1973 Cadillac de Ville, or other classic autos. ◻

I admit to a fascination with suicide notes. Obviously, they're a goldmine for trying to get insight into why people take their own lives and, thus, how we might be able to prevent it. In a completely different vein, writing a note is one of the last acts of a person about to willingly go into the great beyond, and it is a *creative* act—a final burst of thought, self-expression, communication before leaving this vale of tears forever. In some senses, these notes form an unrecognized genre of literature. Below are quotes taken from actual suicide notes.

1

Female, 21-years-old. "I don't want you to think I would kill myself over you because you're not worth any emotion at all. It is what you cost me that hurts and nothing can replace it."

2

Male, 51. "Though I am about to kick the bucket I am as happy as ever. I am tired of this life so am going over to see the other side."

3

Male, 48. "Imagine God playing a dirty trick on me like another life!!! I've lived 47 years—there aren't 47 days I would live over again if I could avoid it....

"Will you see Valerie through college—she is the only one about whom I am concerned as this .38 whispers in my ear."

4

Male, 45. "My darling, May her guts rot in hell—I loved her so much." (This is the entire note.)

5

Male, 74. "I married the wrong nag-nag-nag and I lost my life."

6

Female, 52. "I'm so tired and lonely. There goes a siren. Oh how can I stand being left. I need to go to a Dr. but I am afraid. I'm so cold."

LIST 83 : 19 Suicide Notes

7

Female, 31. "My boss, Kenneth J., seduced me and made me pregnant. He refuses to help me. I had not had intercourse in two years. He says that I will have to suffer through it by myself."

8

Male. "I love you you stupid head."

9

Male. "God I don't know why in the hell it has taken me all these years to be able to tell you I love you. You needed this all this time. My heart is puring out for you now. I can only hope its not to late."

10

Female. "The negatives of all the pictures I took in Germany and Holland (for 10 years) are in the large metal box on the shelf; the prints themselves are in one of the soft sided bags on the shelf in the closet."

11

Male. "Bury or Burn me as cheap as possible I don't care where."

12

Male. "Buy a Steak, Dope, Booze and go out with a BANG! (And see a couple of ladies first!!!)

"Discussion closed!——————"

13

Female. "Don't let the kids in the bedroom I'm dead."

14

Male. "If your interested you are welcome to what ever you want in the garage."

15

Male. "The grass is greener on the other side."

16

Female. "I don't want those assholes Jane & Joe to get my car."

17

Male. "I am tired of failing. If I can do this I will succeed."

18

Male. "What a rotten sham to pull. It's too bad I don't have enough personality to be ashamed of myself."

19

Female. "The Art of Listening
Be Patient—listen to the whole question
Don't start thing @ your response
Listen to Nature/God
Listen" ⬚

The definition of what magick is and what magick *is not*, seems to me to need redefining in the public eye. Magick isn't some sort of hocus-pocus sleight of hand; it's manifesting something extraordinary in your life or in the culture. Here's a list of twentieth century "magicians" using what I think is a more appropriate description of what magick is really all about.

1

Pablo Picasso

In the history of art there is "Before Picasso" and "After Picasso," meaning that no other single figure changed the way we *see* things like Pablo Picasso did. There is a documentary film called *The Mystery of Picasso* and in it, you can watch him paint—he's painting on a glass pane for the camera to see. It's one of the most astonishing things I have ever seen in my life. If you want to see real magick in action, check this film out. While you are watching it, keep in mind that it took him years to develop his talent to the point where he could do something like that in a matter of minutes. It didn't just happen overnight!

LIST 84 | 10 Top Magicians of the Twentieth Century
Richard Metzger

2

Aleister Crowley

Crowley, of course, was magick's Picasso. Crowley came along and wiped the chessboard clean of the archaic hoodoo of the previous era, installing himself along the way as the prophet of *Thelema* (Greek for "will") and as the Great Beast 666—the Antichrist—in the popular imagination. Whether that last part is true or not remains to be seen, obviously, but certainly Uncle Al changed the face of the occult forever with his potent synthesis of Eastern and Western magical traditions and techniques. (Hint: To make any sense of Crowley, you must start with either a biography or his autobiography, *The Confessions of Aleister Crowley*. His magical texts are incomprehensible unless you have a working knowledge of his life before you begin.)

3 **4**

William Burroughs and Brion Gysin

Burroughs and Gysin collaborated for many years on the literary "cut-ups" method of rearranging text on the page like a collage artist would to see what would *happen* and what was *really being said*. They wrote a book together called *The Third Mind*, which shows in detail how a magician using literature as his or her magical medium can *write things into existence* (a lesson not lost on Grant Morrison, see below). *The Third Mind*

is both a manual and a "book of shadows" record of the work they did. For that and many other reasons requiring too much detail for our purposes here, they make the list, hands down.

5

Kenneth Anger

Anger was the first magician to really use cinema as his magical medium and in doing so opened the minds of so many people to the power and lure of the occult. One of the things I find fascinating about his work is how he would use human "stand-ins" for the gods and goddesses he was evoking and his uncanny knack for choosing just the right people, such as casting Marianne Faithfull as Lilith in *Lucifer Rising* or witchy Marjorie Cameron as the Scarlet Woman in *Inauguration of the Pleasure Dome*. Another interesting aspect of his work is that his spells, by virtue of being on celluloid, can be watched over and over again, exponentially charging his intent each time they are screened.

6

Genesis P-Orridge

When I was a teenager, I read and will never forget something Genesis said about how a modern magician would use the tools of the time, meaning forget about the Latin, the robes, and the wands, and pick up a computer, a video camera, or an electric guitar. Founding father of industrial music and rave, now using his own body as a sigil in an effort to "break sex"—one of the most complex, creative, and courageous people ever to walk the face of the earth. When God made Gen, he threw away the cast!

7
Salvador Dalí

The "monstrous ego" of *Le Divine Dalí* insured that he was constantly in the media eye during his time, but if not for his prodigious artistic talents, would we still care? Study of the "paranoiac-critical" method of Dalí's creativity is a must for those seriously interested in magick.

8
Timothy Leary

One of the greatest minds of this or any other century, Leary took seriously the Great Work of alchemy—the cosmic perfection of mankind. In doing so he risked his sanity and the sanity of many others to boot! He was called "the most dangerous man in America" by Nixon and Hoover. By turning on the world, or trying to, with LSD, Leary joined the ranks of the great magi and liberators of human history. It may take another century before the good doctor gets his due, though. But it will happen, mark my words. (Hint: *All* the "secrets" of magick are neatly encoded within the pages of Leary's "Future History Series" of 1970s books. But coded they are: He wrote these books whilst in jail; if he'd have come right out and said in plain English

what he was hinting at, they'd have thrown away the key.)

9
John Coltrane

Music as mantra. John Coltrane isn't merely *playing* his saxophone on "A Love Supreme," he is *praying* with it. If you don't see the practical magical lesson that can be learned here, think harder.

10
Miles Davis

Well, Miles might have been a total asshole, true, but he did manage to change the direction of music several times during his lifetime, and if *that* ain't magical, I don't know what is! (And eat your heart out Brian Eno—it was *Miles* who invented "ambient music," as one listen to his eerie 1975 elegy to Duke Ellington, "He Loved Him Madly," will prove)

Honorable mention goes to **Grant Morrison**, whom I have called "the heir to William Burroughs" for years. Morrison's *meisterwerk*, *The Invisibles*, smuggles magical thought into the minds of comics readers like a Trojan horse, a true magical initiation disguised as an adventure series. It's one of the most subversive things ever to be funded by a major corporation and a spell the reverberations of which will still be felt for some time to come. ⚊

1

The Alcohol Tarot

By the Cult of the Drunken Prophet. Some people who really, really like booze have come up with a full Tarot deck devoted to a different kind of "spirit." The four traditional suits have been replaced by Beer, Wine, Lager, and Spirits. "The Magician" is, of course, the bartender, who can combine all kinds of alcohol and other beverages into an endless variety of yummy concoctions. "The Hanged Man" is a guy puking in a toilet, while "The Star" is a dartboard. The images are in the form of photographs. The heavily Photoshopped major arcana are so-so, but the minor arcana are elegant.

2

The Bosch Tarot

By *A. Atanassov*. Many decks use the style of famous artists to reinterpret the Tarot. In this case, Atanassov employs many images straight from Renaissance painter Hieronyomous Bosch, whose bizarre, labyrinthine works detail the joys of heaven and the horrors of hell. "The Chariot," for instance, shows a

LIST 85

17 Tarot Decks

man in reptilian body armor riding a chariot made of a saddle on a giant fish. Two dogs wearing sweaters appear to be pulling the odd contraption. It only gets weirder from there....

3

Chaos Tarot

By *John Berger*. In this gorgeous deck, every card is a radiantly colorful fractal. Although it may not always be immediately apparent, each image has been carefully selected to correspond to the meaning of the card: the isolated feel of "The Hermit," the merging of "The Lovers," the fiery explosion of "Strength." Some of the Major Arcana have been changed—"The High Priest" has become "Progenesis"—and two have been added to the end: "Hyperspace" and "Eschaton." One of the most beautiful Tarot decks ever created.

4

Cosmic Tribe Tarot

By *Stevee Postman*. One of the most popular recent decks, these phantasmagoric, psychedelic images show the possibilities when Photoshop is used by the right person. Influences include Alex Grey, the Grateful Dead, collage art, butterflies, flowers, LSD, sacred geometry, and attractive, naked people. Perhaps the most talked-about aspect of this deck is "The Lovers" card, which comes in three flavors: gay, lesbian, and het. I can't help thinking that the originators of the Tarot would be surprised but pleased.

5

Erotic Tarots of Milo Manara

Taking a different approach to the idea of a sexual Tarot, legendary erotic comic Euro-artist *Milo Manara* fills the deck with his trademark pouty, slinky women.

6

Erotica Tarot

By *Ylva Trollstierna, Patrik Carlsson, and Pierre Brawin*. From Sweden, this deck takes its cue from sex magick, Tantra, and other traditions that merge flesh and spirit. The black-and-white line drawings display only a medium level of sophistication, but there are many interesting ideas here. "The World" is represented by a daisy chain of people performing oral sex on each other, overlaid with the symbols of the zodiac. "The Lovers" sit entwined in a lotus position on a flaming heart. The phallic symbolism of "The Tower" is made blatant when it becomes a gigantic penis cracking in half.

7

Glow in the Dark Tarot

The Major Arcana have been taken from the Rider-Waite deck, reproduced in black and white, and printed with ink that glows in the dark.

8

H.R. Giger Tarot

The biomechanical work of artist *H.R. Giger*—best known for giving the *Alien* movies their sinister look—has been selected to represent each of the 22 Major Arcana. Dark and fearsome.

9

Hello, Tarot

By Joe Rosales. Comic artist Rosales has designed a black-and-white line art Tarot featuring scenes from the Rider-Waite deck but with the hypercute characters from the "Hello Kitty" universe replacing the traditional figures. Naturally, Kitty is "The High Priestess," while Pochacco the puppy is "Death," striking down other saccharine characters with his scythe.

10

Physical Egg Tarot

By Dirk Gillabel. The image for each card (Major Arcana only) was painted on the shell of a brown egg, which was then photographed on sand. In a similar vein, Gillabel's Oak Tarot is a series of photographs showing the Major Aracana painted on slices of a young oak tree.

11

Rock and Roll Tarot

by Chris Paradis. Photoshopped images show how rockers fit the Tarot archetypes: Frank Zappa is "The Magician"; Tina Turner is "The High Priestess"; Kurt Cobain is "The Hanged Man"; and Elvis is "The Emperor." The "Guitar" suit features Eric Clapton, Jimi Hendrix, and Carlos Santana. Tori Amos, Aretha Franklin, and Bob Marley appear in the "Voice" suit.

12

The Silicon Valley Tarot

By Thomas Scoville. This deck is basically a vehicle to spoof dot-com culture. The Minor Arcana's suits are disks, cubicles, networks, and hosts. The Major Arcana includes "The Hacker," "Venture Capital," "IPO", "Spam," and "The Layoff."

13

Tarot Art Quilt Project

In this collaborative project, 42 fiber artists created all 78 Tarot cards, each as a full-size quilt. The entire set was displayed at the 2003 International Quilt Festival.

14

Tarot of Baseball

By Robert Kasher and Beverley Ransom. The illustrations have the style and coloring of the Rider-Waite deck, but they poke gentle fun at America's Pastime. "The Fool" is a rookie, "Death" is a general manager running over people in his big car, and "The High Priestess" is the girlfriend or wife forced to watch the games. Gloves, caps, balls, and bats make up the Minor Arcana.

15

Tarot of the New Vision

By Pietro Alligo, R. Cestaro, G. Cestaro. Three Italian artists had a brilliant idea: Take the familiar images of the Rider-Waite deck, and paint them from the opposite perspective, showing what was previously "out of the frame." Thus we see that the Magician, with his candle burning at both ends, is performing for an audience in a garden, while a small monkey behind him tugs on his red robe. In the Nine of Swords, the anguished man in bed is actually being attacked by a demon, and two women behind the imperial Justice are nestling a baby into a basket.

16

Tarot Universal Dalí

By Salvador Dalí. Although many decks are retroactively done in the *style* of master artists, very few famous artists have directly taken up the challenge. Supreme Surreal-ist Salvador Dalí did, and the result—as you might expect—is a wild, phantasmagoric deck that is often considered one of the most stunning ever published.

17

The Thoth Tarot

By Aleister Crowley and Lady Frieda Harris. Using concepts from the Kabalah and the Golden Dawn combined with his own wild insights, the world's most famous occultist directed Harris to paint the surreal, abstract-ed images that adorn the cards.

Honorable Mentions: **The Tarot of Oz, Lord of the Rings Tarot, PoMo Tarot, Stick Figure Tarot, Wonderland Tarot, Ferret Tarot, Gummibear Tarot, Fantastic Medical Tarot, Tiny Tarot, Vampire Tarot, Gay Tarot, Nightmare Before Christmas Tarot.**

The Wonders of Modern Medicine, part one

In the medical procedure called enteral feeding, a nutrient in liquid form is piped directly into the digestive system. To see if the fluid leaks into the patient's respiratory system, it is sometime colored with blue food coloring (specifically, FD&C Blue #1, the same type used in M&Ms). Problem is, it sometimes turns the patient's shit and piss blue. Even worse, some people have been smurfed (i.e., their skin turns blue). But that's small potatoes compared to the dozen people who have died from the azure liquid as of September 2003.

1. **acetyl-L-carnitine**
2. **adrafinil**
3. **aniracetam**
4. **arginine**
5. **beta-carotene**
6. **choline**
7. **deprenyl**
8. **dehydroepiandrosterone** (DHEA)
9. **dilantin**
10. **dimethylaminoethanol** (DMAE)
11. **fatty acids**
12. **fipexide**
13. **gerovital** (GH-3)
14. **ginkgo biloba**
15. **glutamine**
16. **hydergine**
17. **KH3**
18. **L-glutamine**
19. **L-lysine**
20. **L-tryptophan**
21. **lecithin**
22. **melatonin**
23. **milacemide**
24. **modafinil**
25. **oxiracetam**
26. **phenylalanine**
27. **piracetam**
28. **pramiracetam**
29. **pregnenolone**
30. **propranolol hydrochloride**
31. **pyroglutamate** (PCA)
32. **selegiline**
33. **tryptophan**
34. **vasopressin**
35. **vinpocetine**
36. **vitacel**
37-43. **vitamins B_1, B_3, B_5, B_6, B_{12}, C, and E**
44. **xanthinol nicotinate**

44 Substances That Soup up Your Brain

LIST 86

In 2003, the Mount Sinai School of Medicine—in connection with two public interest groups—tested the blood and urine of nine people for the presence of 210 chemical pollutants. They found a total of 167 of these toxic substances in the volunteers. The average volunteer was carrying 91 of these compounds; the lowest number was 77, and the highest was 106.

Journalist Bill Moyers—the host of *NOW* on PBS and the interviewer who made mythologist Joseph Campbell famous—was one of the people tested. The following are among the witch's brew of 84 contaminants found in Moyers' body. (For more information, check out the Body Burden website at [www.ewg.org/reports/bodyburden/].)

LIST 87 | 24 Toxic Chemicals in Bill Moyers

1. **lead**

2. **methylmercury**

3. **pentafuran** (2,3,4,7,8-PeCDF)

4. **hexafuran** (1,2,3,4,7,8-HxCDF)

5. **heptadioxin** (1,2,3,4,6,7,8-HpCDD)

6. **octadioxin** (1,2,3,4,6,7,8,9-OCDD)

7. **PCB-8**

8. **PCB-99**

9. **PCB-196/203**

10. **3-methylcyclopentanol**

11. **meta-xylene**

12. **11,14-methyl ester eicosadienoic acid**

13. **methyl isobutyl carbinol**

14. **octadecanal**

15. **(E)-3-eicosene**

16. **cis-9-tricosene**

17. **palmitic acid**

18. **cyclohexane**

19. **O-methyloxime 3,5-dimethyl-2-Cyclohexen-1-one**

20. **1-heneicosyl formate**

21. **di-n-butyl phthalate**

22. **dimethylphosphate** (DMP)

23. **4,4'-DDT**

24. **methoxychlor**

ᗡ

The Wonders of Modern Medicine, part two

An unknown number of people have died from overdoses of morphine because of sloppy prescribing and filling. Roxanal—an oral solution of morphine sulfate—is sold in concentrations measuring in milliliters. Unfortunately, prescriptions are often written without specifying the type of measurement, which is sometimes assumed to be milliliters, instead of the much smaller milligrams. The result: Some poor slobs who should be getting, say, five milligrams of morphine actually end up taking five milliliters, which is 100 milligrams.

Some amount of insects, rodent hair, and mold in our food is inevitable. In 1986, the Food and Drug Administration was told to figure out how much filth is too much. They set limits at which the food was deemed unfit for human consumption; anything under that amount is A-OK. So if seven rat hairs per 10 grams of food are considered defective, then six hairs are fine.

Canned asparagus: 40 or more thrips in 100 grams.

2

Canned mushrooms: More than ten percent of the 'shrooms are decomposed.

3

Canned spinach: two or more caterpillars whose aggregate length is at least twelve millimeters in 24 pounds.

12 Acceptable Levels of Filth in Food

4

Canned tomatoes: two or more maggots *or* ten or more fly eggs in 500 grams.

5

Chocolate: three or more rodent hairs *or* 90 or more insect fragments in a 100-gram sample.

6

Chopped dates: ten or more dead insects in 100 grams.

7

Ginger: three or more milligrams of mammal shit per pound.

8

Ground cinnamon: 400 or more insect frag-ments in 50 grams.

9

Ground oregano: 1,250 or more insect parts in ten grams.

10

Macaroni and noodle products: "Average of 225 insect fragments or more per 225 grams in 6 or more subsamples."

11

Raisins: five percent or more of the raisins is infested with mold.

12

Wheat: nine milligrams or more of rat shit in a kilogram. ◻

The Powerdeath Girls

What could be more harmless than pink lotion from the Powerpuff Girls? A lot of things. The goo that came in some kind of "kit" adorned with the three cartoon girls had to be recalled nationwide in February-March 2003 because it was contaminated with a nasty bacterium. Pseudomonas aeruginosa primarily nails people with weaker than average immune systems, which includes most kids. The University of Wisconsin-Madison Department of Bacteriology says that the bug is "notorious for its resist-ance to antibiotics and is, therefore, a particularly dangerous and dreaded pathogen." Among the diseases it caus-es: pneumonia, meningitis, brain abscesses, untreatable acne, eye infec-tions "that can lead to loss of the entire eye," and infections of the ear, bones, joints, urinary tract, soft tissue, and gastrointestinal tract.

LIST: 88 | 12 Acceptable Levels of Filth in Food

Cathy Wilkinson Barash's colorful, lavishly illustrated 1993 cookbook looks in many ways like a lot of other coffee-table cookbooks. Except that it's titled *Edible Flowers*. In it, the lifelong flower-eater gives recipes, complete with scrumptious photos, for dishes you can prepare with 66 types of flower. Among them:

1

Tulips often taste like peas or beans, Barash tells us from experience, "occasionally with a green apple overtone." They make great salad dressing and tuna salad.

2

Pansy petals taste mildly sweet, while the entire flower has "a wintergreen overtone." Grinding them with granulated sugar in water makes pansy syrup.

3

As for **roses**, Barash recommends old varieties and fragrant hybrids. In general, roses have varying flavors, "all on the sweet side, with overtones ranging from apple to cinnamon to minty."

4

Chrysanthemums are tangy and go well with lamb.

5

When young, **dandelions** "have a sweet, honeylike flavor." Combine them with sugar, yeast, and juice from freshly-squeezed lemons and oranges to make the fabled dandelion wine.

6

Honeysuckle is especially yummy; Barash lavishes praise on this "floral, nectarous delectation." Like all flowers, it can be candied, jellied, or used to infuse vodka.

7

Sunflower buds taste like artichoke, while the petals of the flower are bittersweet. ◻

LIST 89 | 7 Edible Flowers

REFERENCES

3 States Where Cockfighting Is Legal

The Pit Master Website [www.pitmaster.com] § United Poultry Concerns Website [www.upc-online.org]

3 Uncommon Sources of Power

1. Paul, Peralte C. "The Power Is in the Manure." *Atlanta Journal-Constitution*, 5 Oct 2003. § Unsigned. "Manure-powered Energy Plant Opens." *Business Journal* (Milwaukee), 20 Jun 2001. **2.** Office of the Biomass Program, Office of Energy Efficiency and Renewable Energy, US Department of Energy. "Multiyear Plan 2003 to 2008 [draft]." 15 Jan 2003. **3.** Cascades Volcano Observatory (Vancouver, Washington), US Geological Survey. "The Plus Side of Volcanoes - Geothermal Energy." 6 Jun 2001.

4 Unreleased Raunchy Songs (selected sources)

Heylin, Clinton. *Bootleg: The Secret History of the Other Recording Industry*. St. Martin's Press, 1995. § Dean Martin's FBI file. § Various fan websites.

5 Designations of Importance Used by the CIA

Kessler, Ronald. *Inside the CIA*. Pocket Books, 1994.

5 "Family-Safe" Bibles

Green, Jonathon. *The Encyclopedia of Censorship*. Facts on File, 1990.

6 Bands That Are the Subject of FBI Files
(selected sources)

FBI FOIA website [foia.fbi.gov]. § The Smoking Gun website [www.thesmokinggun.com] § Various articles from the defunct website APBNews.com.

6 Celebrities Involved with the Church of Satan
(selected sources)

Various literature from the Church of Satan. § The Religious Movements Homepage Project, University of Virginia. "The Church of Satan."

6 Illegal Substances That Occur Naturally in Our Bodies

Joseph, Miriam. *Speed: Its History and Lore*. Carl-ton Books, 2000. § Concar, David. "Attack of the Munchies." *New Scientist* Website, 11 April 2001. § "The Endorphin Collection." Molecular Expressions Website, Florida State University [micro.magnet.fsu.edu]. § "Endorphins." *Columbia Encyclopedia*, Sixth Edition. Columbia University Press, 2001. § Faculty homepage of Samuel T. Christian, Department of Physiology and Biophysics, University of Alabama. [www.physiology.uab.edu/wyss/faculty/christia.htm] § Joseph, Miriam. *Speed: Its History and Lore*. Carlton Books, 2000. § Linda Rightmire. "Candace Pert's comments." Posting to MAPS forum, 5 Feb 2001. § National Institutes of Health. "Researchers Discover Function for Brain's Marijuana-Like Compound." 22 Mar 1999. § Lycaeum website [www.lycaeum.org.]

6 Sex Acts That Are Illegal

Posner, Richard A., and Katharine B. Silbaugh. *A Guide to America's Sex Laws*. University of Chicago Press, 1996. § Criminal codes of various states online.

7 CIA Plots to Kill Castro

CIA Inspector General. "Report on Plots to Assassinate Fidel Castro." 23 May 1967. Reprinted in *CIA Targets Fidel: The Secret Assassination Report*. Ocean Press, 1996.

7 Edible Flowers

Barash, Cathy Wilkinson. *Edible Flowers: From Garden to Palate*. Fulcrum Publishing, 1993.

8 Books That Didn't Make It Into the Bible

Platt, Rutheford H., Jr. *The Forgotten Books of Eden: Lost Books of the Old Testament*. Bell Publishing, 1980. § Unsigned. *The Lost Books of the Bible*. Bell Publishing, 1979. § Wesley Center for Applied Theology, Northwest Nazarene University. "Non-canonical Literature." Wesley Center Online. [wesley.nnu.edu/noncanon/].

8 Handmade Prison Objects

Angelo. *Prisoners' Inventions*. WhiteWalls, 2003. § Fausset, Richard. "Illegal Brew Gives Calif. Prison Officials Headaches." *Los Angeles Times*, 5 Jan 2003. § Gillin, Eric. "Make Your Own Pruno and May God Have Mercy on Your Soul." *The Black Table*, 24 Sept 2003.

8 Stupid Politician Quotes

1. "A Rare Glimpse Inside Bush's Cabinet." *60 Minutes* (TV show), 17 Nov 2002. The quote was said while Bush was being interviewed by Bob Woodward for his book *Bush at War*. **2.** "Remarks by the President on the Economy." Midwest Airlines Center, Milwaukee, Wisconsin, 3 Oct 2003. Transcript on White House website. **3.** Grove, Lloyd. "Lowdown." *New York Daily News*,11 Jan 2004. Said to *New Yorker* writer Ken Auletta. **4.** "DoD News Briefing - Secretary Rumsfeld and Gen. Myers." 12 Feb 2002. Transcript on Defense Department website. **5.** Durst, Will. "Liberace of Patronage." *The Progressive*, June 2003. **6.** Associated Press interview, 7 Apr 2003. **7.** "Clinton Pledges to Fight as Combat Soldier With Israeli Army." Newsmax.com, 31 July 2002. Quoting a report from the Canadian Press newswire. **8.** Hu, Winnie. "Clinton and Nadler Seek Inquiry Into E.P.A. Response to Sept. 11." *New York Times*, 27 Aug 2003.

9 Religious Quotes

1. Shaw, George Bernard. *Man and Superman*, 1903. **2.** Thomas Jefferson to Horatio G. Spafford, 1814. ME 14:119. **3.** Brant, Beth. "Physical Prayers: Spirituality and Sexuality." In *Ritual Sex*, edited by Tristan Taormino and David Aaron Clark. Masquerade Books, 1996. **4.** Podolsky, Robin. "Dirty." In *Ritual Sex*, edited by Tristan Taormino and David Aaron Clark. Masquerade Books, 1996. **5.** Mencken, H.L. *Living Philosophies*. Ed. by Will Durant. 1931. **6.** Robinson, Spider. "Praise the Lord and Pass the Ammunition," *Globe and Mail* (Toronto), 6 May 2002. **7.** Mencken, H.L. *Minority Report: H.L. Mencken's Notebooks*. 1956. **8.** Hitchens, Christopher. *Letters to a Young Contrarian*. Basic Books, 2001. **9.** Saint John Chrysostom (347-407), *De sacerdotio*.

9 Things That Will Disqualify You From Employment with the FBI

FBI form FD-140: "Application for Employment, Federal Bureau of Investigation."

9 US Companies Allowed to Manufacture Illegal Drugs

US Drug Enforcement Administration. "Manufacturer of Controlled Substances, Notices of Registration," 2003.

9 Visitors Who Died at Disneyland

Berkman, David. "Youth Killed by Disneyland Ride." *Los Angeles Times*, 8 June 1980, p 3. § Holley, David, and Marcida Dodson. "Woman Killed on Bobsled Ride at Disneyland." *Los Angeles Times*, 4 Jan 1984. § Koenig, David. *Mouse Tales: A Behind-the-Ears Look at Disneyland*. Bonaventure Press, 1994, pp 170-5. § Smith, Steven C. "Mickey Mouse Suits." *Los Angeles Times*, 28 Sept 1975, p 1. § Woodyard, David. "Death in Disneyland on the Matterhorn." *Los Angeles Herald-Examiner*, 4 Jan 1984. § Pfeifer, Stuart, Daniel Yi, Jennifer Mena. "Disneyland Rider Dies in Roller Coaster Accident." *Los Angeles Times*, 6 Sept 2003. § Yi, Daniel, and Robert Ourlian. "Man Dies 2 Days After Being Injured at Disneyland." *Los Angeles Times*, 27 Dec 1998. § *Los Angeles Times*, 5 June 1983, p 3. § "Man Killed at Disneyland Bled to Death, Autopsy Says." *Los Angeles Times*, 10 Sept 2003.

10 CIA Front Companies

Goulden, Joseph C. *The Death Merchant: The Rise and Fall of Edwin P. Wilson*. Bantam Books, 1985. § Kerber, Ross, and Bryan Bender. "Apparent CIA Front Didn't Offer Much Cover." *Boston Globe*, 10 Oct 2003. § Sturkey, Marion F. *Warrior Culture of the U.S. Marines*. Heritage Press International, 2001.

10 Oldest Still-Classified Documents at the National Archives

"10 Oldest Document Dates in ADRRES." National Archives and Records Administration, 5 Jan 2004. Document released in response to FOIA request NGC04-003 by Michael Ravnitzky.

10 Reasons Why Cars Suck

Hawken, Paul, Amory Lovins, and L. Hunter Lovins. *Natural Capitalism: Creating the Next Industrial Revolution*. Back Bay Books, 2000. § Kay, Jane Holt. *Asphalt Nation: How the Automobile Took Over America and How We Can Take it Back*. Crown Publishers, 1997. § Transportation Alternatives website [www.transalt.org]. § Coaltion for Appropriate Transportation website [www.car-free.org].

10 Unusual Forms and Genres of Music

All Music Guide website [www.allmusic.com] § Associated Press. "Underwater tunes draw divers," 13 July 2003. § Clark, M.A. "Genetic Music: An Annotated Source List." 1997-2004. [www.whozoo.org/mac/Music/Sources.htm] § Delio, Michelle. "Brain Music: Not Much to Dance To." Wired News, 27 March 2003. § Dye, Lee. "Brain Music." ABCNEWS.com, 28 Aug 2002. § Gresham, Mark. "In the Key of Life." *Creative Loafing* (Atlanta), 24 July 2003. § Kirk Nurock website [www.kirknurock.com] § Maurer, John A., IV. "Research in Underwater Sound" [webpage]. [ccrma-www.stanford.edu/~blackrse/h2o.html] § Mulatta Records website [www.mulatta.org] § The Pi Project website [www.microsound.org/pi/] § Rammel, Hal. "Joe Barrick's one-man band: A history of the piatarbajo and other one-man bands." *Musical Traditions* #8 (1990). § Rolling Stones, The. *According to the Rolling Stones*. Chronicle Books, 2003. § The Sound of Mathematics website [www.geocities.com/Vienna/9349/] § Underwater Music website [www.playalongathome.com/underwater/] § "When Nature Speaks." Jim Nollman interviewed by Derrick Jensen. *The Sun*, #253. [www.interspecies.com/pages/sun.html] § Winchester, Ashley. "Chelsea composer is searching for pets with pipes." *The Villager* (New York), 22-28 Oct 2003.

11 Godly People

1. Danton, Eric R., and David Owens. "'Voice' Tells Mom to Kill." *Hartford Courant*, 15 Aug 2001. **2.** Associated Press. "Father Cites Bible in Child-Chaining Case." 24 Oct 2000. **3.** Bunyan, Nigel. "'Deal with Jesus' Led to Bomber's Hate Campaign." *Daily Telegraph* (London), 22 Sept 2001. **4.** Griggs, Brandon. "Lafferty to Sheriff's Deputy: 'If God Asked Me to, I'd Kill You Right Now'." *Salt Lake Tribune*, 20 Aug 2000. **5.** Shiel, Tom. "Man Hacked Horse to Death for Eating Grass." *Irish Independent*, 2000. **6.** BBC News. "Father Kills Son in Ritual Sacrifice." 26 Feb 2002. **7.** Morris, Chris. "Former Nun Not Remorseful." Canadian Press, in *Toronto Star*, 8 Nov 2002. **8-9.** Ellis, Guy. "Suspects in St. Lucia Church Attack Say God Told Them to Do It." Associated Press, 1 Jan 2001 **10.** "Serial Killer 'Not Sorry' About 13 Murders." Ananova newswire (London), 12 Nov 2000. **11.** Christian, Carol, and Lisa Teachy. "Yates Believed Children Doomed." *Houston Chronicle*, 6 Mar 2002. **12.** McGraw, Seamus. "Cops: Son Attacked for Skipping Sunday School." APBNews, 7 Nov 2000.

11 Materials That Have Been Made Into Guns

Minnery, John. *"Kill Without Joy!": The Complete How to Kill Book*. Paladin Press, 1992.

11 Quotes About Politics and Government

1. *I.F. Stone's Weekly* (documentary), 1974. **2.** Hernandez, Nelson. "Md. Voting Machines Vulnerable, Firm Says." *Washington Post*, 30 Jan 2004. **3.** Disraeli, Benjamin. *Vivian Grey*, 1824. **4.** *The Columbia World of Quotations*. Columbia University Press, 1996. **5.** "Mr. Mencken Sounds Off." *Life*, 5 Aug 1946. **6.** Nathan, George Jean, and H.L. Mencken. *Interpretation of the National Mind*. 1920. **7.** Thoreau, Henry David. "Civil Disobedience." 1849. **8.** Kaufmann, Bill. *America First!: Its History, Culture and Politics*. Prometheus Books, 1995. **9.** "Idiot Whistle." Written by Tony Fitzpatrick. Performed by Jonboy Langford & the Pine Valley Cosmonauts on *The Executioner's Last Songs*, 2002. **10.** George, John, and Laird Wilcox. *Nazis, Communists, Klansmen and Others on the Fringe: Political Extremism in America*. Prometheus Books, 1992. **11.** Orwell, George. *Nineteen Eighty-Four*. 1949.

11 Whistle-blowers (selected sources)

Bouza, Anthony V., Police Chief (Ret.). *Police Unbound: Corruption, Abuse and Heroism by the Boys in Blue*. Prometheus Books, 2001. § Butler, Smedley D. *War Is a Racket*. Feral House, 2003. § Ephron, Dan. "Muzzling a Whistle-Blower." *Newsweek* (International Edition), 12 Jan 2004. § "For Telling the Truth" by Norman Solomon, *Baltimore Sun*, 14 Dec 2003. § Jeffrey Wigand website [www.jeffreywigand.com] § "Karen Silkwood – Campaigner." BBC h2g2 website. § "The Katherine Gun Case." Institute for Public Accuracy website [www.accuracy.org/gun/] § Kick, Russ. *Psychotropedia: A Guide to Publications on the Periphery*. Critical Vision, 1998. § Levitt, Martin Jay, with Terry Conrow. *Confessions of a Union Buster*. Crown, 1993. § Los Alamos National Laboratory. "The Karen Silkwood Story." *Los Alamos Science*, 23 Nov 1995. § Levitt, Martin Jay, with Terry Conrow. *Confessions of a Union Buster*. Crown, 1993. § Stiglitz, Joseph E. *Globalization and Its Discontents*. Norton, 2002. § The US Campaign to Free Mordechai Vanunu [www.serve.com/vanunu/] § US Marine Corps website [www.usmc.mil]

12 Acceptable Levels of Filth in Food

Center for Food Safety and Applied Nutrition, US Food and Drug Administration. "The Food Defect Action Levels." May 1995; revised May 1998.

12 Arguments Against the Police State at Guantanamo Bay

Text of the *amicus curae*, which are posted at the website of the Center for Constitutional Rights [www.ccr-ny.org].

12 Erotic Works by Well-Known Writers

Pitt-Kethley, Fiona. (Ed.) *The Literary Companion to Sex*. Random House, 1992. § Quasi Official Robert Silverberg Home Page [www.majipoor.com] § Zacks, Richard. *An Underground Education*. Anchor, 1999. § The text of the works themselves.

12 Olde-Timey Porn Books (selected sources)

Green, Jonathon. *The Encyclopedia of Censorship*. Facts on File, 1990. § Perkins, Michael. *The Secret Record*. Rhinoceros, 1992. § Rasmussen, R. Kent., *et al*. (Eds.) *Censorship* (3 volumes). Salem Press, 1997. § Zacks, Richard. *History Laid Bare*. HarperCollins, 1994.

12 Songs About Drugs (selected sources)

Digital Tradition Database [www.mudcat.org] § Indiana Prevention Resource Center at Indiana University. "References to Drugs in the Lyrics of Songs from the 1930's and 1940's."

12 Strange Drugs

1. Inaba, Darryl S., Pharm. D., and Cohen, William E. *Uppers, Downers, All-Arounders: Physical and Mental Effects of Psychoactive Drugs* (second edition). CNS Productions, 1993. § US Marine Corps, the Basic School, Training Command. "B1321.1 Student Handout: Engineering Skills Field Firing Exercise." **2.** Provonsha, Jack, M.D., Ph.D. "Exploring the Edges of Death." *Signs of the Time*, March 1999. § Stolaroff, Myron. "Carbogen." 20 Aug 2002, Multidisciplinary Association for Psychedelic Studies forum. **3.** Lycaeum website [www.lycaeum.org.] **4.** McLean, D., R.G. Forsythe, and I.A. Kapkin. "Unusual side effects of clomipramine associated with yawning." *Canadian Journal of Psychiatry*, vol 28 (Nov 1983). **5.** "Mickey Slim." Wikipedia

[www.wikipedia.org]. **6.** Borkhane. "More Tripping & Revelations." Erowid website, 5 Sept 2003. § Shulgin, Alexander and Ann. *TIKHAL: The Continuation*. Transform Press, 1997. **7.** Elmer, Bob. "Was Napoléon a Junkie?" NapoleonSeries.org. § Mandel, Jerry. "The Mythical Roots of US Drug Policy: Soldier's Disease and Addicts in the Civil War." Schaffer Library of Drug Policy [www.druglibrary.org/schaffer]. § Unsigned. "Nations Uniting to Stamp out the Use of Opium and Many Other Drugs." *New York Times*, 25 July 1909. § Von Bibra, Baron Ernst. *Plant Intoxicants: A Classic Text on the Use of Mind-Altering Plants*. Healing Arts Press, 1995, pp 214-5. **8.** Rudgley, Richard. *The Encyclopedia of Psychoactive Substances*. St. Martin's, 1998. § Erowid website. **9.** Rudgley, Richard. *The Encyclopedia of Psychoactive Substances*. St. Martin's, 1998. **10.** Kozorog, Miha. "Salamander Brandy: 'A Psychedelic Drink' Between Media Myth and Practice of Home Alcohol Distillation in Slovenia." *Anthropology of East Europe Review*, 21.1. **11.** Miller, Steven L. "Plants, Fungi and Shamanism." Website of Steven L. Miller, associate professor of botany, University of Wyoming [asuwlink.uwyo .edu/~fungi] § Morgan, Adrian. "Father Christmas Flies on Toadstools." *New Scientist*, 25 Dec 1986, p 45. **12.** Anonymous. "An Extremely Expensive High." Lycaeum website, 10 Oct 2000. **HM.** Warren, Ellen. "Could It be That Old Books Are Really, uh, Mind-Altering?" *Chicago Tribune*, 21 Sept 1996.

12 Things to do With Your Body After You're Dead

De Vancy, Scott. "Alternative Funeral Resource Guide." *The Wave* (San Francisco), 2003. § Scheeres, Julia. "Ashes to Ashes, Dust to Diamonds." Wired News, 19 Sept 2002.

1. "Dead Mum's World Tour." BBC, 29 May 2001. **2.** Website of Eternal Reefs, Inc. [www.eternalreefs.com]. **3.** Website of Celestis, Inc. [www.celestis.com] § "Space Final Frontier for Timothy Leary." CNN, 20 Apr 1997. **4.** Website of LifeGem [www.lifegem.com]. **5.** Website of Eternally Yours Everlasting Memorial Art [www.memorialart.com]. **6.** Harris, Ron. "Dead Designer Will Become Frisbee." Associated Press, 15 Aug 2002. **7.** Website of Kelco Supply [www.kelcosupply.com]. **8.** Website of AKRA/Ecopod [www.ecopod.co.uk]. **9.** Website of Alternative Ceremonies [www.alternative-ceremonies.co.uk]. **10.** Website of the Natural Death Centre [www.naturaldeath.org.uk]. **11.** Website of Summum [www.summum.org]. § Kelly, David. "Man Finds There's Money to be Made in Mummies." *Los Angeles Times*. Reprinted in *Post & Courier*

(Charleston NC), 5 Jul 2003. **12.** Websites of Motorcycle Funerals [motorcyclefunerals.com], Carriage for Occasions [www.horsedrawnservices.com], and Classic and Vintage Funeral Coaches [www.funeralcoaches.com.au].

---

12 Unorthodox Sex Practices (selected sources)

Cassell. *Sex and Sexuality: A Thematic Dictionary of Quotations*. Cassell Publishers Ltd., 1993. § Gates, Katharine. Deviant Desires: Incredibly Strange Sex website. [www.deviantdesires.com] § Love, Brenda. *Encyclopedia of Unusual Sex Practices*. Barricade Books, 1992. § Stoller, Robert J., MD. "Erotic Vomiting." *Archives of Sexual Behavior* 2.4 (1982): 361-5.

A Dozen US Politicians Who Have Smoked Pot (selected source)

Cass, Connie. "Past Marijuana Use No Longer A Political Stigma." Associated Press. In *Sun News* (Myrtle Beach, SC), 30 Nov 2003. § *Pumping Iron* (film). 1977.

---

12 Ways to Alter Your Consciousness Without Drugs (selected sources)

Califia, Pat. "Shiny Sharp Things." In *Ritual Sex*, edited by Tristan Taormino and David Aaron Clark. Masquerade Books, 1996. § Vale, V., and Andrea Juno. Interview with Fakir Musafar. In *Modern Primitives: An Investigation of Contemporary Adornment and Ritual*. RE/Search Publications, 1989. § Weil, Andrew, M.D. *The Marriage of the Sun and the Moon*. Houghton-Mifflin, 1998. § Williams, Donna. *Nobody Nowhere: The Extraordinary Autobiography of an Autistic*. Avon, 1994. § "Therapeutic Benefits of Laughter." Holistic Online [www.holistic-online.com].

---

13 Exotic Guns and Knives

David A. Cushman website [website.lineone.net/~dave.cushman/] § Evans, Colin. *The Casebook of Forensic Detection: How Science Solved 100 of the World's Most Baffling Crimes*. Wiley, 1998. § Metal Storm Limited website [www.metalstorm.com]. § Minnery, John. *"Kill Without Joy!": The Complete How to Kill Book*. Paladin Press, 1992. § Stinger Manufacturing website [stingerpengun.com]. § Taggart, Stewart. "New Gun Fires 'Laser of Lead'." Wired News, 28 Sept 2001.

---

13 Innocent People Who Went to Prison

Innocence Project website [www.innocence project.org]

---

13 Last Meals Requested by Executed Texas Prisoners

"Final Meal Requests." [www.tdcj.state.tx.us/stat/finalmeals.htm]. A now-deleted page from the Texas Department of Criminal Justice website. Now mirrored at The Memory Hole [www.thememory hole.org].

---

13 Nuclear Tests That Spread Radiation into Civilian Areas

Nevada Operations Office, US Department of Energy. *Radiological Effluents Released from US Continental Tests, 1961 Through 1992*. DOE/NV-317 (Rev. 1). UC-702. Aug 1996.

---

13 Programs From DARPA's Defunct Information Awareness Office

From a saved version of the now deleted website for the Information Awareness Office [www.darpa.mil/iao/].

---

14 Criminal Cops and Their "Punishments"

1. Akin, Paige. "Officer Resigns, Pleads Guilty: Mark Bolger, Originally Charged With Sodomy, Agrees to Lesser Charge." *Times-Dispatch*, 16 Jan 2004. **2.** Associated Press. "Former Sheriffs Deputy Sentenced for Child Pornography." *Circa* 23 Jan 2004 **3.** Fulkerson, Martha. "Officer Sentenced." *Times* (Frankfort, IN). 22 Jan 2004. **4-9.** Hogben, David, and Neal Hall. "Two Vancouver Police Officers Sentenced to House Arrest." *Vancouver Sun*, 6 Jan 2004. § Tanner, Adrienne. "Criminal Records for 4 Officers." *The Province*, 6 Jan 2004. **10.** Carlile, Jordan. "Deputy Pleads Guilty to Child Abuse." Brigham Young University NewsNet, 15 Jan 2004. § Helps, Shana. "Former Sheriff's Deputy Sentenced to up to Life in Prison in Sodomy Case." *Daily Herald* (Provo, UT), 8 Jan 2004. **11.** Kelleher, Jennifer Sinco. "Ex-NYPD Cop Gets Jail for Deaths." *Newsday* (NY), 15 Jan 2004. § Pulitzer, Lisa, and Andy Geller. "Jail for DWI Cop." *New York Post*, 16 Jan 2004. **12.** Morse, Janice. "Ex-officer Enters Guilty Plea." *Cincinnati Enquirer*, 4 Dec 2003. § 9News. "Former Police Officer Sentenced To Six Years." WCPO (Cincinnati), 14 Jan 2004. **13.** "Former

Police Officer Sentenced in Child Molestation Case." Associated Press, 7 Aug 2003. **14.** "Ex-trooper Gets Light Sentence in Child Porn Case." *Observer-Reporter* (Washington, PA), 6 Aug 2003. **HM.** Fazlollah, Mark. "3 Say Abusive Police Got Slaps on Wrist." *Philadelphia Inquirer*, 16 Jan 2004.

---

15 Things That Cause or Mimic "Mental Illnesses" (selected sources)

Giller, Robert M., M.D., and Kathy Matthews. *Natural Prescriptions*. Carol Southern Books, 1994. § Marohn, Stephanie. *The Natural Medicine Guide to Bipolar Disorder*. Hampton Roads Publishing Company, 2003. § Marohn, Stephanie. *The Natural Medicine Guide to Depression*. Hampton Roads Publishing Company, 2003. § Marohn, Stephanie. *The Natural Medicine Guide to Schizophrenia*. Hampton Roads Publishing Company, 2003. § Quicksilver Associates. *The Mercury in Your Mouth: The Truth About "Silver" Dental Fillings*. Quicksilver Press, 1996.

---

16 Legal Substances That Can Cause False Positives on Drug Tests (selected sources)

Daniel, Lisa. "Officials Involved in Workplace Drug Testing Get a Chilling Reminder of the Hazards of False Readings." *Federal Times*, 26 Jan 1998. § Gombos, Justin. Drug Testing FAQ 4.12, 15 Mar 1998. § Nightbyrd, Jeffery. "Conquering the Urine Tests." [www.nodrugwar.com/html/booklet/booklet.htm]

---

16 Movies Banned in the US

Goodridge, Michael. "The Best Films You Can't See." *The Advocate*, 23 July 2002.§ Green, Jonathon. *The Encyclopedia of Censorship*. Facts on File, 1990. § Internet Movie Database website [www.imdb.com] § Ledes, Richard. "'Let There Be Light': John Huston's Film and the Concept of Trauma in the United States after WWII." Lecture presented at the Apres-Coup Psychoanalytic Association, 13 Nov 1998. § The Profit website [www.theprofit.org] § Rasmussen, R. Kent., *et al.* (Eds.) *Censorship* (3 volumes). Salem Press, 1997. § Subterranean Cinema website [www.subcin.com]

---

17 Questions You'll be Asked When Applying to Become an FBI Agent

FBI form FD-140: "Application for Employment, Federal Bureau of Investigation." § FBI form FD-190: "Special Agent Interview Form."

---

17 Tarot Decks (selected sources)

Aeclectic Tarot Website [www.aeclectic.net] § Artof-tarot.com § The Tarot Garden [www.tarotgarden.com]

---

18 Biblical Atrocities

Ball, Mark D., Ph.D. "Best-Selling Errancy: An Essay on Inconsistencies in the Bible." Internet Infidels Website [infidels.org]. § Bible, various versions. § Morgan, Donald. "Bible Atrocities." Internet Infidels Website [infidels.org]. § Walker, Jim. "The Dark Bible: The Atrocities." NoBeliefs.com.

---

18 Celebrities Involved With the Church of Scientology (selected sources)

Hausherr, Tilman. "Scientology Celebrities FAQ." 1 Jan 2003. § Scientollywood website [www.scientollywood.org].

---

19 Profanely-Named Bands (selected sources)

All Music Guide website [www.allmusic.com]. § Websites of various bands.

---

19 Suicide Notes

Alverez, Alfred. "Appendix B: Suicide Notes: 1983-1984." In *The Savage God*. Random House, 1972, 1990. § Kleiner, Art. "How Not to Commit Suicide." *News That Stayed News—1974-1984: Ten Years of CoEvolution Quarterly*. North Point Press, 1986.

---

20 Famous Drinkers of Absinthe

Baker, Phil. *The Book of Absinthe: A Cultural History*. Grove Press, 2001. § Conrad, Barnaby, III. *Absinthe: History in a Bottle*. Chronicle Books, 1988. § Lanier, Doris. *Absinthe: The Cocaine of the Nineteenth Century*. McFarland & Company, 1995. § Wittels, Betina J., and Robert Hermesch. Ed. by T.A. Breaux. *Absinthe: Sip of Seduction*. Corvus Publishing, 2003.

---

20 Mishaps That Might Have Started Nuclear War (selected sources)

Britten, Stewart: *The Invisible Event: An Assessment of the Risk of Accidental or Unauthorised Detonation of Nuclear Weapons and of War by Miscalculation*. London: Menard Press, 1983. § Calder, Nigel:

Nuclear Nightmares. London: British Broadcasting Corporation, 1979. § *Peace Research Review*, 9.4 (1984), 9.5 (1984), 10.3 (1986), 10.4 (1986). Dundas, Ontario: Peace Research Institute. § Sagan, Scott D.: *The Limits of Safety*. Princeton University Press, 1993.

---

21 Biblical Contradictions

Ball, Mark D., PhD. "Best-Selling Errancy: An Essay on Inconsistencies in the Bible." Internet Infidels [infidels.org]. § Bible, various versions. § Merritt, Jim. "A List of Biblical Contradictions." 24 July 1992. Internet Infidels [infidels.org]. § Morgan, Donald (compiler). "Biblical Inconsistencies." Internet Infidels [infidels.org]. § Walker, Jim. "The Dark Bible: The Atrocities." NoBeliefs.com.

---

21 Natural Aphrodisiacs

Meyer, Clarence. *Herbal Aphrodisiacs From World Sources*. Meyerbooks, 1993.

---

23 Early Cases of Involuntary Human Experimentation

Lederer, Susan E. *Subjected to Science: Human Experimentation in America Before the Second World War*. Johns Hopkins University Press, 1995. § Except item #21: Goliszek, Andrew. *In the Name of Science: A History of Secret Programs, Medical Research, and Human Experimentation*. St. Martin's Press, 2003.

---

23 Quotes Regarding the 2003 Invasion of Iraq

1. Powell, Secretary Colin L. "Press Remarks with Foreign Minister of Egypt Amre Moussa," Cairo, Egypt (Ittihadiya Palace), 24 Feb 2001. Posted on the State Department website [www.state.gov]. **2.** Condoleezza Rice on *CNN Late Edition With Wolf Blitzer*, 29 July 2001. Transcript from Lexis-Nexis. **3.** *Time*, 31 March 2003. **4.** Veterans of Foreign Wars 103rd National Convention, 26 Aug 2002. **5.** Bumiller, Elisabeth. "Bush Aides Set Strategy to Sell Policy on Iraq." *New York Times*, 7 Sept 2002. **6.** FOX News Sunday interview with Tony Snow, 8 Sept 2002. **7.** Central Intelligence Agency. "Iraq's Weapons of Mass Destruction Programs," Oct 2002. **8.** Rose Garden, 2 Oct 2002. **9.** Address to the Nation, 17 Mar 2003. **10.** Press conference, 25 March 2003. **11.** Gellman, Barton. "Special Search Operations Yield No Banned Weapons." *Washington Post*, 30 Mar 2003. **12.** "This Week with George Stephanapolous." ABC, 30 Mar 2003. **13.** Agence France-Presse. "Blix: Iraq War Planned Long in Advance." 9 April 2003. **14.** *New York Times*, 14 Apr 2003. **15.** Interview with TVP, Poland, 29 May 2003. **16.** Thomas, Evan. "Groping in the Dark." *Newsweek*, 1 Sept 2003. **17.** Kamen, Al. "Misdirected Military E-Mail Spills the Beans." *Washington Post*, 15 Oct 2003. **18.** "Jessica Lynch Laments Military Portrayal." Associated Press, 7 Nov 2003. **19.** Burkeman, Oliver, and Julian Borger. "War Critics Astonished as US Hawk Admits Invasion Was Illegal." *Guardian* (London), 20 Nov 2003. **20.** Filkins, Dexter. "Tough New Tactics by US Tighten Grip on Iraq Towns." *New York Times*, 7 Dec 2003. **21.** Associated Press. "Rice: No Evidence Iraq Moved WMD to Syria." 9 Jan 2004. **22.** "The Man Who Knew." *60 Minutes II*, 4 Feb 2004. **23.** *Uncovered: The Whole Truth About the Iraq War*. Produced and directed by Robert Greenwald. 2003.

---

24 Toxic Chemicals in Bill Moyers

Body Burden website [www.ewg.org/reports/body-burden/].

---

25 Iranian Rock Bands

TehranAvenue Music Open website [www.tehran 360.com]

---

25 Tips for Interrogating a Prisoner, From the CIA

"KUBARK COUNTERINTELLIGENCE INTERROGATION." Central Intelligence Agency, July 1963. Declassified January 1997. Copy obtained by Russ Kick on 14 Jan 2004 through FOIA request F-2004-00596.

---

31 Products Containing Hard Drugs

Booth, Martin. *Opium: A History*. St. Martin's, 1996. § Hodgson, Barbara. *In the Arms of Morpheus*. Firefly Books, 2001. § Karch, Steven B. *A Brief History of Cocaine*. CRC Press, 1998. § Plant, Sadie. *Writing on Drugs*. Picador, 2001. § Addiction Research Unit, Department of Psychology, University at Buffalo, State University of New York. "Before Prohibition." [wings.buffalo.edu/aru/preprohibition].

---

32 Cigarette Additives

Indiana Prevention Resource Center, Indiana University. "Additives Found in American Cigarettes," 2 Aug 1998. [www.drugs.indiana.edu]

32 Famous People Involved in Triads

Foster, Barbara, Michael Foster, and Letha Hadady. *Three in Love: Ménages à Trois from Ancient to Modern Times.* HarperSanFrancisco, 1997. § Thomson, David. *Rosebud: The Story of Orson Welles.* Vintage, 1997.

33 Names of Defense Department Internal Investigations

From documents released under a Department of Defense FOIA request filed by Michael Ravnitzky. Full list posted at The Memory Hole [www.thememoryhole.org].

34 CIA Cryptonyms (selected sources)

"Abbreviations and Cryptonyms." In *Foreign Relations, Guatemala, 1952-1954.* Office of the Historian, State Department. § "CIA cryptonym." Wikipedia [www.wikipedia.org].

36 Botched Executions

1. Denno, Deborah W. "Is Electrocution an Unconstitutional Method of Execution? The Engineering of Death over the Century." William & Mary Law Review, 35: 551, 664-665 (1994). **2.** For a description of the execution by Evans' defense attorney, see: Canan, Russell F. "Burning at the Wire: The Execution of John Evans." In *Facing the Death Penalty: Essays on a Cruel and Unusual Punishment.* (Michael L. Radelet, ed.). 1989. § See also *Glass v. Louisiana,* 471 U.S. 1080, 1091-92 (1985). **3.** Bruck, David. "Decisions of Death." *New Republic* (12 Dec 1984): 24-5. § Solotaroff, Ivan. "The Last Face You'll Ever See." *Esquire,* 124 (Aug 1995): 90, 95. **4.** "Two Charges Needed to Electrocute Georgia Murderer." *New York Times,* 13 Dec 1984: 12. § Editorial, *New York Times,* 17 Dec 1984: 22. **5.** "Murderer of Three Women is Executed in Texas." *New York Times,* 14 Mar 1985: 9. **6.** "Killer's Electrocution Takes 17 Minutes in Indiana Chair." Washington Post, 17 Oct 1985: A16. § "Indiana Executes Inmate Who Slew Father-In-Law." *New York Times,* 17 Oct 1985: 22. **7.** "Killer Lends a Hand to Find a Vein for Execution." *Los Angeles Times,* 20 Aug 1986: 2. **8.** "Addict Is Executed in Texas For Slaying of 2 in Robbery." *New York Times,* 25 June 1987: A24. **9.** "Drawn-out Execution Dismays Texas Inmates." *Dallas Morning News,* 15 Dec 1988: 29A. § "Landry Executed for '82 Robbery-Slaying." *Dallas Morning News,* 13 Dec

1988: 29A. **10.** "Witness to an Execution." *Houston Chronicle,* 27 May 1989: 11. **11.** Applebome, Peter. "2 Jolts in Alabama Execution." *New York Times,* 15 July 1989: 6. § Archibald, John. "On Second Try, Dunkins Executed for Murder." *Birmingham News,* 14 July 1989: 1. **12.** Barnett, Cynthia. "Tafero Meets Grisly Fate in Chair." *Gainesville Sun,* 5 May 1990: 1. § Barnett, Cynthia. "A Sterile Scene Turns Grotesque." *Gainesville Sun,* 5 May 1990: 1. § Moss, Bill. "Chair Concerns Put Deaths on Hold." *St. Petersburg Times,* 18 July 1990: B1. § Ritchie, Bruce. "Flames, Smoke Mar Execution of Murderer." *Florida Times-Union* (Jacksonville), 5 May 1990: 1. § Ritchie, Bruce. "Report on Flawed Execution Cites Human Error." *Florida Times-Union* (Jacksonville), 9 May 1990: B1. **13.** "Niles Group Questions Execution Procedure." United Press International, 8 Nov 1992 (Lexis/Nexis file). **14.** Allen, Mike. "Groups Seek Probe of Electrocution's Unusual Events." *Richmond Times-Dispatch,* 19 Oct 1990: B1. § Allen, Mike. "Minister Says Execution Was Unusual." *Richmond Times-Dispatch,* 20 Oct 1990: B1. § Brown, DeNeen L. "Execution Probe Sought." *Washington Post,* 21 Oct 1990: D1. **15.** Haywood, Karen. "Two Jolts Needed to Complete Execution." *Free-Lance Star* (Fredericksburg, VA), 23 Aug 1991: 1. § "Death Penalty Opponents Angry About Latest Execution." *Richmond Times-Dispatch,* 24 Aug 1991: 1. § "Virginia Alters its Procedure for Executions in Electric Chair." *Washington Post,* 24 Aug 1991: B3. **16.** Clinesmith, Sonja. "Moans Pierced Silence During Wait." *Arkansas Democrat-Gazette* 26 Jan 1992: 1B. § Farmer, Joe. "Rector, 40, Executed for Officer's Slaying." *Arkansas Democrat-Gazette,* 25 Jan 1992: 1. § Farmer. Joe. "Rector's Time Came, Painfully Late." *Arkansas Democrat-Gazette,* 26 Jan 1992: 1B. § Frady, Marshall. "Death in Arkansas." *New Yorker,* 22 Feb 1993: 105. **17.** Howe, Charles L. "Arizona Killer Dies in Gas Chamber." *San Francisco Chronicle,* 7 Apr 1992: A2. § Kwok, Abraham. "Injection: The No-Fuss Executioner." *Arizona Republic,* 28 Feb 1993: 1. § "Gruesome Death in Gas Chamber Pushes Arizona Toward Injections." *New York Times,* 25 Apr 1992: 9. **18.** Greene, Wayne. "11-Minute Execution Seemingly Took Forever." *Tulsa World,* 11 Mar 1992: A13. **19.** "Another U.S. Execution Amid Criticism Abroad." *New York Times,* 24 Apr 1992: B7. **20.** Graczyk, Michael. "Convicted Killer Gets Lethal Injection." Herald. (Denison, TX), 8 May 1992. § Wernsman, Robert. "Convicted Killer May Dies." *Item* (Huntsville, TX), 7 May 1992: 1. **21.** Rodriguez, Alex, and Scott Fornek. "Gacy Lawyers Blast Method: Lethal Injections Under Fire After Equipment Malfunction." *Chicago Sun-Times,* 11 May 1994: 5. § Chapman, Rich. "Witnesses Describe Killer's 'Macabre' Final Few Minutes." *Chicago Sun-Times*, 11 May 1994: 5. § Karwath, Rob, and Susan Kuczka. "Gacy Execution Delay Blamed on Clogged IV Tube." *Chicago Tribune*, 11 May 1994: 1 (Metro Lake Section). **22.** Because they could not observe the entire execution procedure through the closed blinds, two witnesses later refused to sign the standard affidavit that stated they had witnessed the execution. § "Witnesses to a Botched Execution." *St. Louis Post-Dispatch*, 8 May 1995: 6B. § O'Neil, Tim. "Too-Tight Strap Hampered Execution." *St. Louis Post-Dispatch*, 5 May 1995: B1. § Slater, Jim. "Execution Procedure Questioned." *Kansas City Star*, 4 May 1995: C8. **23.** "Store Clerk's Killer Executed in Virginia." *New York Times*, 25 Jan 1996: A19. **24.** The involvement of this anonymous physician violated rules of both the American Medical Association and the Indiana State Medical Association. § Edwards, Sherri, and Suzanne McBride. "Doctor's Aid in Injection Violated Ethics Rule: Physician Helped Insert the Lethal Tube in a Breach of AMA's Policy Forbidding Active Role in Execution." *Indianapolis Star*, 19 July 1996: A1. § McBride, Suzanne. "Problem With Vein Delays Execution." *Indianapolis News*, 18 July 1996: 1. **25.** Martin, Doug. "Flames Erupt from Killer's Headpiece." Gainesville Sun, 26 March 1997: 1. § Medina was executed despite a life-long history of mental illness, and the Florida Supreme Court split 4-3 on whether to grant an evidentiary hearing because of serious questions about his guilt. This puts to rest any conceivable argument that Medina could have been guilty "beyond a reasonable doubt." *Medina v. State*, 690 So.2d 1241 (1997). The family of the victim had joined in a plea for executive clemency, in part because they believed Medina was innocent. *Id.*, at 1252, n. 6. Even the Pope appealed for clemency. Martin, *op. cit.* **26.** Overall, Michael, and Michael Smith. "22-Year-Old Killer Gets Early Execution." *Tulsa World*, 8 May 1997: A1. **27.** "Killer Helps Officials Find a Vein at His Execution." *Chattanooga Free Press*, 13 June 1997: A7. **28.** Cannon was executed for a crime committed when he was 17 years old. § "1st Try Fails to Execute Texas Death Row Inmate." *Orlando Sentinel*, 23 Apr 1998: A16. § Graczyk, Michael. "Texas Executes Man Who Killed San Antonio Attorney at Age 17." *Austin American-Statesman*, 23 Apr 1998: B5. **29.** Graczyk, Michael. "Reputed Marijuana Smuggler Executed for 1988 Dallas Slaying." Associated Press, 27 Aug 1998. **30.** Whaley, Sean. "Nevada Executes Killer." *Las Vegas Review-Journal*, 5 Oct 1998: 1A. **31.** "Davis Execution Gruesome." *Gainesville Sun*, 8 July 1999: 1A. § *Provenzano v. State*, 744 So.2d 413, 440 (Fla. 1999). § Melone, Mary Jo. "A Switch Is

Thrown, and God Speaks." *St. Petersburg Times*, 13 July 1999: 1B. **32.** Moore, Ron. "At Last I Can be With My Babies." *Scottish Daily Record*, 4 May 2000: 24. **33.** Bragg, Rick. "Florida Inmate Claims Abuse in Execution." *New York Times*, 9 June 2000: A14. § Long, Phil, and Steve Brousquet. "Execution of Slayer Goes Wrong; Delay, Bitter Tirade Precede His Death." *Miami Herald*, 8 June 2000. **34.** Rimber, Sarah. "Working Death Row." *New York Times*, 17 Dec 2000: 1. **35.** Scott, David. "Convicted Killer Who Once Asked to Die is Executed." Associated Press, 28 June 2000. § Letter from attorney Cheryl Rafert to Missouri Governor Mel Carnahan, 30 June 2000. **36.** Cook, Rhonda. "Gang Leader Executed by Injection: Death Comes 25 Years After Boy, 11, Slain." *Atlanta Journal Constitution*, 7 Nov 2001: B1.

---

36 Corporations That Ripped off the US Government

Corporate Crime Reporter. "The Top 100 False Claims Act Settlements." Report issued 30 Dec 2003. § Taxpayers Against Fraud, Education Fund. *False Claims Act and Qui Tam Quarterly Review*, various issues 1995-2004.

---

39 Famous People Who Used Drugs
(selected sources)

Booth, Martin. *Opium: A History.* St. Martin's, 1996. § Palmer, Cynthia, and Michael Horowitz. *Shaman Woman, Mainline Lady: Women's Writings on the Drug Experience.* Quill (William Morrow), 1982. § Plant, Sadie. *Writing on Drugs.* Picador, 2001. § Rudgley, Richard. *The Encyclopedia of Psychoactive Substances.* St. Martin's, 1998. § "Opium Throughout History." Part of the Website for the Frontline program "The Opium Kings." PBS, May 1997. www.pbs.org/wgbh/pages/frontline/shows/heroin/

7. Coleridge, Samuel Taylor. H.J. Jackson (ed.). *Samuel Taylor Coleridge: The Major Works.* Oxford Press, 2000, pp 519-21. § Hill, John Spencer. *A Coleridge Companion.* Macmillan Press, 1983. Chapter 3: "Kubla Khan." **8.** Cover, Arthur Byron. "Vertex Interviews Philip K. Dick." *Vertex*, Feb 1974. § Margot, Joel. "PKD FAQ." 1993. **9.** Kaplan, Fred. *Dickens: A Biography.* Johns Hopkins University Press, 1998. **10.** Hall, Donald, and Dock Ellis. *Dock Ellis: In the Country of Baseball.* Fireside, 1989. § Mikkelson, Barbara and David P. "Dock Ellis." Urban Legends Reference Pages [snopes.com]. **15.** Grinspoon, Lester. *Marihuana: The Forbidden Medicine.* Yale University Press, 1993. **16.** Donaldson, Maureen and William Royce. *An Affair to*

Remember: My Life with Cary Grant. Putnam, 1989. § Harris, W.G. *CG, A Touch of Elegance.* Doubleday, 1987. § Grant, Cary "Archie Leach." Currently available at [www.carygrant.net/autobiography/]. **19.** James, William. Bruce Kuklick. (Ed.). *William James: Writings 1902-1910.* Library of America, 1988. § Tymoczko, Dmitri. "The Nitrous Oxide Philosopher." *Atlantic Monthly*, May 1996. **20.** "Traveling Down the Information Highway With Mitchell Kapor." *Tricycle*, summer 1994. **24.** Mullis, Kary. *Dancing Naked in the Mind Field.* Pantheon Books, 1998. **28.** Paz, Octavio. Translated by Helen R. Lane. Introduction to *Miserable Miracle* by Henri Michaux. New York Review of Books, 2002. **34.** The Walter Scott Digital Archive, Edinburgh University Library [www.walterscott.lib.ed.ac.uk]. **35.** Interview with Susan Sontag. The Staff of High Times. *High Times Greatest Hits.* St. Martin's, 1994. **37.** Lemmo, Robert. "Pot, Pesants and Pancho Villa." The Staff of High Times. *High Times Greatest Hits.* St. Martin's, 1994. **HM.** Dalby, J. Thomas, Ph.D. "Sherlock Holmes's Cocaine Habit." *Irish Journal of Psychological Medicine* 1991; 8: 73-74. Reprinted on the Website of The Singular Society of the Baker Street Dozen [www.bakerstreet dozen.com]. § Doyle, Arthur Conan. *Sign of the Four.* 1890. Reprinted at literature.org.

42 Famous Drinkers of Vin Marini
(selected sources)

Pendergrast, Mark. *For God, Country, and Coca-Cola.* Basic Books, 2000. § Plant, Sadie. *Writing on Drugs.* Picador, 2001. § Zacks, Richard. *An Underground Education.* Anchor, 1999.

42+ Things That Have Been Made Out of Hemp
(selected sources)

Herer, Jack. *The Emperor Wears No Clothes* (revised and expanded 1995 edition). HEMP/Queen of Clubs Publishing, 1995. § Robinson, Rowan J. *The Hemp Manifesto.* Park Street Press, 1997. § US Department of Agriculture. *Hemp For Victory* (film). 1942. § USA Hemp Museum [hempmuseum.org]

44 Substances That Soup up Your Brain

Dean, Ward, M.D. and John Morgenthaler. *Smart Drugs and Nutrients.* Smart Publications, 1991. § Dean, Ward, M.D., John Morgenthaler, and Steven Wm. Fowkes. *Smart Drugs II.* Smart Publications, 1993. § Potter, Beverly, and Sebastian Orfali. *Brain Boosters: Food and Drugs That Make You Smarter.* Ronin Publishing, 1993. § Erowid website [www.erowid.org].

47 Nuclear Tests by the US

Nevada Operations Office, US Department of Energy. *United States Nuclear Tests, July 1945 through September 1992.* DOE/NV—209-REV 15. Dec 2000.

52 Items from the Delta Collection of the Library of Congress

Various Library of Congress documents pertaining to the Delta Collection, as archived by the Manuscript Division, Library of Congress. (Uncovered by Michael Ravnitzky. In possession of the author.) This includes the article "The World's Lewdest Library" by John Gardener Race from an unknown, undated magazine.

55 Companies Reportedly Doing Business With Enemy Nations

"Civil Penalties Information," related by the Office of Foreign Assets Control, Department of the Treasury, 2003 through Feb 2004. § Conflict Securities Advisory Group website [www.conflictsecurities.com] § Iraq's statement regarding weapons programs, given to UN Security Council in December 2002.

56 Pulp Novels

Bianco, David. "The Heyday of Lesbian Pulp Novels." PlanetOut website, 19 July 1999. § Book Em Books website [www.bookembooks.com]. § BookScans website [www.bookscans.com]. § Vintage Paperbacks & Digests website [www.vintagepbks.com].

63 Gay Animals

Bagemihl, Bruce, Ph.D. *Biological Exuberance: Animal Homosexuality and Natural Diversity.* St. Martin's Press, 2000.

82 Brands of Heroin

Booth, Martin. *Opium: A History.* St. Martin's, 1996. § National Drug Intelligence Center, US Department of Justice. "Heroin Distribution in Three Cities." November 2000 § Office of National Drug Control Policy, Executive Office of the President. *Pulse Check: Trends in Drug Abuse.* Various issues. § Unsigned. "Smashing Pumpkins' Keyboardist Dies of Heroin Overdose in New York Amid Music Industry's Anti-Drug Drive." National Drug Strategy Network, Summer 1996.

87+ People Mormons Have Baptized by Proxy

Associated Press. "Mormons Meet With Jews Over Baptizing Holocaust Victims." 11 Dec 2002. § Donovan, Gill. "Mormons Renew Pledge to End Proxy Baptism of Jews." *National Catholic Reporter*, 27 Dec 2002. § Ostling, Richard N., and Joan K. Ostling. *Mormon America: The Power and the Promise*. Harper SanFrancisco, 1999. § "Prominent People Mormons Have Baptized by Proxy." Website of Mormonism Research Ministry [www.mrm.org]. § Moore, Carrie A. "Proxy Names Stir up Lively Debate." *Deseret Morning News*, 6 Dec 2003.

Top 100 Corporations Laying off US Workers Due to NAFTA

Congressional Research Service. Memorandum: "Re: Top 100 Companies Reporting and Certified as Suffering NAFTA-Related Job 'Losses' (based on the Department of Labor Database)." 1 Dec 2003. Published on the website of US Senator Byron L. Dorgan [dorgan.senate.gov].

111 People Who Are the Subject of FBI Files
(selected sources)

FBI FOIA website [foia.fbi.gov]. § O'Reilly, Kenneth. *Black Americans: The FBI Files*. Carroll and Graft, 1994. § Robins, Natalie. *Alien Ink: The FBI's War on Freedom of Expression*. Rutgers University Press, 1992. § Various articles from the defunct website APBNews.com by Janon Fisher, Joe Beaird, Tami Sheheri, and Michael Ravnitzky.

815 People Killed by Religious Rituals and Objects

1. Wallechinsky, David. *The People's Almanac Presents the 20th Century*. Overlook Press, 1999. **2.** Reuters. "Girl Crushed by Cross at Brother's Grave." 21 Nov 2001. **3.** Associated Press. "Elderly Priest Crushed by Heavy Iron Gate." 21 Dec 2001. **4.** Celona, Larry, and Angelina Cappiello. "Priest Is Fatally Stricken at Pulpit." *New York Post*, 11 Feb 2002. **5-6.** Associated Press. "Couple Charged in Possible Exorcism Death." 20 Jan 2004. § Associated Press and CBS News. "Minister Charged in Exorcism Death." 27 Aug 2003. **7-185.** Rageh, Rawya. "Stampede Kills 244 at Hajj Pilgrimage." Associated Press, 1 Feb 2004. **HM.** Kennedy, Les, and Vanessa Wilson. "Lightning Hits Catholic College Girls After Mass." *Sydney Morning Herald*, 26 Sept 2001.

Bush Family Values
(selected sources)

Grove, Lloyd. "Lowdown." *New York Daily News*, 1 Jan 2004.

Classified Quotes 1 & 2

McCutcheon, Chuck. "Lawmakers Take Aim at Excessive Government Secrecy." Newhouse News Service, May 2003.

Corporate Quote #1

Newsweek International, February 1, 1999

Corporate Quote #2

Unsigned. "Flak for Imperial Tobacco at AGM." *Evening Post* (Bristol, UK), 4 Feb 2004.

Drug Quotes

1. Weil, Andrew, M.D. *The Marriage of the Sun and the Moon: A Quest for Unity Consciousness*. Houghton Mifflin, 1998. **2.** King, Stephen. *On Writing*. Scribner, 2000. **3.** Plant, Sadie. *Writing on Drugs*. Picador, 2001. **4.** Staff of High Times. *High Times Greatest Hits*. St. Martin's 1994. **5.** *Op cit.,* Weil. **6.** Stolaroff, Myron. *Thanatos to Eros: 35 Years of Psychedelic Exploration*. Berlin: Verlag fur Wissenschaft und Bildung, 1994. **7.** *Op cit.,* High Times. **8.** Fisher, Carrie. *Postcards from the Edge*. Simon & Schuster, 1987. **9.** *Op cit.,* Weil.

Federal Investigative Priorities 1 & 2

Associated Press. "9/11 Panel Faces Time, Money Pressure." 21 Jan 2003.

Judge Lambastes Police Abuse of Protestors

Driscoll, Amy. "Judge: I Saw Police Commit Felonies." *Miami Herald*, 20 Dec 2003.

Law Quotes

1. Thoreau, Henry David. "Civil Disobedience." 1849. **2.** France, Anatole. *Le Lys rouge*. 1894. **3.** Publius Cornelius Tacitus. *Annales*.

Number of Civilians Killed by Bombing During World War II

Knell, Hermann. *To Destroy a City: Strategic Bombing and Its Human Consequences in World War II*. Da Capo Press, 2003.

The Powerdeath Girls

US Food and Drug Administration. "FDA Enforcement Report," 8 Oct 2003.

Scorecard for the Domestic "War on Terror"

Transactional Records Access Clearinghouse, Syracuse University. "Criminal Terrorism Enforcement Since the 9/11/1 Attacks." 28 Dec 2003.

Stupid Government Trick

MacKenzie, Debora. "US Develops Lethal New Viruses." *New Scientist*, 29 Oct 2003.

Unusual Band #1

Agence France-Presse. "'Burqa Band': The Afghan Girl Band Made in a Day." 3 Aug 2003.

Unusual Band #2

Transplant Band's Website [www.transplantband.com] § Website of Michael Coleman [www.miqel.com]

Unusual Band #3

Sabbatum website [www.sabbatum.com]

The Wonders of "Herbal" Medicine

MedWatch, US Food and Drug Administration. "Medical Product Safety Information." [www.fda.gov/medwatch/safety.htm].

The Wonders of Modern Medicine, parts 1 & 2

MedWatch, US Food and Drug Administration. "Medical Product Safety Information." [www.fda.gov/medwatch/safety.htm].

Worker Safety Priorities, parts 1 & 2

Barstow, David. "US Rarely Seeks Charges for Deaths in Workplace." *New York Times*, 22 Dec 2003. ◨

Everything You Know Is Wrong:
The Disinformation Guide to Secrets and Lies
by Russ Kick (Editor)

Book of Lies: The Disinformation Guide to Magick and
the Occult
by Richard Metzger (Editor)

50 Things You're Not Supposed to Know
by Russ Kick

Abuse Your Illusions: The Disinformation Guide to Media
Mirages and Establishment Lies
by Russ Kick (Editor)

LIST: 6 Other Books and 3 DVDs from the Disinformation Company

You Are Being Lied To: The Disinformation Guide to Media Distortion, Historical Whitewashes and Cultural Myths
by Russ Kick (Editor)

Disinformation: The Interviews
by Richard Metzger

R.I.P.: Rest in Pieces
DVD

Disinformation: The Complete Series
DVD ~ Richard Metzger

Uncovered—The Whole Truth About the Iraq War
DVD

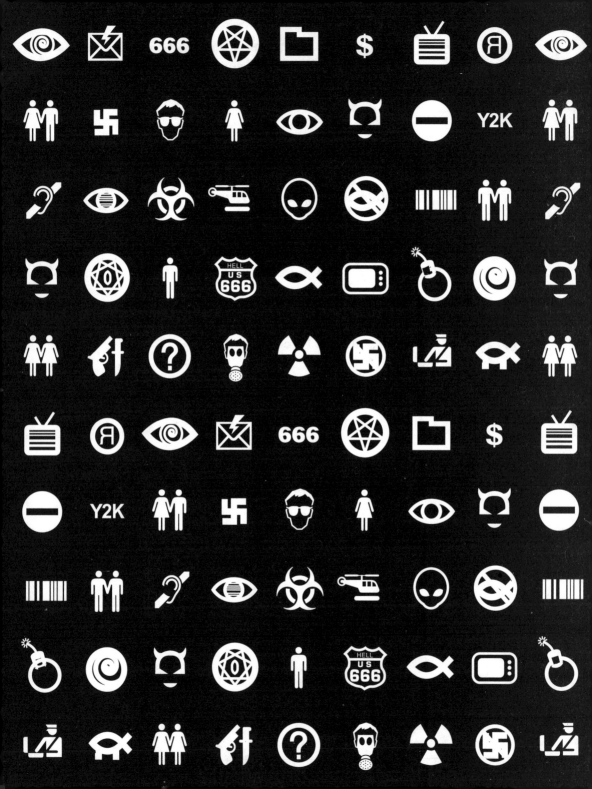